# Spaces of Political Pedagogy

This book examines three sites of pedagogical innovation, all of which are explicitly activisms against the current political and pedagogical climate. Drawing on an interdisciplinary framework including autonomous Marxism, post-anarchism, social movement theories and theories of critical pedagogy, it examines social movements though a pedagogical lens and attempts to understand how connections can be made between social movement learning and other initiatives and forms of higher learning. With studies of the London Occupy! movement; The Social Science Centre, a co-operative higher learning provider that practises popular education in city venues; and a university politically opposing the 'student as consumer' ethos, *Spaces of Political Pedagogy* connects these various projects as a continuum of educational experimentation, offering insights into the ways in which these sites practice pedagogy and the manner in which these practices could be implemented more widely to inform and improve struggles for wider social justice. As such, it will appeal to scholars of education and sociology with interests in pedagogy, social movements and activism.

**Cassie Earl** is a lecturer in Education at the School of Education, at the University of Bristol, UK.

# Spaces of Political Pedagogy

Occupy! and other radical experiments in adult learning

Cassie Earl

LONDON AND NEW YORK

First published 2018
by Routledge
2 Park Square, Milton Park, Abingdon, Oxon OX14 4RN

and by Routledge
711 Third Avenue, New York, NY 10017

*Routledge is an imprint of the Taylor & Francis Group, an informa business*

© 2018 Cassie Earl

The right of Cassie Earl to be identified as author of this work has been asserted by her in accordance with sections 77 and 78 of the Copyright, Designs and Patents Act 1988.

All rights reserved. No part of this book may be reprinted or reproduced or utilised in any form or by any electronic, mechanical, or other means, now known or hereafter invented, including photocopying and recording, or in any information storage or retrieval system, without permission in writing from the publishers.

*Trademark notice*: Product or corporate names may be trademarks or registered trademarks, and are used only for identification and explanation without intent to infringe.

*British Library Cataloguing-in-Publication Data*
A catalogue record for this book is available from the British Library

*Library of Congress Cataloging-in-Publication Data*
A catalog record has been requested for this book

ISBN: 978-1-138-63321-6 (hbk)
ISBN: 978-1-315-20780-3 (ebk)

Typeset in Times New Roman
by Taylor & Francis Books

I want to dedicate this work to all those people out there who are inconveniencing power to change the world. Those brave people who do things, who act, who put their bodies on the line to create a better future for all of us. Those are the people I wish to support, to help as critical friend; those are the people whose stories I wish to tell, to give yet another echo to their voice. Those are the people that give us all hope, that create a trust in humanity against the backdrop of distrust and despair. Those people have made this work possible and I am grateful to them for that, but more than my gratitude, I offer them my solidarity, my hope and my future efforts.

> These people here on the streets of London, are learning, they are educating and being educated by the very fact of their being here. I wish people understood that, I wish people understood that school is not education and education is not school, for me the two concepts could not have been more different. People have said to me that I might not be interested in their story as they are not educated and would therefore be uninteresting for my study – on the contrary, they have a wealth of education, they are wildly interesting, they have the best education a person could have, they have street smarts, they have, for some reason, been unsuccessful in the system of schooling – for me it was dyslexia and a non-conformist streak a mile wide – for them it could have been anything, a need to work, a racially biased curriculum, a gendered classroom, whatever. But, if they failed at school, yet they are still here, believing they can change things, then they are the most educated people I know.
> (Author's Reflective Fieldwork Journal, 2012)

# Contents

|   | Introduction: defining the moment | 1 |
|---|---|---|
| 1 | Sleeping on the floor and other spaces: the importance of space and place to learning | 12 |
| 2 | Social change and the political academic: creating a place for research in social movements | 28 |
| 3 | Political? Pedagogical? Philosophical?: putting the theory to work in conversation | 53 |
| 4 | Organic education from the ground up: stories from Occupy | 79 |
| 5 | Becoming organised: co-operatively organised education: stories from the Social Science Centre and higher education against neoliberalised consumerism: stories from Student as Producer | 115 |
| 6 | In the beginning Occupy created camps: thinking through the implications | 138 |
| 7 | Capturing future resistance in education | 160 |
|   | *References* | 169 |
|   | *Index* | 190 |

# Introduction
Defining the moment

Paulo Freire once said that

> There is no tomorrow without a project, without a dream, without utopia, without hope, without creative work, and work towards the development of possibilities, which can make the concretization of that tomorrow viable.
> (Freire, 2007: 26)

And the following notion from Williams (1989: 118) adds to Freire's sentiment in a robust way for our times: 'To be truly radical is to make hope possible, rather than despair convincing'. These words from Freire and Williams are the opening sentiments of this book, the projects described and discussed here are seen in this work as the 'development of possibilities', the 'creative work' that makes the dream, the hope and the utopia always more possible. These are words that have inspired the narrative in this endeavour, the exploration of possible models of pedagogical organisation for new ways of thinking and enacting pedagogy; projects that have dreamt, been creative and worked toward a new tomorrow.

This book, then, is an examination of the type/s of pedagogy that were practiced within three 'pedagogic actions' in the UK during 2011–2014. These actions attempted to explore ways of people being pedagogically and personally together 'otherwise'. The book examines the pedagogical social relations within these actions, and the claims being made about them in an attempt to understand what organisational forms might be realised in education in order to create the possibility of a transformative praxis for social justice and emancipatory learning. Each of these actions aims beyond merely anti-capitalist relations by prefiguring different ways of organising society through education. It is argued in each of these three actions, and in this book, that the social relations that are necessary for the continuation of a globalised capitalist society are harmful to human dignity, cooperation, and quality of life, as well as being harmful to the Earth itself in terms of environmental destruction through private ownership of all of nature itself (Graeber, 2013; Hardt & Negri, 2000, 2004, 2009, 2012; Harvey, 2003, 2011, 2012; Holloway, 2010; Smith, 1984; The Invisible Committee, 2009). It is also argued that new sites of struggle need to be identified as, due to the changing nature of production, old theories regarding who can be revolutionary change agents may have to be revised (Fisher, 2009; Gorz, 1997; Hardt & Negri, 2004, 2012; Holloway, 2010; Melucci, 1989; Steinberg, 2007; The Invisible Committee, 2009).

Holloway (2010: 29) insists that 'capitalism, ever since its beginning, has been a movement of enclosure, a movement of converting that which is enjoyed in common into private property'. Today we are becoming increasingly aware that this includes areas of life such as education (Bailey & Freedman, 2011; Couldry, 2011; Crowther *et al.*, 2005; Nixon, 2011; Williams, 2013, etc.). However, this research did not start out as attending to the privatisation or commodification of our education system; it started out as an exploration of the popular pedagogy taking place in the UK Occupy movement, particularly Occupy London and the Stock Exchange (LSX) camp outside St. Paul's Cathedral, in the autumn of 2011 to the spring of 2012.

I was interested in what were being termed the 'post-Seattle' New Social Movements (Castells, 2012; Holloway, 2010; Katsiaficas, 2006; Shantz, 2013). These movements claimed to be practicing a less colonial 'politics of the first person' (Katsiaficas, 2006) than the old social movements of my childhood and it seemed that a new revolutionary subject could be being born and indeed, educated.

This stress on the politics of the first person; living the way you would like the future to be, or prefigurative politics: building a new world in the shell of the old (Holloway, 2010; Katsiaficas, 2006), felt exciting and vibrant – and extremely pedagogical. It seemed they were offering hope, the hope of starting the search for new ways of being. This interested me politically and pedagogically because I agree with Webb (2010: 327) that 'if hope is characterised as a constant search, then the purpose of education is to act as its permanent guide'.

The key questions, then, arose out of a specific interest as to the nature of the pedagogical experimentation discernible within the Occupy movement and how it might relate to other pedagogical experiments occurring nearer or within the formal academy this took me to the Social Science Centre and Student as Producer (discussed later). The questions asked will be discussed as the book progresses, but the main question which became the overarching shape of this work concerned, could a form of 'learning loop', a feedback mechanism, or 'broad action research' type cycle be established between the three different pedagogical actions as a way to connect different forms of learning within in social movements, community groups, and higher education establishments, so that they might support each other and find ways to share and contribute to each other's knowledge and tactics for creating transformative change?

The first thing that caught my attention about the Occupy movement (Occupy) in London was that the largest structure in the Occupy LSX (London Stock Exchange) camp was 'Tent City University' (TCU), a large marquee in which seminars, group discussions and workshops were taking place (Occupy London LSX, 2011). This is where this story started. Having spent some time with Occupy London, questions began to form in my mind, I thought that perhaps more was needed to ensure something robust was built from the project to give more permanence and purpose to the ideas and knowledges already emerging from Occupy. I then sought out other organisational forms that also claimed to be explicitly in opposition to the way things were currently configured in education and in society. Sites which were attempting to address the problems that they perceived through an education that might enable a radically democratic public. This led me to a chance encounter, or a 'serendipitous research event', through which I discovered the Student as Producer project at the University of Lincoln and a co-operative higher education provider, the Social Science Centre. It immediately occurred to me that there may well be potential for some kind of trajectory of popular education within these projects, that gave rise to the possibility of creating a line of solidarity, a support infrastructure and a feedback system, or 'learning loop'. This support could allow teaching and research in these very different situations and circumstances to create a praxis that would lead to a form of 'action research' that allowed support and reflection from these differently organised educational initiatives. This action research cycle might then allow insight into how new and emerging organisational structures within education might be constituted to build these new publics and allow the conditions for a formation of a radical democracy. The project took on a grander ambition, and now remains situated in those spacial and temporal case studies, those happenings that didn't last, but serve as a snapshot of what could be, as creative possibility.

A working definition of popular education is needed here, I am utilising the definition provided by Crowther *et al.* (2005: 2), taken from the Popular Education Network (PEN), which was decided on by all members democratically:

> Popular education is understood to be popular, as distinct from merely populist, in the sense that it is:
>
> - Rooted in the real interests and struggles of ordinary people
> - Overtly political and critical of the status quo
> - Committed to progressive and social change
>
> Popular education is based on a clear analysis of the nature of inequality, exploitation and oppression, and is informed by an equally clear political purpose. This has nothing to do with helping the 'disadvantaged' or the management of poverty; it has everything to do with the struggle for a more just and egalitarian social order.
>
> The process of popular education has the following characteristics:
>
> - The curriculum comes out of the concrete experience and material interests of people in communities of resistance and struggle

- Its pedagogy is collective, focussed primarily on group as distinct from individual learning and development
- It attempts, wherever possible, to forge a direct link between education and social action

Cavanagh adds to this 'popular education is fundamentally anti-authoritarian and challenges dominant power relations.... The processes of popular education are extremely effective for increasing people's capacities to function democratically and with critical mindedness' (Cavanagh in Borg & Mayo, 2007: 43). Throughout this work, I will use the terms critical pedagogy/education and popular education interchangeably. There may be subtle differences between them; however, in the messy reality of the worlds the book inhabits, any differences are permitted here without note.

On examination, Occupy seemed to be combining much of the new politics of prefiguration with a popular education that was being grown from the ground up and this is what had initially interested me. Of course, as Schostak and Schostak (2013: vii) insist,

> no research is ever undertaken without a motive ... at the back of those motives is not just the curiosity of the scientist adopting a stance of 'neutrality' but a curiosity in-mixed with the whole range of emotions of everyday life that in every way subverts the neutrality, the objectivity.

I argue that this subversion of neutrality was not problematic as Schratz and Walker (1995: 5) describe, 'once we admit that, as researchers, we hold values that affect the research that we do, we have to find ways to scrutinise our actions and our motives more closely'. These sentiments have informed many aspects of this work, not least its solidarity with those who contributed by allowing me into their life-worlds and experiences with a generosity that never ceased to amaze me. Here, I acknowledged that I understand 'the role of science as first and foremost a cultural activity' (Kincheloe & Berry, 2004: 9).

It is important here to make a robust distinction between schooling, which aims to train and tame people, into the new neoliberalised industrial reserve army (Marx, 1867/1990) and education, which is to be separated from the notion of schooling. Education, it is argued here, as elsewhere, is the process of critically becoming, of creating the possibilities for imagining and creating alternatives and a safe space, free from judgement and discrimination, to enact those alternatives and create the world that exists not yet. Therefore, I argue here that an examination of what was happening on the streets, when people who wished to change things got together and organised their own educational activities, is necessitated, as our classrooms are perhaps, on the whole, no longer what bell hooks (1994: 12) calls 'spaces of radical possibility'.

This is where I start then, with a study that argues that my research was education; not only for me, but also for others I encounter along the way. From a position which understands that I am applying my own standpoint, my own understandings as an involved researcher, a specific type of learner, a person who is capable of critical thought, but not objectivity.

In addition, I believe, as Darder (2002: 30) does that

> there is no question that in today's world, no authentic form of democratic life is possible for the future without a revolutionary praxis of hope that works for both the transformation of social consciousness on the one hand and the reconstruction of social structures on the other.

Hardt and Negri (2012: 30) add to this that democracy will be realised only when a subject capable of grasping it and enacting it has emerged. This book will argue that this subject, as an intellectual public, began to emerge out of the practices discussed throughout. The social structure that I understand best is education and I will argue that education will be pivotal in the emergence of the subject capable of grasping and enacting democracy.

The book is organised in the way it is in the hope of creating a relationship, an organisational structure, that engages the reader in ideas centred on action and reflection. Hopefully allowing the reader to get the sense of entering the sites under discussion as stranger (Schutz, 1944) and becoming traveller (Kvale & Brinkman, 2009). This is attempted through the bricolage methodology (Kincheloe & Berry, 2004) of the original research. This methodology allowed for an experimental design where the theory is grounded in the data and then the two are put in conversation with each other. This method will be discussed in some detail later in the book as a necessary element of understanding the discussion of the sites and the conclusions the book draws about where we are and how we go forward. However, suffice to say here, that the study took a post-disciplinary approach to its knowledge work and utilised what Kincheloe and Berry (2004) call the fictive and imaginative elements of the bricolage, allowing the me, as researcher to attempt to access the research subjects as equals and often on their terms (Patrick, 1973; Whyte, 1943). The notion of subjects as equals grounds the methodology in democratic theory (Lefort, 1988; Laclau & Mouffe, 1985; Mouffe, 1999, 2005, 2013). In this book, the fictive and imaginative traits of bricolage are utilised to engender the possibility that the work can travel into the imagined future and create potentialities based on the uncovered stories of the sites explored.

It is argued that the bricolage approach revealed the emergence of key protagonists, through whom the initial reading could be theorised: Paulo Freire, who brings to the work an understanding of critical, politically engaged pedagogy; Ira Shor, who provides an example of critical democratic power sharing in an adult classroom; Jacques Rancière, who suggests the notion that it is possible to teach what you do not understand; and John Holloway, whose unique form of open Marxism (see Bonefeld, *et al.*, 1992, 1995) brings to the conversation a potential plan to 'crack capitalism' and escape from enclosure. There are, of course other voices present, however these authors provide the backbone because, I will argue, they echoed the sentiments of the London Occupy movement and our other spaces of hope (Harvey, 2000).

The book will further examine whether a form of pedagogical feedback mechanism could be developed between grassroots, popular education, protest movements and academe that might be practical and transformative. This book then, is an attempt to allow those people practicing forms of popular education, such as that seen at Occupy, to have access to a theorised praxis, a mixture of practice and theory, to underpin their future experiments. This form of witness and recording, critical analysis, dissemination and reimplementation has the traits of action research but on a 'grander scale'. Knowledges, from this text and others, can then be shared to improve practice among many organisations and settings for a singular purpose of creating multiple curricula aimed at strengthening struggles for social justice and creating cracks in the fabric of the capitalism that encloses society. This cycle was envisaged because the stories related to me showed that Occupy had no time for reflection or theorising whilst the occupation was in progress.

Clearly this piece of research for this book was not an action research project – that would have been impractical in such a fluid and fast paced movement. However, this book attempts to give a sense of 'being there' so that the experiences, particularly of the main case study, Occupy, is recognisable to those that were there, in the hope that it will be useful to them and others. In this sense, once the action ended, there would be practical theory, creating the potential for researchers and activists to sit down together and begin to understand all the forces that had acted upon the movement, both internally and externally, to influence future performance and effectiveness. Denzin (2010) calls this being critical secretary to the social movement, here I will attempt to extend this notion to allow a two-way flow of learning. This notion of the two-way flow of learning, could allow for reinterpretation and development of this work in other contexts, another value of the bricolage methodology employed (Kincheloe & Berry, 2004). It is hoped that the questions that emerge throughout this book, developed from the stories of those undertaking this form of curricula design, are seen as issues to think about, and have the potential to contribute to those struggles in a robust manner as they reveal some of the possible pitfalls of these curricula for those implementing them. In this respect, this book hopes to disseminate what Shukaitis and Graeber (2007), among others, call 'Really Useful Knowledge'.

Themes emerged in the original research, which were explored to varying degrees, such as the initial question regarding whether or not Occupy, and the other spaces, were able to practice a transformative critical pedagogy, given their structures. The literature that was examined in light of the initial stories brought up its own questions: can one indeed teach what one did not understand in these circumstances? What possible conditions were needed for a pedagogy to become truly transformative? Was power being shared in teaching spaces and what were the challenges for building socially just organisations of each of these? Further analysis formed questions regarding how each strata of education could assist the others and in what ways could we practice research in order to ensure that our assistance was not delivered in a colonial or patriarchal manner (Burdick & Sandlin, 2010). The research undertaken for this book had grand ambitions in a fluid and shifting period of political activity. As Schratz and Walker (1995: 5) insist, 'lacking the stability of stable paradigms and accepted methods throws the researcher back on personal resources; imaginative, cognitive and moral', adopting bricolage certainly did this (as will be explored throughout), but it led me to an interesting exercise in 'radical openness' (Schostak & Schostak, 2008: 8).

Holloway (2010: 11) argues that

> in this world in which radical change seems so unthinkable, there are already a million experiments in radical change, in doing things in a different way ... there has been a surge in recent years, a growing perception that we cannot wait for the great revolution that we have to start to create something different here and now.

History seems to confirm this; and there were, and continue to be, many experiments in radical change and it has been difficult to limit myself to detailing only three.

Critical educators, such as Darder (2002: 30), argue that 'only through a praxis of hope can alliances across differences be forged – alliances sufficiently strong for teachers and students to "learn together, teach together, be curiously impatient together, produce something together and resist the obstacles" (Freire, 1998: 69)'. In addition, this argument continues in political theory, that democracy is, or should be, a politics of hope (Laclau & Mouffe, 1985; Mouffe, 2005); also, Holloway (2010) insists on trust as a centrally organising principle for any new society. There are many more arguments concerning trust and hope, particularly in terms of forging alliances and ensuring that any 'empty place of power' (Lefort, 1988) created through struggle is not filled by populist leaders (Arditi, 2008), or that consent is not manufactured by elites (Bernays, 1928, 1947; Herman & Chomsky, 1994; Lippman, 1922, 1927). Trust and hope are seen by many to counteract these tendencies. This book attempts to take these two notions, hope and trust, to the core of their necessity, through its examination of hopeful and experimental pedagogies.

In attempting to contribute to hope, I argue that there is indeed the potential for a trajectory of pedagogical 'otherness' that could be utilised as a support network and that there is a necessity for this support network and 'learning loop', or feedback system, in order to build resilience and progression into grassroots popular movements and education projects. I argue, too, that there is also much scope for encompassing a more critical and popular education ethos into our teaching and learning practices in higher education to begin the process of reconstitution, and still greater need for the development and extension of institutions of the commons to enable a democratic, learning and intellectual public to be fostered. All these notions could be seen to support the argument that it is difficult but indeed not impossible to change the world and that transformative pedagogy, instigated by skilled pedagogues could make an escape from the enclosure of capitalist and neoliberal social relations (Holloway, 2010) a possibility. Not only may this be possible, but I argue, necessary, if we are to reverse the privatisation and enclosure of our increasingly atomised selves.

This book is not an attempt to make the familiar unfamiliar, but instead an attempt to disquiet the familiar by allowing the unfamiliar to be known (Burdick & Sandlin, 2010). These were strange times of upheaval and unrest: think for example of the so-called 'Arab Spring' that preceded the global Occupy movement and the seemingly ever continuing protests, revolutions and civil wars in Syria, Ukraine, Latin America and other places. Think for a moment about the very English riots in the summer of 2011 (Arditi, 2012; Bloom, 2012; Tyler, 2013; Žižek, 2013, 2014) and other upheavals brought about by global austerity measures in response to the globalised banking crisis of 2007/2008. Many people seem angry, confused, bitter and are becoming increasingly insurrectional as a result. Which makes more urgent the point that Shantz (2013: 72) insists upon: 'there is a pressing need ... for institutions, organisations, and relations that can sustain people as well as building capacities for self-defence and struggle'. This book, then, explores some of the possibilities of developing such institutions, organisations and relations. In addition, Johnston (2005: 67) argues that 'a key contribution from popular educators might also be to embark on a more intensive attempt at documenting popular education practice.... In this way, popular education praxis can be better understood, promoted, and built upon'. The book attempts, then, to document and witness a microcosm of education that is claimed to be popular and alternative in three very different but potentially important sites. It attempts to connect them, find the lines of continuity between them and offer suggestions as to how they might help support and sustain each other and move forward.

The book is an exploration of a potential trajectory of popular, critical pedagogies, framed around the two different ideas of universal teaching (Rancière, 1991) and critical, democratic power-sharing (Shor, 1996) that may have the potential to engender a popular education from the streets to the academy and back. I will reconnoitre the lines, loops and connections between the three pedagogical spaces and attempt to make sense, as a contribution to on-going debates, of whether there are enough lines of continuity, enough connections and understandings, to enable the creation of a trajectory from one model to another. Creating this feedback system of popular education practice and theory – a learning loop which can cycle as a form of praxis – that one day may have the efficacy to enable a reconstitution of educational establishments into learning commons with revolutionary organisational forms.

This book attempts to reveal situations of oppression within the spaces analysed; as critical friend. There has been an attempt to create a different role for the researcher in unsettled times, a more active role in the battle against enclosure.

My intention here is to contribute to what Shukaitis and Graeber (2007: 11) describe as 'Thoughts. Provocations. Explorations. Forms of investigation and social research that expand possibilities for political action, proliferating tactics of resistance through the constituent power of the imagination'. It endeavours to be a contribution to the thinking about 'the power of the bricolage to expand research methods and construct a more rigorous mode of knowledge about education' (Kincheloe & Berry, 2004: 1), even if in a small way.

Therefore, the overall hope is to make a contribution to other ongoing discussions which examine possibilities, allowing new questions to emerge from the specific context and creating further hope for an educational praxis that could make a difference to where we are now and where we are going. In order to attempt this the book attempts to bring a real sense of 'being there', first to give context to my own reflections and the questions that emerge from my inquiries, and second to enable those who read my work to excavate reflections and questions of their own.

There are two main themes that run through the book: hope and bricolage, both tentative and nebulous, they express my position as onlooker, as subjective activist researcher, as human person, wishing for a world where people understand from a specific place, from a place of understanding and acceptance. A place where knowing is important and the poetics of life are the rhythm that binds us, rather than the flows of spectacle and commerce. This work is an exercise in exploring one of the many possible ways we might find that world.

I have understood the individuals in Occupy through my research journey – despite their words of frustration and despair, which tell a different story – to be of the same disposition. Behind the collapsing in of the paranoia, the frustration of the internal repression in the movement, a thread that ran behind their words, and filled their actions, was hope; as I sat there in those spaces, created by the camp and agreements to converse, I saw their eyes light up when they spoke of their triumphant experience, even months after the disillusionment set in, still, their hope was there, behind those words.

I have attempted to capture this in the books theorising, whilst also attempting to honestly represent the problems, sitting, therefore, often in the interstices between hope and critique. I wanted, through Bricolage, to capture both sides of what was being told: the critique of what happened through their words but also their underlying, but ever-present hope through the theory. This theorising was an ongoing part of the conversations I had with occupiers and others involved in the pedagogic actions, it was theory in action, this was part of the research process. This was the basis for the 'mutually useful conversations' discussed later: each of us dynamically adding to each other's knowledge and ways of knowing.

Whilst I acknowledge that hope and critique may not necessarily be binary poles, I have attempted to set them in contrast. The work wishes to say 'I hear you, there were problems that were probably inevitable, but you had, and gave others, hope and this is the most precious "commodity" of all'. I wanted to recognise and witness that hope and despair are the inevitable two-sided narrative of working for change.

I have attempted to produce a work that allows readers to see both sides of that happening, and gain the understanding from it that, there will always be problems, but we cannot lose the successes that were gained in spite of those problems, because it is moments of joy that allow us to continue to believe, to look forward, and to hope.

As for my methods, it is true, essentially, that Bricolage is a methodology; a way of thinking about research. But it is more; it is an ontology, a way of attempting to understand the world and the researcher's place in that world as human subject and potential change agent. Bricolage is an emotional response to the injustices and inequalities we see around us as researchers, watchers of people, it allows for sociological theorising in ways that position the researcher as 'in service' to the sometimes beaten down aspects of the research subjects accounts. In the case of this work their desires, their immense learning, their courage, and, yes, again, their hope.

Bricolage is indeed a disposition, the bricoleur has to desire, almost need, to conjure this aspect of their craft, otherwise Bricolage becomes an empty signifier, another empty label for collecting stories and freely interpreting their meaning. The Bricoleur has to understand the subtext of human activity: what is it that makes people get involved? What makes them spend their time and tolerate a questioning intrusion into their lives to say, 'we did it, but this is how it went wrong'? In my understanding, the bricoleur cannot extract this and say 'yes, it went wrong' and merely represent, the bricoleur must accept the failures and voice them in their work, for sure, but add to those voices others, others who inspire people to try again, to reflect with their assistance and never lose hope.

This, in essence, is what the story of this book has always been about – how can we maintain a genuine hope for the future in current times? We cannot wait, we cannot leave the changes to future generations, we must educate ourselves and each other to understand the necessity of changing our social relations. It is my understanding, through theorising and observing, that this cannot be done through formal institutions alone, if at all. The research indicates that it must be done on the streets, in the Social Centres, and the community halls – this is what Occupy did, what they told us.

However, they also exposed the pitfalls of this, they laid bare the problems and complexities of their experiment. They did this by talking to researchers, more than in any other way, because the people who talked to me were the people who exposed the internal problems, despite fear of retribution; they were the people who attempted to get the message out from the sometimes repressive atmosphere in the camp.

It is interesting to me that the people who gave their time and stories all had a similar message: we did something amazing, but here is how it failed and why. That message coupled with the ecstatic expression on their faces, the enthusiasm in their words, when they talked of their accomplishments, spoke to me of a hope that this 'stage' of Occupy could teach, so that others might learn. Why else bother?

My disposition as Bricoleur, as sociological theorist, as desirer of change, as human subject in frightening times responded to them with this book, in my own hope that it will help in some way in that learning. Hope can be infectious, but so can despair – in some ways this book has been a battle between the two and an offering of a possible trajectory out of one and into the other. In other words, I return to one of the opening sentiments of this book: to be truly radical is to make hope possible, rather than despair convincing (Williams, 1989: 118).

# 1 Sleeping on the floor and other spaces
## The importance of space and place to learning

I want to introduce the pedagogic actions, to understand the situatedness of the work, because the rest of the book, including theoretical exploration, has to be grounded on an understanding of the sites, particularly Occupy London. This situatedness comes from the socio-political climate of the time that gave rise to the Occupy movement and their educational response, the dissatisfaction with the neoliberal university and the responses from the two other sites; the notion that all three sites are connected by their stated desire to do education differently and to teach politically. The situatedness is also temporal, situated in that time, a snapshot of the action.

The three sites in this book are not given equal weighting as the rare opportunity of studying the organic and popular education of Occupy remains my central focus and the place where my theory is grounded. I wanted to understand what was happening pedagogically in Occupy, I did not initially know where the boundaries of my study would be. I wanted to get to know the phenomenon that Chomsky (2012) had described as 'unprecedented' and allow the emergent questions that would inevitably come from that exploration to guide the boundaries of the case study. Allowing this organic interpretation to happen, I began by exploring Occupy London and the London Stock Exchange (LSX) camp outside St. Paul's Cathedral specifically.

For these purposes, in this chapter I present the sites in a purely descriptive manner; to encourage a 'picture' of the phenomena under investigation to emerge. In the hope that this will enable a more detailed understanding of how the theory was generated. First then, an introduction to Occupy LSX:

> Walking around the site, with its convivial atmosphere and bustling activity was inspirational. A few things stood out immediately that gave the whole site a jovial aspect. There were banners and flags, some banners had serious messages: 'capitalism is crisis' or 'the banks got bailed out, we got sold out'. Some more tongue in cheek: an English Heritage style blue plaque with 'Real democracy reborn here October 2011' displayed upon it, a street sign saying 'Tahir Square EC4M, City of Westminster' and a giant 'Monopoly' board (rumoured to have been dropped off in the night by the infamous artist Banksy). There was the big Tent City

University marquee off to one side and a large info tent welcoming you into the square. I could hear the constant noise of conversations, drums, music, the clattering of pots and pans. The camp was a surreal interruption in the lives of those who passed through the square, whilst I was there I saw people in smart suits who looked so incongruent but had obviously gotten used to the camps presence; tourists taking pictures; people discussing and debating with the Occupiers and even a wedding party that pulled up in a stretch limousine, the woman in an expensive full white gown, going to get married in St. Paul's and stopping as she went to have her wedding photos taken in Tent City.

(Fieldwork Notes, 2011)

Occupy, globally, intrigued me. It is said that it 'happened' in September 2011; the exact date of the beginning of the global movement is ambiguous, as is its origin. Globally, Occupy was initially thought to have been launched in the U.S.A. by a Canadian activist magazine: Adbusters (Gamson & Sifry, 2013: 159), with their question 'are you ready for a Tahrir moment?' referring to the protest camp, or the movement of the Squares, in Tahrir Square, Egypt. Another, less spectacular explanation is that a meeting was held in New York with a multi-national group of anti-capitalist activists planning an action of physical occupation of public space (Kroll, 2011: 16) that would later catch on in 'over 951 cities in 82 countries' (Jaramillo, 2012: 67; Thorpe, 2013: 226–7). The first Occupy encampment was in Zucotti Park, New York City as close to Wall Street as was possible (see Chomsky, 2012; Jaramillo, 2012; Pickerill & Krinsky, 2012; Van Stekelenburg, 2012, among others). Noam Chomsky (2012) described Occupy Wall Street, as this first encampment was called, as 'an extremely exciting development. In fact, it's kind of spectacular. It's unprecedented. There has never been anything like it that I can remember' (Chomsky, 2012: 24), an opinion that seemed to resonate widely, and made investigation of Occupy even more inviting. Occupiers and commentators alike insisted that it had taken at least some inspiration from other encampment protests around the world, including the student occupations of 2010 against the fee rises in the UK; the so-called 'Arab Spring' movements and the M15 and *Indignados* in Spain and the uprisings in Greece (Glasius & Pleyers, 2013; Pickerill & Krinsky, 2012; Thorpe, 2013; etc.). Some of the global camps lasted for 'less than a day, some of them for months ensuring that Occupy has become, if not a new political force per se, at least a new socio-political problematic that demands attention' (Thorpe, 2013: 226–7). According to Halvorsen (2012: 427), 'Occupy London represents one of the longest lasting examples of Occupy camps in the world', stressing it was the physical encampment that was one of the longest lasting, whether Occupy London endured in any other way is often hotly debated.

Occupy were insisting, at the time of my engagement with them, that the point of reference for the discontents was not the state or politics conventionally defined. There seemed to be no desire to take over the state or to create a new party. The Occupy movement claimed to reject this form of representative politics, focussing instead on people taking control of their own lives and expanding the democratic spaces in which they live and work (Sitrin, 2012: 75). Therefore, a question emerges regarding what the 'Occupy movement' signifies. Was the 'movement' an empty signifier for a multitude of discontents? Was Occupy a movement, or an event? And what, apart from the physical place, was actually being 'occupied' by taking part?

According to Pickerill and Krinsky (2012: 279 and backed up by my own interviews), for many people who joined a camp or Occupy group, the movement started at the

> moment when resistance to the inequalities of capitalism finally emerged: a tipping point in which the unfairness of bank bailouts juxtaposed against rising personal poverty triggered a moment of clarity of the absurdity of the current economic and political system.
> (Pickerill & Krinsky, 2012: 279)

Chomsky describes the Occupy movement as 'the first major public response to thirty years of class war' (Chomsky, 2012: 9). Even if the notion of 'thirty years of class war' is accepted, questions still emerge here about the 'public'. Who are this 'public', how are they constituted and where did they come from? Are they a homogenous 'mass' as in 'the masses', or are they 'the people'? Debates about the nature of the 'public' that responded through Occupy can be seen in Hardt and Negri's book *Declaration* (2012), which builds on the work in *Multitude* (2004). Hardt and Negri's view of the new 'multitude' described in *Declaration* goes some way to answering this question, other debates (for example, Lippman, 1927; Schostak and Schostak, 2013) regarding how publics are constituted and what their collective power may or may not be are also of interest, as this is a problematic concept. However, for now a working definition of what I mean by 'public Space' may be useful: Public spaces are the areas seen as being designated for public use, that is that they allow for freedom of passage through a place, where people can meet, assemble and travel without contravening any laws, even when they are often privately owned.

Occupy globally claimed to, and indeed seemed to, illuminate issues about 'public space', whether such a thing exists anymore, and how these contested spaces are managed and controlled. This is partly because most of (but not all) the Occupy movements around the world confront power by occupying this so called public space with urban tent camps (Van Stekelenburg, 2012). Of course, this work concentrates on the encampment at St. Paul's known as Occupy LSX, therefore it is worth emphasising that this is the Occupy action that I am talking about throughout as the larger, globalised movement, was, of course, much more complex in the multi-various actions and attitudes it displayed (for example see literature written about Occupy such as Byrne, 2012; Lunghi & Wheeler, 2013; van Gelder, 2011; Khatib, *et al*, 2012; collections of stories from various Occupy camps and actions).

The Occupiers who set up the Occupy LSX camp made a failed attempt to occupy Paternoster Square outside the London Stock Exchange, which facilitated a realisation, at least among the activists and their supporters, that 'the financial corporate world was not only off limits to most, economically and socially, but also quite literally' (Pickerill & Krinsky, 2012: 280). The failure was due to the closure of the 'public' Paternoster Square, or the 'fortifying of the space with police, private security and metal barriers', was a moment when, to some, the 'real nature of this "public" space was revealed – only a very specific type of public is welcome, and their activities are restricted to those of work and consumption' (Köksal, 2012: 447). This failed attempt at setting up the encampment in the desired, and most politically strategic, site also shows the extent to which privatised areas of the city which normally remain open for public access, are being controlled not by law enforcement officers, but by private security firms employed by the financial institutions, revealing the extent to which the use of laws and their enforcers can be utilised by a new order to protect private property. These restrictions on movement and interruption are enforced, in this case by private security guards, but also more generally by the state police through the use of militarised tactics and 'non-lethal' weaponry, the use of which, such as Pepper Spray, has been highly publicised, for example in the Occupy Oakland protests (USA Today, 2011), where peaceful activists were pepper sprayed whilst sitting on the ground.

By disturbing the normal flows and uses of space, the Occupiers went some way to bringing to light the underlying force of the police order (Rancière, 2011) by publicising the denial of public access across Paternoster Square and by interrupting the flow of business and commerce across the Square outside St. Paul's Cathedral as well as creating counter cartographies, discussed below. In addition, this exposed the legal structures and mechanisms used to control these flows. In turn, it then disrupted and illuminated the discourses of 'rights' to public spaces and of manufactured 'publics' that show what is at stake for states, elites and those citizens that attempt to develop democratic politics, policies and ways of organising (Hardt & Negri, 2004, 2009, 2012; Harvey, 2000, 2012; Lefort, 1998). Occupy's examination of this included producing counter-cartographies, in which cityscapes were used and mapped for activities alternative to that of commerce and control (Köksal, 2012), city tours (Occupy London LSX, 2011) and protests wherein the space would be put to an alternative use, such as dancing, picnicking or teach-outs (Chomsky, 2012; Köksal, 2012; Occupy London LSX, 2011).

As can be assumed, just from these two central points about Occupy, 'it is not a simple movement, not a single issue, but instead embodies the frustration and energy that many of us have with the way society is organised' (Pickerill & Krinsky, 2012: 286), suggesting that it may be possible/desirable for a more emancipatory and communal 'police order', in Rancière's terms, to be brought to bear. The complexity seems to arise further when attention is turned toward how the LSX camp was physically organised: the largest structure on site was a marquee, displaying the words, *Tent City University* (TCU) in large letters. This marquee had a space for workshops and a library. Halvorsen (2012: 428), who was active within Occupy London as well as researching it, adds that 'Tent City University ... has provided a diverse range of seminars and discussions, as well as the facilitated "teach outs" in front of banks', there were indeed a large number of speakers and guests, from many professions at TCU, their diversity, when it comes to political standpoints, however, is perhaps in doubt. However, education was a large aspect of the camp, as my interviews with Occupiers revealed: 'we wanted to get educated about the issues as well as educating others' (Jane); 'TCU was a priority as people wanted to know more about what was going on and an alternative university seemed like a really good thing to have on site' (Hannah); 'I've learnt loads, TCU has been really good for creating the space for that learning to happen' (John).

For many of the people, it seemed, learning was a defining aspect of the camps; having the power and freedom to know, to reflect, to think, but also to enact. It seemed that personal stories were being 'uploaded' to the collective knowledges to assist the understanding of the crisis and how it affected people. Therefore, according the stories told in my study, the issues being protested and the Occupiers' enactment of learning became central in their experiments with democracy, referred to variously as direct/deliberative/consensus democracy, all these labels technically correct for the decision-making processes that occurred in the camps. This potential enactment of learning through direct and participatory democracy made possible in Occupy implied the question of whether the assertion of the right to free association is the best way to learn new social relationships. Does this allow for real reflection, and although the learning about democracy is taking place, what else is being learnt/(re)created/(re)established? The discussion on this point will be picked up later.

The main tool of this enactment of learning, this trialling of alternative forms of democracy seemed to be the General Assembly (GA), I heard many stories about how influential the GAs were in people's thinking. On the surface at least, they seemed to work very well as a democratic tool:

> in the first few weeks of the camps, the daily general assemblies of Occupy London Stock Exchange became efficient enough to disseminate information, discuss and adopt practical decisions during the first part of the meeting, by then attended by over 200 people, while the second part of the meeting was dedicated to broader political or strategic issues
> 
> (Glasius & Pleyers, 2013: 557)

The GAs were well attended from the start of Occupy LSX (as can be seen from the GA minutes available on the Occupy London Website and from the many photographs that circulate on Internet feeds and can easily be found through Google Images) and, although they had their problems, at face value they were generally convivial and productive. According to several Occupiers, the GAs were 'exciting places to be, where you felt anything could happen' (Danny); 'GAs allowed people to express their political opinions, we got a lot of things decided about the camp and about what it was we wanted' (Hannah), and 'I really found my voice at the GAs, they were what made Occupy different' (John). These views about the GAs were supported by the minutes (Occupy London LSX, 2011), which were taken during the GAs and later uploaded onto the web site, although these minutes may not give a complete picture of the full proceedings. Even so, one of the striking aspects about the GAs was the practice of the 'human microphone': the words of any speaker were re-spoken in waves across the crowd in order for everyone present to hear; which became one of the visible and moving forms of cooperation within the movement in both London and New York. As Chomsky (2012: 57) reports,

> one of the striking features of the movement has simply been the creation of cooperative communities – something very much lacking in an atomised, disintegrated society – that include general assemblies that carry out extensive discussions, kitchens, libraries, support systems and so on. All of that is a work in progress leading to community structures that, if they can spread out into the broader community and retain their vitality, could be very important

Halvorsen (2012: 428) explains that, 'Occupy London ... formed dozens of autonomous working groups, focussing on everything from practical issues, such as kitchens and first aid to groups discussing alternative economic models and links between the financial crisis and the environment'. It was apparently these working groups that formed the backbone of the movement and brought proposals to the GAs for deliberation and decisions. This prefiguration of alternative politics was felt to be one of the most exciting aspects of the movement, this was because as Sitrin (2012: 74) identifies,

> the Occupy movements ... purpose is not to determine 'the' path that a particular country should take but to create a space for a conversation in which all can participate and in which all can determine together what the future should look like. At the same time these movements are trying to prefigure that future society in their present social relationships

This included providing services, such as the ones mentioned earlier: libraries, first aid, kitchens and education, etc. as Pickerill and Krinsky (2012: 283) explain,

> many camps explicitly sought to circumvent traditional providers of services and rather than make demands simply to create alternatives. By establishing temporary tent communities ... they recreated new spaces of provision: prefigurative alternative communities with very few resources.... In particular, there was significant focus on alternative education.

The provision of these services however, did reportedly lead to friction in the movement as certainly some of the people I spoke to thought that Occupy were providing (or creating anew) services that the government ought to supply. For some, however, this was part of the reason that they came to the camps in the first place: the cuts to public services through austerity measures imposed by the UK Conservative/ Liberal Democrat coalition government (Pickerill & Krinsky, 2012). This issue arose partly because the camps attracted many homeless people and people with mental health or drug issues. These people were not turned away because the Occupiers acknowledged that for the camp to be fully inclusive, it had to cater for anyone that came along. One Occupier, Adam, told me that

> we have some problems with people who are mentally ill, or have drug or alcohol problems, but if we ask them to leave, we are not being inclusive are we? But if we let them stay, we're providing services that we're not really equipped to provide, it's really complicated to know how to feel …

The albeit problematic inclusion of these services and the reported inclusivity of the camp itself meant that what Occupy were potentially doing, in effect, was to create 'institutions operating on anarchist principles of mutual aid and self-organisation – a genuine attempt to create the new society in the shell of the old' (Graeber, 2011: 4). These principles, were apparently carried further by the political organisation of the camp, its main identity, one might say, that of horizontalism: the desire to put an end to all hierarchies and authority – the state, capitalism, patriarchy, racism – and establish a truly free and equal society. Horizontalism has, on the surface, been a key aspect of many post-Seattle movements according to several scholars (Solnit & Solnit, 2010; Thomas, 2000). As Gitlin (2013: 8) explains,

> at the core of Occupy was an identity, however absurd it appeared to be to the outside. It prided itself on a famously horizontal style, a will towards cooperative commonwealth, a repertory of rituals and repertoires of playful, sometimes confrontational action.

Sitrin (2012: 74) adds that '[horizontalism] was seen as a tool to create more participatory and freer spaces for all – a process of awakening and empowerment', this speaks to the inclusivity aspect of the movement, as does probably their most famous slogan, that of 'We are the 99%'.

It is argued here, as elsewhere, that the 'we are the 99%' slogan, whether accurate or not, was an incredibly powerful slogan as it 'immediately created a sense of inclusion and majority' (Pickerill & Krinsky, 2012: 281) because it 'resonated with the larger public that was severely disillusioned with political-economic establishments widely seen as having superintended the economic breakdown of 2008 and then having thrived with impunity' (Gitlin, 2013: 10). Gitlin also reminds us however, that

the Occupy movements terminology (1%, 99%) entered into popular lore so readily because it summed up, albeit crudely, the sense that the wielders of power are at once arrogant, self-dealing, incompetent, and incapable of remedying the damage they have wrought; and that their dominance constitutes a moral crisis that can only be addressed by a moral awakening
(2013: 9)

Chomsky (2012: 69–70) argues that 'one of the really remarkable and almost spectacular successes of the Occupy movement is that it has simply changed the entire framework of discussion of many issues'. Or perhaps, as Arditi (2012: 1, my italics) comments, these types of events *are the plan* in the sense that they make a difference by moving the conversation, they are political performatives – participants start to experience what they strive to become – and vanishing mediators or passageways to something other to come'. Chomsky goes on to say that, this is because 'there were things that were sort of known, but in the margins, hidden, which are now right up front – like the imagery of the 99 percent and the 1 percent'. This, coupled with 'the dramatic facts of the sharply rising inequality over the past roughly thirty years, with the wealth being concentrated in actually a small fraction of the 1 percent of the population', meant in just that one slogan Occupy had potentially unveiled an issue that included such a large majority that it was almost completely inclusive. Chomsky asserts that 'this has made a very heavy impact on the ridiculous maldistribution of wealth'. Perhaps it would be more accurate to say that it has had an impact upon *the debate about* the maldistribution of wealth, as Gitlin (2013) and others would argue. For example, one Occupier wrote that

> what the Occupy movement COULD do was to start conversations. We, the people, could just ignore the 1% for a minute, get together for a chat and say, 'This isn't really working out for us, is it? What kind of world do we want to live in? and how do we get there?' And that is what seemed to be happening quite naturally. People wanted to come and tell us their stories, and we listened (some of us) ... they talked about their hopes for the future. We felt the mood was growing, and it was with us
> (Anonymous, 2012: 442)

Moreover, as Van Stekelenburg (2012: 227) insists,

> one should not only consider the relatively small number of people who camped out, but also the much larger number of people who came to the protest site for a rally, or made a donation on line, or sent a petition supporting the activists right to remain on the site. These people shared a collective identity with the protesters, one they gained from blog entries, Facebook posts, YouTube videos, online newspaper stories and television reports. Digital media made an imagined community possible

Occupy, like other post-2010 movements, also made extensive use of the Internet, which as current debates suggest, may have produced new forms of politics and for the purposes here, an 'Occupy politic' especially (see, for example, Castells, 2012; Hardt & Negri, 2012; McNair, 2011). This was also reported as being instrumental in gaining notoriety for the movement and providing a feeling of global solidarity. However, as Hardt and Negri (2012: 18) state,

> the encampment and occupations of 2011 have rediscovered this truth of communication ... that physical proximity matters.... Facebook, Twitter, the Internet, and other kinds of communication mechanisms are useful, but nothing can replace the being together of bodies and the corporeal communication that is the basis of collective political intelligence and action.

Therefore, although this was an important part of the movement it will not be discussed at great length in this work as the use of social media in this context is a complex issue which could not be done justice here, and has been extensively written about by others (see, for example Gamson & Sifry, 2013). Suffice to acknowledge here that, as Gamson and Sifry (2013: 159) say, 'the Occupy movement has made extensive use of a whole panoply of user-generated social media and social networking', which enabled the movement to become supported by various actions globally under the one Occupy signifier and create a positive feeling of global solidarity and many ideas shares, at least for a time during the encampments of 2011/2012 and for some Occupiers, long after the camps had gone. There are also discussions to be had regarding the use of technology intended to further the control and repression by the 1% being used to bring down that system of social organisation by turning the technology against them. In this work, however, the attention is on the notion, as Hardt and Negri attest, that the truth of communication is that physical proximity matters, the spaces created by bodies coming together created the movement and the learning that emerged from it. However, what these notions of a global movement with global solidarity existing under one 'name' or 'label' that of Occupy, do evoke, are questions of how solid was Occupy as a political actor and did it in the end 'melt into air' (Berman, 1982; Marx, 1848/2003)?

Solidarity was reportedly very important for Occupy; it was this aspect, along with the learning that took place, which was a constant theme within the movement itself (Occupy London LSX, 2011) and in my interviews. The solidarity, encompassing the (re)connection of people outside capitalist social relations was apparently evident in the LSX camp, at least on the surface:

> I was excited about the idea of a protest where we would not go home at the end of the day, but where we would remain for as long as we deemed

necessary. Where we would create a space where capitalism could not intrude and real democracy was practiced and where we could plan further actions in an attempt to reclaim our present and the future that we felt was being hijacked

(Köksal, 2012: 446)

we build spaces where you find freedom of imagination.... When St. Paul's was there, I was able to avoid money, universities ... and all the things people tell me I have to do to have a happy life

(Occupy interviews in Glasius & Pleyers, 2013: 556)

This notion of avoidance, of escapism from what this Occupier calls 'all the things people tell me I have to do' is interesting and poignant as on the one hand it speaks of mere escapism, which does not constitute a countervailing practice. On the other hand, it speaks of having the space and freedom to associate differently, of providing thinking room, where those countervailing democratic practices and plans can be hatched.

Jaramillo (2012: 69) expresses those feelings and the impression I certainly absorbed from my visits to the camp like this:

there is a message that the Occupy movement clearly conveys: we generate strength in conviviality, reciprocity and mutual support ... it signals a break, we could say, a breach from ordinary life occurrences. This break jolts the collective unconscious from its dormant state of mind and through collective displays of protest, creates the conditions for individuals to barreldown the unknown path of revolt, that is, if a tear gas canister does not stop them dead in their tracks.

I now move on to the other spaces explored in this book, again a descriptive account to give the reader a taste of what is to come. These two, supplementary spaces, are not given the weighting of Occupy in the story that unfolds in this book, but are important to it nevertheless. The predominant reason for examining the practices of the Social Science Centre, Lincoln, UK (SSC) was to understand its potential to become an institution of the commons (Hardt & Negri, 2012; Shantz, 2013), to attempt an understanding of whether it can be seen as a new organisational form where education can flourish without the fear of becoming schooled. There is a caveat here: it was difficult at the time to get any real access to the SSC without disrupting its activities, therefore a great deal of what follows on the Centre is taken from writings and interviews with its founder members and particularly Mike Neary. This must be viewed as rhetoric, as it has been said at other times that the account given by Neary often does not accurately reflect the lived experience of some of the members, therefore a cautious scepticism should be adopted when reading the account. However, based on the rhetoric and stories included here, the SSC could well be considered an emergent institution, consisting of emergent procedures, practices and mechanisms, if taken at face value and with acceptance of the group's rhetoric. Therefore, it is important for the purposes of this work to understand whether it was, or even could be, an emergent institution which not only has the potential to support movements such as Occupy, but gives a countervailing approach to the university in order that it might bridge the gap between the two, through an emerging praxis of theories of radical political practice and a practice of radical political theories. Could it even one day become the normative way of practicing popular education that connects what the university might one day become and sites of struggle in robust and powerful ways?

The Social Science Centre (SSC) describes itself as 'a not-for-profit co-operative ... organised on the basis of democratic, non-hierarchical principles, with all members having equal involvement in the life and work of the SSC' which 'offers opportunities to engage in a co-operative experience of higher education' (Social Science Centre, 2012). It has been described by others in various ways; as, for example, a 'radical attempt to forge an alternative model of higher education, able to stand independently without being subject to the whims of marketising politicians and managerial bureaucracies' (Carrigan, 2011). Its own web site describes it as an attempt 'to create alternative spaces of higher education whose purpose, societal value and existence do not depend on the decisions of the powerful'. One might be wary of such high ideals and blustery rhetoric; however, the reality seemed, on the surface to at least reflect this in some key ways.

The SSC was very small; it started its first year (the year this study was conducted) with nine students, everyone giving their time freely, on a voluntary basis, which, according to Neary (conversation, 2013), a founder member, can be both problematic and limiting and I would argue brings up issues about volunteerism. However, Neary also told me that the small size of the Centre makes it very productive, as every person involved can feel that they are a valuable part of the Centre's work and life. He adds:

> [a] sense of imagination and the imaginary extends to the way in which the centre is managed and run, with time set aside to consider the meaning and purpose of the Centre, using the critical concepts developed in the SSC sessions: gender, ethics and power, to build our own sense of collective activity. These critical reflections can lead us to challenge our own working practices, including, and in particular, how power is distributed across the collective and whose knowledge within the group is privileged
>
> (Neary in Class War University, 2013)

These are high ideals; indeed, this begs the question of how successful they are at this. However, Neary and other members of the SSC claimed that the often problematic relationship between 'teachers' and 'students' is attended to: 'we refer to all members as "scholars" as a way of dissolving the distinction between academics and students' (conversation, 2013), this tension, it seems, was not fully resolved however, as members were actually referred to as either 'student scholars' or 'teacher scholars' (SSC conversations, 2013), suggesting that even though a resolution was perhaps attempted, there is still some essential divide between the two. However, the web site suggests that 'one key guiding principle of the centre is that "teachers" and "students" have much to learn from each other' (Social Science Centre, 2012), a principle that if practiced should allow at least the *problematisation* of subjugated/privileged knowledge. They also claim that 'decisions at general meetings shall be made by consensus' (Social Science Centre, 2012), which extends all the way from the running of the Centre to planning the curriculum.

The SSC also insisted that members see and enact the importance of connecting with space and place as an essential criterion. In an interview in *The Times Higher Education*, Neary insisted that '"place is the key", bonding teachers and learners' (Bonnett, 2013). In conversation with me, he expressed this importance as 'I like to think we are reclaiming our right to the city, or occupying the city as a new pedagogy of space and time' (conversation, 2013) and McAleavey, a founder member of the SSC, argues that 'the centre needs to be understood as "an active part of the city" rather than a "discrete entity"' (Bonnett, 2013). This idea links in with what Neary calls 'an essential characteristic' of the SSC and its activities is that it is 'based on direct and personal engagement' (Neary in Class War University, 2013). This engagement, according to Neary and Amsler (2012), extends from the relationships between the scholars in the SSC to the City itself, reclaiming not only the right to the city, but also the public nature of inquiry into the social, how this works in practice seemed unclear to those student scholars I spoke to, but they do often hold their meetings in cafes and other spaces accessible to the public. These principles give rise to the claim on the web site that 'our work in co-operative higher learning has the potential to transform the way in which higher education is being imagined, designed and undertaken' (Social Science Centre, 2012).

In addition to the apparent localised relationship to the City of Lincoln and the criteria of connection to space, the constitution states that while 'it is important that the Centre works in real places at the heart of its local community' and works in 'a variety of public space across the city' and is 'orientated towards work in the social sciences', it also states that they 'hope and expect that similar projects of small-scale, self-funded higher education will be created for different subject areas and in different locations nationally and internationally' (Social Science Centre, 2012). It is then expected by the members of the SSC that 'these multi-various Centres can provide a supportive network to further advance such sustainable and resilient forms of higher education', in other words, in addition to the physical connections to space, place and each other, they hope that, at some future point, connections will be made through networks of others around the country and indeed the globe.

So, what exactly do the SSC scholars do?

> [w]e've run an entry level evening class called 'The Social Science Imagination' (after C. Wright-Mills's 1957 book The Sociological Imagination), which is an open course run by and for people who want to develop a critical understanding of the social world through social-scientific inquiry. The class proceeds from scholars' everyday problematics to theoretical critique. Through this emerging curriculum, we take up Mills's key challenge: how can individuals who appear powerless change and transform wider social structures in ways that are progressive and humanizing?
> (Members of the Social Science Centre, 2013: 66)

It can be seen from the initial project that this does not seem to be a simple HE course. The course does seem to support the argument that they are practicing a 'higher learning orientated towards intellectual values of critical thinking, experimentation, sharing, peer review, co-operation, collaboration, openness, debate and constructive disagreement point towards a better future for us all' (Social Science Centre, 2012). Note the description of 'higher *learning*' as opposed to 'higher *education*'; this is because, as Neary insists,

> we don't claim to be a university. The title Social Science Centre links us directly to the Social Centre movement that emerged in Europe from the 1970s as radical spaces that sought to provide community based and collective alternatives to state provision, or to the lack of it.
> (Mike Neary in Class War University, 2013)

In addition, the SSC web site states that

> the SSC was born in 2010, out of a desire to preserve public space for social science education and research after the present Conservative-Liberal Government withdrew funding for the teaching of social science and other forms of knowledge deemed 'non-essential' in English Universities.... We are also concerned that the promises of the university are being impoverished by a system of higher education that is increasingly orientated towards satisfying the perceived needs of business and industry, and that embraces short-termist, highly competitive, profit-driven motives of the capitalist market
> (Social Science Centre, 2012)

And Neary further qualifies this by adding that

> the SSC is not a demand for the state to provide higher education, but a recognition that revolutionary education cannot be provided by the

capitalist state; and, therefore, we have no other option but to establish our own necessary revolutionary alternative form of higher education.
(Conversation, 2013)

On that point, I will now introduce the Student as Producer (SaP) initiative at the University of Lincoln; this initiative was of particular interest to the story of this work as the University posited it as a way of being and teaching in political opposition to the student as consumer model of higher education, thus it claimed to be practicing a countervailing ideology to the increasingly normative one. This means that, for the project here, it potentially had the possibility of enacting a trajectory of learning from the street to the university and back again. However, the initiative did not go that far, nor did it claim to, however, the potential was there to practice higher education otherwise, and introduce a solidarity loop required to complete a type of 'action research' cycle that is explored within these pages. It is also worthy of note at this point to point out that the main protagonist on the introduction of this initiative to the University was, again, Professor Mike Neary. This may be thought of as a contradiction, however, Neary described to me how he felt that the SSC and SaP were two ends of the same project, a project to dissolve the walls of the university.

The Student as Producer project (2010) at the University of Lincoln was described on the web site as

> Restat[ing] the meaning and purpose of higher education by reconnecting the core activities of universities, i.e., research and teaching, in a way that consolidates and substantiates the values of academic life. The core values of academic life are reflected in the quality of students that the University of Lincoln aims to produce. Student as Producer emphasises the role of the students as collaborators in the production of knowledge. The capacity for Student as Producer is grounded in the human attributes of creativity and desire, so that students can recognise themselves in a world of their own design.

It claimed to be, moreover, a 'policy of ... research-engaged teaching' that was *encouraged* throughout the University's teaching activities and as such was not enacted by all members of the teaching staff. According to the web site (Student as Producer, 2010), there were eight key features of the program:

- Discovery: Student as Producer
- Technology in Teaching: Digital Scholarship
- Space and Spatiality: Learning Landscapes in Higher Education
- Assessment: Active Learners in Communities of Practice
- Research and Evaluation: Scholarship of Teaching and Learning
- Student Voice: Diversity, Difference and Dissensus

- Support for research based learning through expert engagement with information resources
- Creating the Future: Employability, Enterprise, Beyond Employability, Postgraduate

The explanation of these features could be found in full on the web site, but for the purposes of this book, an overview of what was meant by them is sufficient. The key features were, it was claimed, aimed at variously creating work that is 'collaborative', 'driven by challenging, open ended questions', making use of formal and informal spaces and ensuring inclusivity and enhanced experience for all involved. Teachers become facilitators of learning and students take ownership of and responsibility for their own work. In this sense, it was claimed that commons were created, both physical and virtual, to enhance opportunities for collaboration and engagement with others outside of the university. Students were encouraged to carry out activities that demonstrated their research skills for assessment, and staff were asked to engage in research into their own pedagogy. According to the literature they produced, there was a great emphasis on student voice, which is 'dedicated to developing a community of learners and teachers which is respectful of diversity and difference, allowing for the space of dissensus and disagreement, driven by engaged and participatory pedagogies'.

It should be remembered that SaP was a funded project[1] at a traditionally organised university. That is, The University of Lincoln still operated under a top-down hierarchical structure. Students were still paying £9000 per year tuition fees and the University still had traditional admissions policies for its type. As mentioned, the project was made possible by Professor Mike Neary, the then Dean of Teaching and Learning and the Centre for Educational Research and Development. It also required the agreement of the University Vice Chancellor, it was not instigated by the will of the students themselves. It is therefore, a very different organisation and pedagogical structure than the other sites and therefore its potential to be more than it was, was perhaps inevitably very limited. However, it was important to include it as firstly, it claimed to be politically part of the same project as the SSC, that of resistance to the neoliberalisation of the university (Neary & Amsler, 2012). Second, it could potentially have been an emergent form of top-down critical and popular education due to its claimed ethos of resistance, interruption into the normative pedagogical flow, and its potential to introduce a more revolutionary form of teaching and learning into existing institutions.

Now with an understanding of the three sites under investigation I would like to turn to an examination of the role of research itself in 'Making Hope Possible', in creating a robust and resilient movement for change by contributing to a 'grand action research type cycle', and examine the question of how might the researcher understand their role in making change? The next chapter, then, rethinks the role of the researcher and of research, framing the politically underpinned constructivist grounded theory into a bricolage methodology in order to better understand the three sites and their potential in the struggle for a better world.

**Note**

1 The project was funded by the Higher Education Academy under the National Teacher Fellows Project programme.

# 2 Social change and the political academic
## Creating a place for research in social movements

> Walking around the camp at St. Paul's it seems that there must be so many stories, so many justifications for being here, so many reasons to come. People are here to learn, that's for sure, but they're also here to commune, to have relationships of whatever kind develops. They are here because their stories need to be told, to each other, to the wider population, and yes, even to researchers. It is a duty then, surely, for us as researchers to capture the stories, to give them flight, to marry them with theory, to validate them in the only way researchers know how, to turn them into knowledge.
>
> (Fieldwork Journal, 2012)

The above thoughts from my original fieldwork journal speaks of the role of the researcher in these actions, the role as witness and as disseminator of knowledges that otherwise might be flightless. Therefore, discussed in this chapter are thoughts on what that means, on what academics can do to be feathers in the wings of the voices of those trying to change the world? The questions asked in the previous chapter bring up these issues concerning the very structure of the research. Notions such as what Occupy actually signified and what was being occupied, the idea that the SSC could have the potential to be a revolutionary space of learning and what the possible potential of an initiative like Student as Producer was.

Pertinent here is the question that Schostak & Schostak (2013: *vii*) ask: 'So what today is frightening? There is much. And in their writing people either address it directly, indirectly or ignore it as if it were not there'. This book tries not to ignore what is frightening and attempts to address it directly as positioned researcher. The initial interest of the research was the pedagogy in Occupy, this seemed to me to warrant a type of case study approach as the space inhabited by the Occupiers seemed to create an intrinsic case (Stake, 1978, 1995, 2000) for study, as the 'case' was what was interesting. However, in studying Occupy in terms of a single case, a great deal was learnt about the potentials and possibilities of other cases of alternatively organised pedagogy. An additional attraction of using a case study approach was that as Sturman (1994: 26) insists, 'the distinguishing feature of case study is the belief that human systems develop a characteristic of wholeness or integrity and are not simply a loose collection of traits'. However, it may be important to think anew about these notions of 'wholeness' and 'integrity' here. The bounded site here, as well as being a physical place, bounded in a practical sense, is a space of contested discourses, a 'bounding' of debates, within the physical space. And, on the nature of wholeness, it is the constitution of integrity and contestation of the idea of set human systems. Therefore, the 'belief' assumed about human systems becomes contested and vibrant, rather than static, assured and able to colour the research process.[1]

Within the bounded case of the Occupy LSX encampment, I wished to seek, as Star (2007: 77) describes, a 'methodological place that was faithful to human experience and that would help me sift through the chaos of meanings and produce the eureka of new, powerful explanations', in the newly imagined case this notion of human experience becomes experiences *in reaction* – in reaction to injustice, to agonism, to difference, where wholeness and integrity melt away to be replaced by countervailing discourses and the utopian imaginary. This description confirmed, in my mind, Kemmis' (1980: 119) point that case study 'always reminds us of the active and interventive character of the research process' and further indicated that case study was the appropriate way to think of this project. This was supported, in my opinion, by Adelman *et al.*'s (1980: 60) insistence that 'case studies are a "step to action". They begin in a world of action and contribute to it. Their insights may be directly interpreted and put to use'. In specific educational settings, Stenhouse (1988: 50) has this to add:

> many researchers using case study methods are concerned ... with the understanding of educational action.... They are concerned to enrich the thinking and discourse of educators either by the development of educational theory or by refinement of prudence through the systematic and reflective documentation of evidence.

For me this explanation is important for the 'case study' of Occupy London, but also in the overall argument in this book, as what is implied here is that the case study of Occupy London allows us to understand educational action and the subsequent extended thought experiment, developed through the other sites, and the creation of an imagined 'action research type cycle' from one to the other. In addition, it allows what is described here as enriching the thinking and discourse of educators by the development of educational theory. It also uncovers questions about the nature of the educational act, the political implications of that act and how delimited the thinking about education and its intimate relationship to politics could be.

This chapter, then, serves as an extended exploration of an activist methodology. Extended because it sits alongside a justification of researching social movements as outside researcher, rather than as insider activist. I wish to create a method that Bryant and Charmaz (2007: 1) describe as encouraging 'researchers' persistent interaction with their data,[1] while remaining constantly involved with their emerging analysis'.

When Occupy erupted, the people there seemed to be performing an educational experiment. This created a natural field of inquiry for me as a scholar in, and practitioner of, critical pedagogy, as they set up and self-organised education, quite purposefully it seemed, without manipulation from experts. This manipulation would, of course, have rendered the research useless for understanding *organic* and popular pedagogy.

I agree with Clarke and Friese (2007: 364) when they say that 'society as a whole can be conceptualised as consisting of ... arenas that are constantly in flux' although for the purpose here, it might be helpful to think more in terms of 'process' rather than 'flux'. Clarke and Friese go on to say that 'the arenas framework offers a way of understanding the *ongoing* and *situated organisation of negotiations:* unstable, contingent, hailing how things can be otherwise and maybe soon'. Adelman *et al.* (1980: 59) say 'the best case studies are capable of offering support to alternative interpretations'; this I have taken to mean both the interpretations the research makes and the interpretations of social relations being attempted through the pedagogy of Occupy. I would argue that this framing can be understood here as a way of grounding theory, through a specific method. However, what this research has attempted to do is to borrow from constructivist grounded theory method in order to create theory that is grounded through an iterative process within the written theory, and data – or 'living theory' (Shukaitis & Graeber, 2007; Suoranta, 2010). However, it is more the spirit of grounded theory method that has been adopted than the actual method (Bryant & Charmaz, 2007), as it is framed in a political manner and takes into account the messiness of life, social action and research as only forms of radical research, here termed as bricolage, can.

If we view the social world/arena of Occupy as a layer, or mosaic, as Clarke and Friese suggest, it is possible that the internal layers might be initially be made visible through the exploration of issues such as, *how* one researches a quickly emerging and evolving phenomenon such as Occupy, from a pedagogical point of view. How can that be done without ignoring such issues as the motivation for the initiation of the project (Graeber, 2011), the politics of such an education (Neary & Amsler, 2012) and the surrounding public and organic pedagogy that was encompassed in the educational space that was being produced (Lefebvre, 1991)? In addition, I argue that if this emergent pedagogy were to be usefully witnessed, the theories, questions and answers it produced had to be of some *ongoing* use (Jardine, 2006). I felt that the precise research questions would come as I proceeded, grounded in the data, emerging from a critical interest in the pedagogy as a whole. This would happen through reading and re-reading the data and the associated theory, juxtaposing their messages and stories, and keeping track of the thoughts they provoked and the emerging themes they contained. If the social world was as messy and complex as Occupy seemed to suggest it was, I felt that the research needed a paradigm that encompassed the unveiling of the individual life worlds and an ability to juxtapose those stories without subjugating the context of these evolving and intensified subjectivities. A radical way of looking at research was needed.

Of course, as Kincheloe and Berry (2004: 31) point out, 'no research act or interpretive task begins on virgin territory. Countless acts of meaning-making have already shaped the terrain that researchers explore', so I acknowledge that the decisions made about the research were driven by my own experiences of schooling and education and the tensions that reside there, my experience of social movements and my hope that Occupy was, indeed, something pedagogically and politically different.

I saw the process of this research as useful witnessing. It has been an empirically grounded thought journey. A journey that takes a line through the entire education spectrum, in snapshot, looking, as Holloway (2010) insists should happen, for the lines of continuity, the cracks between the explosive and easily seen moments of interruption in the normative practices of what education is often assumed to be. Attempting to connect the dots in the way that the experiences, conversations and fortuitous meetings led me to connect them. This is part of the beginning of the practice of what some (Denzin & Lincoln, 2000; Kincheloe & Berry, 2004; Kincheloe, *et al.*, 2011) call 'the bricolage'.

This chapter, then, critically engages with the form of radical research that was employed, in the hope that it makes sense of the standpoint and of the utopian thinking behind the dual narratives mentioned in the introduction to this text. The story of this book, then, is based on a bricolage approach, which encourages multiple ways of seeing from different disciplines, creating a post-disciplinary ethos, and potentially allowing more voices to be heard within the research through a juxtaposition of storytelling and experience. I would argue that this ethos supports the notion of radical democracy as it allows for complexity, contention, imagination and the temporality of knowledges. This form of radical research was employed because it allows an exploration of a mix of the politics and pedagogy that are essential to the way the sites work. It also allows the use of a variety of critical tools, such as the mixture of pedagogical and political theory, imagination and creativity, and a rigorous, radical openness, in order to interpret the politics and pedagogy so that their potential for creating new forms of organisation can be imagined. I will begin here with an exploration of what it means to begin the life long process of becoming a bricoleur (Kincheloe & Berry, 2004).

Marx, writing with Engels, once famously said, 'the philosophers [and here we might include much social science research] have only *interpreted* the world, in various ways: the point, however, is to *change* it' (Marx & Engels, 1846/ 2007, p. 123). This point from Marx illustrates the aims of both research activism and bricolage. This notion of assisting, or perhaps even initiating, change, led me to an exploration of bricolage as a research methodology that claims at its centre a desire for and a commitment to social change (Denzin & Lincoln, 2000; Kincheloe & Berry, 2004; Kincheloe, *et al*, 2011). Bricolage is the name for just one of the methodologies that claims this commitment; there are other modes of radical research (see, for example, Brydon-Miller, 2009; Denzin, 2010; Schostak & Schostak, 2008, 2013; Shukaitis, et al., 2007). I also felt that the research method should complement the phenomena under investigation (Earl, 2013) and thus turned to this radical approach to create symmetry between object and method.

It is a *beginning* of bricolage I have attempted and I will continue to develop on this journey. Kincheloe and Berry (2004) insist, to be a bricoleur one must be fully conversant with multiple methodologies and multiple ways of viewing, adding theoretical and empirical knowledges along the way. They also stress that 'bricolage implies the fictive and imaginative elements of the presentation of all formal research' (p. 1), elements that I have utilised, as shall be seen. This approach lies at the heart of carrying out a bricolage study as Kincheloe and Berry (2004: 3) state:

> bricoleurs understand that their interaction with the objects of their inquiries is always complicated, mercurial, unpredictable and, of course, complex. Such conditions negate the practice of planning research strategies in advance. In lieu of such rationalisation of the process, bricoleurs enter into the research act as methodological negotiators.

Bricolage, as conceived here, is a *multidisciplinary* approach (Denzin & Lincoln, 2000; Kincheloe & Berry, 2004; Kincheloe et al, 2011), or what Schostak and Schostak (2008) might call 'post-disciplinary', as the research hoped to 'maintain a radical openness ... a more encompassing approach' (p. 8). It attempts to be a pursuit that it is 'inquiry-driven rather than discipline driven', with 'the stress on the construction of knowledge' and 'the focus on the interrelationship between knowing, doing, being and relating' (Montuori, 2008: *xi*). I have attempted, as Schostak and Schostak (2013: 15) suggest should be done, to allow the 'discourses that could only be heard elsewhere', in the spaces between the tents in Tent City, or the under the canvas of TCU, to be heard in my work in order to 'bring to the fore a newly opened space, a new agenda'. These voices were the voices of individuals who wanted change, who began with Holloway's (1995, 2003, 2005) scream and moved into the square outside St. Paul's. They began to constitute a Multitude, in Hardt and Negri's (2004) terms, wherein they expressed the desire for a world of equality and freedom. They not only called for an open and inclusive democratic society but also experimented with the means for providing it. They became what Schostak and Schostak (2013) call a textual public, a public that creates its own intertextuality through the spaces it creates and the discourses it explores. Those spaces are further composed in writing, such as this book, and it is the hope that those spaces will be further (de/re)composed in other and future texts: infiltrating the conversations, discussions and debates of everyday life, creating a juxtaposition between the politics of dissent and the politics of everyday life. This is the intertextual composition of this work, by necessity it is inter/post disciplinary in order to (de/re)compose the public text of Occupy.

It is due to these efforts, this attempt; the multidisciplinary approach with a trans/post-disciplinary ethos, and the commitment to assisting change and creating countervailing discourse through reporting the voices absent from the normative discourse, that I feel justified to declare that I have begun the journey towards bricoleur and to endeavour to capture what Kincheloe and Berry (2004: 17) call generating 'questions previously unimagined', unimagined by those providing the case study and other sites and unimagined at the start of this enquiry. I have chosen, here, to refer to the elastic boundaries of bricolage as post-disciplinary, considering the context.

Learning in social movements has, of course, been studied before, most notably by authors such as John Holst (2002), Griff Foley (2004) and Bud Hall (2012) and subsequently scholars such as Choudry (2015) and others. However, this research attempts to take this type of study in a different direction to look at the flow lines (Holloway, 2010), the attempts at change and the nature of the apparently politicised pedagogy, between the organic pedagogy in Occupy, the claimed cooperative pedagogy in the SSC and the institutionalised productive ethos to the pedagogy of Lincoln University as parts of a line of continuity. The exploration of this line of continuity is the reason bricolage was chosen as a guiding methodology because I would argue, as Denzin (2010: 15) does, that we are all, indeed, 'interpretive bricoleurs stuck in the present working against the past as we move into a politically charged and challenging future'. Bricolage, as I will argue, allows for this interpretation, allows for the playful and thought-provoking examination of the politically charged and challenging future, thus potentially adding to the discourses on change and becoming an exercise in useful witnessing and producing useful knowledge.

So what *exactly* is bricolage? The etymology of the word from the Oxford English Dictionary (2007: 291) is from the French: the bricoleur who does odd jobs, who tinkers about, or bricolage: 'construction or creation from whatever is immediately available for use'. Bricolage as methodology however goes beyond the dictionary definition, it has that element of the activist using whatever is at hand; and thus similarly, the researcher uses whatever is at hand in the fieldwork experience to focus research activity and construct understandings through engaging with a multiplicity of sources. It contains the elements of what Shukaitis and Graeber (2007: 11) call 'militant co-research', in that it has 'Thoughts. Provocations. Explorations.' and is a form of 'investigation and social research that expand[s] possibilities for political action, proliferating tactics of resistance through the constituent power of the imagination'. These are some common aspects of various descriptions of bricolage: imagination, provocations, explorations and possibilities for political action (Denzin, 2010; Kincheloe & Berry, 2004; Kincheloe *et al.* 2011; Kincheloe & Tobin, 2006; Lincoln, 2001; Pinar, 2001 among others). They are also constituents of other radical research methodologies (Denzin, 2010; Howe & MacGillivary, 2009; Schratz & Walker, 1995; Schostak & Schostak, 2008, 2013; Whitehead & McNiff, 2006, to name but a few). Due to the eclectic nature of bricolage, I will attempt to encompass the thinking of several authors of radical research methods under the title of bricolage for expedience and simplicity, and of course, continuity. I argue that I am 'permitted' to do this, as bricolage is both subversive (Kincheloe & Berry, 2004) and transgressive:

> transgression generally refers to discursive actions which cross boundaries or violate limits.... Transgressions that are permitted or escape the notice and discipline of boundary-policing authorities push the boundaries further (toward those resisting or away, depending on the eventual response of the authorities). In other words, transgression redefines lines of distinction, giving new meaning to identities and social practices
> (Foust, 2010: 3)

It is my view that the bricoleur needs to be open to being both subversive and transgressive in bricolage's post-disciplinary approach as 'the strict disciplinarian operating in a reductionistic framework chained to the prearranged procedures of a monological way of seeing is less likely to produce frame shattering research than the synergised bricoleur' (Kincheloe & Berry, 2004: 76). I would argue that it is necessary, at this continuing socio-political juncture that 'frame shattering' research is produced, that the background is framed in order to transgress that frame (Schostak & Schostak, 2013); otherwise, research potentially becomes a reproductive endeavour and loses its radical edge. However, Schostak and Schostak (2008: 14) ask, 'is it really possible to see radically?' The question is pertinent because as Schostak and Schostak go on to say,

> being radical implies some counter-stance to the world as it is, a stance that is active, engaged and committed to bringing about change. But this demands some conception of the world as it 'should' be and where 'I' am in it.

This research, carried out under bricolage's post-disciplinary ontology, attempts this. This vision of the counter-stance starts at the point where the topic for research is chosen:

> even the decisions researchers make about what to study reflect ... political and ideological dynamics ... the problems and issues that are chosen by researchers are marked by subjective judgements about whose problems are deemed important
> (Kincheloe & Berry, 2004: 34)

In my case, my understanding was that Occupy told the social world that the problems of the 99% were important and that we should do something *educational* about it – that to me was worth exploring, ideologically and politically. I understood this unfolding 'event', 'protest', 'occupation', whatever you wish to call it, as an organic curriculum, unfolding in public, with a dynamic that was worth listening to, observing, studying and understanding. Not just for itself but also for its wider implications about, and tensions with, schooling. So what does a person, failed by the school system do – a person who has felt the blow of inequality and misfitting (Hardt & Negri, 2012; Holloway, 2010; Merrifield, 2011a) in the system that is provided to help us conform? Perhaps they raise campaigns about their unequal status – I know I did –perhaps they feel a 'calling' to join others who misfit. Perhaps the very system that fails so many people creates Hardt and Negri's (2004) Multitude, the very people that can, and may, make a difference. Perhaps. However, perhaps, for many there is no such calling, just a future of trying to better conform? The mantras of control and hegemony fixed in their minds; consume and accumulate until you are full, which we will make sure you never are. My answer was to turn to researching those who join the Multitude and attempt to become revolutionary subjects (Hardt & Negri, 2012) and attempt to share their stories and assist their development.

The study of Occupy, seemed to suggest that schooling, or a lack of it, was at least in part producing the very Multitude that Hardt and Negri talk about as the revolutionary subject. As one Occupier put it 'you probably don't want to talk to me, I've had no education at all really. Mind you I was reading Chomsky and thinking about what Castells said the other day ...' (John). I met many people at Occupy who had not been 'successful' enough at school to be taught not to question, not to be non-conformist, not to be critical thinkers, so they did not know it was 'wrong'. Perhaps it is their stories that can create that juxtaposition between politics and education? However, there is a caution here, not to romanticise Occupy as a movement of the unschooled. A great many of the Occupiers were graduates of the system, students from all levels of formal educational, however, as shall be discussed later, there were differences between the successfully schooled and the (mis)educated.

Denzin (2009: 215) insists that 'it is necessary to re-engage the promise of qualitative research as a form of radical democratic practice.... Today we understand that we write culture and that writing is not an innocent practice'. I would always similarly argue that writing cannot be innocent; writing is done for a reason, to convince, to explore, to convert. In this case, my narrative hopes to encourage thoughts of alternatives, to create debate, to 'identify a transgressive alternative [which] invites us to consider more (or robustly debate) a broader range of effective resistance at a time in which resistance is becoming more eclectic and more necessary' (Foust, 2010: 9). From my point of view, my individual experience, education and research acts are an attempt to be part of that 'effective resistance' and the post disciplinary nature of bricolage allows exploration of education to be 'eclectic' therefore potentially rendering it 'more necessary'.

## Grounding the theory

> Going into the field, as methodological negotiator was difficult, I didn't really know exactly what I wanted to know. It was a strange feeling, I wanted to

know what they knew, what they were experiencing and then I wanted to put that together with what I knew, what others knew, what thinkers had thought. There just seemed to be too much going on for me to fence it in with theoretical judgements, I wanted to understand their experience through my human senses. I wanted to use those senses, rather than my intellect to understand. And what an assault on the senses it was, there was a feeling of being lost and found all at the same time. A feeling of things in flux, in process, it was edgy and exciting, but the progress was slow and the debates sometimes heated, sometimes stinted. They knew so much, more than I did about politics, about economics, sometimes it was frightening. The job of sifting through the experiences I was hearing and having myself for something coherent was going to be a real task. It looked like the theories I call home are at work, coming alive, being real. But what theories, and how? In general the theories I was hearing through the stories of lived experience were those of a broad critical pedagogy, but there was sometimes more, sometimes less. I would have to find a few in-depth theories and paradigms just to make sense of what was going on.
(Fieldwork Journal 2012)

The process of engaging in the research and attempting to follow the bricolage methodology was complex. I borrowed a grounded theory principle at the beginning, that of entering the field without first deciding on a theoretical framework. I knew roughly what I was looking for, and wanted to be open to finding, or discovering something else, so I entered the field with that as my plan. I was armed with a camera to record the visual images, in case they were the most telling medium; a voice recorder to capture, not only voices but also ambient sound in case that was illuminating; a note pad and pen, to write, to draw, to doodle if necessary what I felt, heard, saw and experienced, and I wondered/wandered in. This, I felt was the freedom of bricolage, I could discover as a stranger, with no vested interest in this piece of information or that. I wondered/wandered around, I took photographs (these images served as a personal memory jogger in the end), I made notes and I was able to conduct interviews because people wanted to talk.

After this first round of 'getting lost' in order to find something unexpected, I started to look more seriously at the theory, what theory was it that gave me the most insight into what I had discovered. I felt that bricolage allowed me to understand the theory through the data and the data through the theory as I mixed the collecting and collating of each, right through the research period, in this way I attempted to ensure that the exploration of each was grounded in the other. One event/discovery/happening led me onto the next and I was able to understand that I could never reach the end of the discovery, but that what I had discovered was important to the study and would tell me where to look next, what methods to put into practice, what was a scintillating tangent and what was relevant to the story the research was producing. I allowed serendipity to be a guide as much as my planning and careful consideration of where the research was leading. Bricolage allowed me the freedom to wonder/wander and to take every opportunity that presented itself to learn more. Kincheloe and Tobin express an important factor of this way of conducting research thusly:

> In this complex context we understand that even when we use diverse methods to produce multiple perspectives on the world, different observers will produce different interpretations of what they perceive. Given different values, different ideologies, and different positions in the web of reality, different individuals will interpret what is happening differently
> 
> (Kincheloe & Tobin, 2006: 7)

And serendipity intervened with the process of bricolage in many ways:

> I was informed of a conference where some Occupy people were speaking in London. The people that spoke from the movement were instrumental in setting up Tent City University (TCU) so I was excited to hear them speak. Their presentations were interesting but it felt as if there was a great deal more to hear about the processes they went through during the encampment, so I set up a meeting with one of them a few weeks later. That meeting turned into a series of meetings with various people on various topics, the person from the conference set me up with interviews from people who understood Occupy as pedagogical, as well as people who did not and never attended any workshops or talks at TCU, and one person who had left the movement disillusioned with the whole thing. This meant I was able to look at what was being learnt from several points of view. Some of the interviews were online, either email or Skype, some face to face over a coffee.
> 
> (Fieldwork Journal, 2011–2013)

Glaser and Strauss (2009: 4) state, 'theory based on data can usually not be completely refuted by more data or replaced by another theory. Since it is too intimately linked to data, it is destined to last despite its inevitable modification and reformulation'. What Glaser and Strauss are saying here is that their theory is linked to data through a continual process of testing and refining. Employing processes of comparison and contrast, the theory that emerges is the product of systematic testing and therefore grounded in the empirical data. In this study, I did not use a full grounded theory approach, as I shall explore. There is, again, a complex ontology at work here; the study did indeed attempt to create theory that is 'intimately linked to the data', both pre and post full analysis, and one hopes that it is, indeed 'destined to last' in some guise. However, I would also welcome its 'inevitable modification and reformulations' because one accepts Kincheloe and Berry's (2004: 100) question of 'if reality is shaped by the interaction of countless factors, then how can the bricoleur account for them all?' Further, their answer that 'there is no way to account for them all and no way the bricoleur should attempt such a Sisyphean task. Only a radical reductionist would claim such a feat is possible in her quest for a single, universal truth'. Not only that, but also, 'bricoleurs must realise that knowledge is always in process, developing, culturally specific and power-inscribed' (Kincheloe & Berry, 2004: 79). Therefore, one of the main reasons for grounding the theory in the data for this research was that as Kincheloe and Berry (2004: 16) insist, bricoleurs should 'commit their knowledge work to helping address the ideological and informational needs of marginalised groups or individuals'. This meant that for this study, one of the essential tasks was to try to understand a way in which the experimental, prefigurative politics and the emergent pedagogy could be integrated together in a coherent way. In effect, the review of the pertinent literature was not so much a traditional literature review but more an attempt to gain insight into the thinking from literature that seemed to illuminate the thinking in the movements and to attempt to build a realm of possible practices, organisational structures and their implications, utilising the fictive and imaginative elements of bricolage mentioned earlier. This attempted exploration was achieved through a general reading of the interview transcripts and other data sources to attempt to understand what pedagogy was underpinning the immanent politics. Another reason this was felt necessary was the non/post-ideological stance that Occupy was making (see particularly Occupy LSX, 2011a, 2011b), which made understanding which political theory to use to identify the ideology behind the pedagogical methods and curriculum open to interpretation. This led me to the open Marxism of Holloway (2010) and others (for example, Backhaus, 1992; Bonefeld, 1992, 1995; Clarke, 1992; Cleaver, 1992; Dalla Costa, 1995; Gunn, 1992 and others) and to theories of commonism (see for example Hardt & Negri, 2009; Neary & Winn, 2012; Shantz, 2013) and also explorations of pedagogy from critical pedagogy (see Freire, various; Giroux, 1988, 2001, 2011; Macrine, 2009; Shor, 1992, 1996; Shor & Freire, 1987 among others) through critical thinking and social movement learning (Brookfield, 2001, 2005; Brookfield & Holst, 2011; Hall, 2012; Holst, 2002 and others), right to the musings of Rancière (1991), in order to attempt to understand and contextualise the happenings in the movement and see any lines of continuity throughout the case studies. These theorists have been used to explain and be exemplars of the pedagogy that was witnessed and as extensions, allowing for the more in-depth analysis of the pedagogy and experiences of the Occupiers in this book. This attempt to understand, from the struggles of the subjects of the inquiry, wishes to pay homage to their voices as well as being a method of theory generation, because as Shukaitis and Graeber (2007: 37) say about protests and movements, 'these moments embody not just practices to adapt and creatively redeploy, but are in themselves ways of understanding the world and forms of research in action'. It therefore made sense to me to explore theory from *their* understanding, or at least my interpretation of it, because both the movement and the research were trying to generate a 'politics of the local, and a utopian politics of possibility (Madison, 1998) that redress social injustices and imagine a radical democracy that is not yet (Weems, 2002: 3)' (Denzin, 2010: 15). It is also argued here, as in Kincheloe and Berry (2004: 6), that 'while empirical research is obviously necessary, its process of production constitutes only one step of a larger and more rigorous process of inquiry. Bricolage subverts the finality of the empirical act'. In this work, this subversion, initiates a 'conversation' between the data and the immanent theory, creating a dialectic relationship, an intertextuality, wherein one dialogues with the other, until some sense of understanding is reached. This acceptance of 'some sense' of understanding is encompassed by the notion that 'the most important social, psychological and educational problems that confront us are untidy and complicated' (Kincheloe & Berry, 2004: 33). In addition, Whitehead and McNiff (2006: 41) insist 'the work needs to show its own generative potential, in that new learning emerges from previous learning, and any new learning already holds within itself its own potential for improved learning'. In other words, the research theory generation employs itself as only a stage of the learning that is already taking place within the groups and individuals whose struggle and experience is generating the theory grounded in their doings. It is my argument that this posits the research as a 'grand scale' action research project, for example:

> the core values of action research have been defined as respect for people and for the knowledge and experience they bring to the research process, a belief in the ability of democratic processes to achieve positive social change, and a commitment to action
> (Brydon-Miller, 2009: 244)

Or this from Kindon *et al.* (2010: 11):

> Today, Action Research ... [is] the most common term used to describe research that involves: a participatory, democratic process concerned with developing practical knowing in the pursuit of worthwhile human purposes, grounded in a participatory world view ... [and bringing] together action and reflection, theory and practice, in participation with others in the pursuit of practical issues of concern to people, and more generally the flourishing of individual persons and communities.
> (Cited in Reason & Bradbury, 2006: 1)

Obviously, this piece of research was not action research traditionally constituted, the main difference between this bricolage research and action, or participatory action research, is that the 'participants' are participating in a different way. They are still positioned as research subjects, but their doings, their experience, their voices ground the research in order for it to be of use to them at another time – unlike the immediacy contained within normative action research. For example, one of the Occupiers I talked to said that when the occupation of St. Paul's began, they 'hit the ground running' and that they had 'no time for reflection about what they were doing or to think about the actions and consequences'. She said that they felt that 'anything was possible, we could and would change the world, the feeling was so positive, we didn't think of the need to record anything about our practice, we just ran to keep up with things as they were happening' (Angie). In my envisioning of this broader cycle this is where the researcher comes in as part of the 'action research cycle', to record, to witness, to reflect. It is this grounding of the theory for a 'grand' action research cycle which also necessitated the questions being emergent from that process. I did not have a 'freshly pressed' set of clean questions when I began, another case of the transgressive and subversive behaviour of bricolage. In my view and method, the questions had to emerge from the research process in order for them to be less about my research and more about the usefulness of the whole endeavour; what questions, when an answer was attempted, would lead to theories and possible suggestions for further development of the pedagogy being practiced. This is because, as Kincheloe & Tobin (2006: 8) insist, 'social theory viewed in relation to pedagogical theory ... profoundly enhances the ability of educators as critical thinkers to evaluate the worth of particular educational purposes, public knowledge policies, articulations of the curriculum, and evaluation practices', and, I would argue, this includes learning for change and resistance. Kincheloe and Berry (2004: 26) have this to add:

> knowledge in this process orientated context has a past and a future; researchers have traditionally viewed a phenomenon in a particular stage of its development. Bricoleurs operating on a terrain of complexity understand that they must transcend this tendency and struggle to comprehend the process of which an object of study is part.

I understand this as important as it speaks to the politics of the movements – the revolutionary moment (protest) versus the revolutionary process (prefiguration) – and reflects the processness of the commonist (Shantz, 2013) anarchism (Graeber, 2011) seemingly practiced by most of the social actors examined here. Therefore, there are no claims of single truth in this work, no great proclamations of final answers, only a recognition that it attempts to be part of a reflective and evolving process from one point of view (Coffey, 1999; Kincheloe & Berry, 2004; Whitehead & McNiff, 2006) and an attempt to engage with ongoing conversations about revolutionary pedagogy and its necessity for social change (Cowden & Singh, 2013; Darder, 2002; Peters & Freeman-Moir, 2006; The Edu-Factory Collective, 2009; Trifonas, 2000). There is humility in bricolage that allows the researcher to appreciate this via an understanding of the 'power-saturated' nature of any knowledge: 'This is a political and ethical position.... It understands that knowledge is power' (Denzin, 2010: 26). However, as Kincheloe and Berry (2004: 71) argue, this is also an essential ingredient in the post disciplinary ethos of bricolage itself:

> in confronting the regressive dynamics of mainstream disciplinarity bricoleurs push those within the disciplines to consider modes of understanding

that fall outside the traditional conventions. Drawing upon critical theory, bricoleurs work towards an evolving criticality that melds several social-theoretical traditions in the effort to understand the way power operates to perpetuate itself.

I would argue that this understanding must pertain not only to the topic of the research, but also be attentive to the way in which research is written and what the research wishes to achieve in the longer term. A warning then concerning writing this way:

> the objective knowledge and the validated research processes used by reductionists are always sociologically negotiated in a power saturated context. Assertions that knowledge is permanent and universal are undermined [by bricolage] and the stability of meaning is subverted. Forces of domination will often reject such historically conscious and power-literate insights, as such awarenesses undermine the unchallenged knowledge assertions of power wielders. Critical hermeneutics, bricoleurs come to understand, can be quite dangerous when deployed in the sacred temples of knowledge production.
> (Kincheloe & Berry, 2004: 12)

And as Schostak and Schostak (2013: 20) add,

> what is at stake in writing is the overlooked perspective, absent from the articulations of histories when written by the powerful. It is there that the revolution resides, not as a finalised or finalisable vision but as the voice to be heard.

This speaks to bricolage's dialectical approach to research narratives as it 'lends the word "tentative" to the bricolage – the knowledge produced by bricoleurs is tentative rather than final' (Kincheloe & Berry, 2004: 94). Kincheloe and Berry add that

> since in the zone of complexity no fact is self-evident and no representation is 'pure', any knowledge worker who believes research narratives are simple truths is operating in a naïve domain. Thus, bricoleurs assert that there are fictive elements to all representations and narratives.
> (Kincheloe & Berry, 2004: 28)

I concur and argue that there need to be fictive elements, acts of imagination and furtive thought experiments; this is what gives new theories, new knowledge, new understanding, and allows the process to continue. It allows the practice of radical research that 'implies a radical politics because it raises questions that make the powerful feel uncomfortable, even threatened' (Schostak & Schostak 2008: 1).

Another element of thinking through bricolage brought me to a feeling that the ethics of my research needed close examination. One area of this examination was that the legalistic relationship that researchers enter into when they ask the subjects of research to sign informed consent forms was inappropriate in this context. It seemed that this would produce an unequal relationship (Brydon-Miller, 2009) from the start, where my 'expertise' and standing as a researcher may have been interpreted as putting me in a superior position to the research subjects. In addition, I felt that it took away any power that they had as subjective storytellers or individuals with experience worth sharing into mere informants. This feeling was amplified when the people I spoke to welcomed me into what was essentially their community and were pleased to tell me their stories and explore their experiences with a third party, despite the repression they often suffered and the hostility they were experiencing from the media. My thinking about how the ethics of the research worked was further developed by the number of people I spoke to asking if they too could record our interaction, more on this later. I explored ideas on ethics and whilst according to Kincheloe and Berry (2004) bricolage is at its heart an ethical pursuit, as it gives voice to subjugated knowledges and places the subjective life worlds of its subjects at its core, something more solid was needed for the operational ethics of the work. Creating the usual legalistic framework from standard guidelines felt wrong to me, as enclosing those stories that were enjoyed and experienced in common into private property felt like the practice of a form of academic capitalism (Holloway, 2010; Neary, 2012), and it was capitalism that was being fought against and therefore any notion of capitalist ideals had to be avoided. I turned to the work of Brydon-Miller (2009) for a discussion on covenantal ethics, which, although often associated with action research, seemed to offer a more appropriate set of guidelines for this research:

> rather than approach the determination of ethics using current contractual discourse that regards research as commodity and ethics as a legalistic exchange, we adopt a covenantal ethics founded on the establishment of caring relationships among community research partners and a shared commitment to social justice
>
> (Brydon-Miller, 2009: 244)

This notion of caring relationships and shared commitments speaks to the ethos of bricolage in that these notions were common to all of the aspects in the work; a bricolage methodology, a focus from critical pedagogy and of course the focus of the research topic itself: education against the enclosure of capitalism. Hilsen (2006: 27) describes a model of covenantal ethics thus; 'the unconditional responsibility and the ethical demand to act in the best interest of our fellow human beings'. This statement certainly seemed to ring true with bricolage and I feel should surely be at the top of the list for all ethical guidelines, especially in research committed to social justice. However, there is, as always, a note of caution with vague notions such as 'the best interest' of others, as we understand from history that what is considered in someone's 'best interest' changes both with the times and of course, from person to person, group to group. Kvale and Brinkman (2009: 68) pose a series of questions to be asked at the beginning of any interview study. I have reproduced the ones that seem pertinent:

- What are the beneficial consequences of the study?
- How can the study contribute to enhancing the situation of the participating subjects? Of the human condition?
- How can the informed consent of the participating subjects be obtained?
- How will the researcher's role affect the study?
- How can the researcher avoid co-option from the funding of the project or over identification with his or her subjects, thereby losing critical perspective on the knowledge produced?

Kvale and Brinkman (2009: 69) do stress however, that 'rather than seeing these as questions that can be settled once and for all in advance of a research project, we conceptualise them as fields of uncertainty (i.e., problem areas that should continually be addressed and reflected upon throughout an interview inquiry)'. These were indeed, reflected upon throughout my inquiry, therefore, it is my hope that some, if not all of them will be addressed in what follows.

During the study I came across The Occupy Research Collective (ORC), a working group set up to examine the research being done on Occupy and other social movements and especially, it seemed, to explore the ethics of researching social movements. One of the pressing issues was to draft a response to the issue of the number of requests for interviews Occupiers were receiving and concern over how the material that emerged from them was being used. The ORC held a convergence to address these issues collectively. Most of the people who attended the convergence were researchers of one type or another, all were sympathetic to Occupy's causes and some were actively involved in Occupy's activities. However, there were some attendees that were not actively engaged in research but only within Occupy. The conversation started with a discussion about insider/outsider perspectives and it became clear that those who were not researchers, but active in Occupy, were quite adamant that people who were not active in Occupy should not be able, or indeed allowed, to research it. This was unexpected as my previous experience with Occupiers was that they wanted to tell their stories and have as much information in the public realm as possible. This issue was not resolved despite discussions on the power of research, critical distance, academic discourse and other pertinent issues. However, the reason for this objection may have been present in what followed. A list of guidelines for researching Occupy and other social movements was drawn up (Occupy Research Collective, 2012).

These were the guidelines:

1 Anyone researching a social movement or activist group should, whenever possible, make those groups aware of the fact.
2 The researcher(s) should send examples of previous work and/or describe their political interests and motivations for researching.
3 If there are any concerns, the researcher(s) should make an effort to meet with the activist group to discuss further before continuing.
4 The researcher(s) should ask the activist group what research they consider useful and if possible collaborate on such endeavours.
5 More generally, the research(s) should, where at all possible, commit to some form of collaboration with the activist group, whether it be helping out at a protest camp (e.g. in the kitchen), a social centre, or on a demonstration, or through online work or more administrative tasks.
6 All research material should be made freely available for anyone to view.
7 Reasonable effort should be made to discuss research findings with activists groups before publication, in particular to try and avoid misrepresentations that could be politically damaging to the group.
8 Any ethical requirements imposed through external institutions should be made clear to activist groups in correspondence with them.

(Guidelines available at http://piratepad.net/XqLMuhCau8)

Of course, some of these guidelines differ little from standard ethical guidelines, such as number 1 and number 8 which are essentially pertaining to informed consent. However, many of the other guidelines could be read as censorship and coercion: ideas such as sending 'examples of previous work and/or describe their political interests and motivations for researching' might be viewed as the movement censoring who gets to write about them and how, ensuring they are always seen in a positive light.

> The researcher(s) should, where at all possible, commit to some form of collaboration with the activist group, whether it be helping out at a protest camp (e.g. in the kitchen), a social centre, or on a demonstration, or through online work or more administrative tasks,

indicates a 'payment' for the 'privilege' of carrying out the research. This could be seen in two ways; first, as the 'collaboration' suggested is generally not using the researchers expertise (with the possible exception of the social centre work), it devalues and ignores the knowledge that the researcher may already have that could be valuable to the camp; second, and most importantly for this work, it assumes that the research is of no value to the individuals or the movements in and of itself, somewhat understandable in times of rife academic capitalism, but problematic nonetheless. Another clause that is very open to misunderstanding is number 7 – 'Reasonable effort should be made to discuss research findings with activists groups before publication, in particular to try and avoid misrepresentations that could be politically damaging to the group'. I concur that it is very rarely a bad idea to ensure that no misunderstandings have occurred, but to ensure that the research is not politically damaging could be (mis)understood as only allowing research that is not politically in opposition or critical of the movement to be published.

Of course, as Schostak and Schostak (2013: vii) say, 'no research is ever undertaken without a motive'. It could be argued that some researchers may come with the express intention of politically damaging the movement, but surely, that is a risk one has to take when one places oneself in the public eye? There are unethical researchers, there are politically motivated journalists and there is always public scrutiny. However, to allow only research that you agree with, and have potentially censored, to be produced seems to me to be a direct paradox with the rest of the Occupy rhetoric. It does seem, therefore, that the production of ethical guidelines – whoever produces them – leads to a stagnant, distanced, open to interpretation, and mistrustful relationship between researchers and the researched. There is also the 'all too common belief' as Brydon-Miller (2009: 246) warns, 'that simple adherence to the specifications of [ethics] documents ensures that the research will be ethical'. She argues that 'rather than consider the broader ethical and moral implications of research, such systems narrow our focus to a minute examination of the precise language of consent forms' or, perhaps, in this case become less ethical because manipulation may be required to gain access. It is recognised that 'an experienced interviewer's knowledge of how to create rapport and get through the participants defences may serve as a "Trojan Horse" to get inside areas of a person's life where they were not invited' (Kvale & Brinkman, 2009: 75), therefore even vetting the researcher prior to access does not guarantee that the research subjects will achieve the kind of censorship that the ethical guidelines produced by Occupy suggest.

I would argue that the majority of the researchers I have met and read that have studied Occupy have done so with the apparent intention of understanding the movement from their disciplinary perspective (for example Chomsky, 2012; Hall, 2012; Halvorsen, 2012; Kroll 2011; Neary & Amsler, 2012, among others). In some of the accounts I have heard and read, I cannot recognise my own experience; some, though, have produced work that creates the sights, sounds and smells in my mind as I recognise theirs. Nevertheless, what all these accounts did is provide food for thought, with more material for discussion and reflection. All of these endeavours have been part of Occupy in one way or another and have encouraged me to wonder as Arditi (2008: 119) does, 'what is it that entices people to involve themselves in this revolutionizing, and, what does it mean to 'get involved' here?'.

Surely, for the researcher this is a question of ethics and of the use-value of her research. Coffey (1999: 57) reminds us that

> [i]t is impossible to differentiate the subjective, embodied self from the socio-political and the researcher-professional. Our own sense of

personhood – which will include age, race, gender, class, history, sexuality – engages with the personalities, histories and subjectivities of others present in the field. Our own subjective personality is part of the research and is negotiated in the field.

I argue here that this is part of Arditi's getting involved. The research can become very much a part of who you are and, I would argue, even more so if you accept a bricolage ethos, the notions of solidarity, of voicing on behalf of the seemingly 'voiceless', or even the critical secretary role espoused by Denzin (2010). As one becomes inseparable from the research in order to engage with those others in the field, and, it is argued, if the relationship between individuals and their contexts is the key to understanding, then the most ethical way to proceed is a dynamic engagement with ethical and moral principles, honesty and negotiation seem to become the key watchwords.

This is also the conclusion that Brydon-Miller (2009) comes to in her exploration of covenantal ethics and as Kvale and Brinkman (2009: 74) suggest,

> being familiar with ethical issues, ethical guidelines and ethical theories may help the researcher to make choices that weigh ethical versus scientific concerns in a study. In the end, however, the integrity of the researcher – his or her knowledge, experience, honesty, and fairness – is the decisive factor.

It could further be argued that this knowledge, experience, honesty and fairness is especially pertinent when considering that researchers come from specific knowledge backgrounds. Kincheloe and Tobin (2006: 7) hold that

> researchers use language developed by others, live in specific contexts with particular ways of being and ways of thinking about thinking, have access to some knowledges and not others, and live and operate in a circumstance shaped by particular dominant ideological perspectives.

This requires recognition of how much there is to give at every stage of the research process as well as how much there is to gain. In other words, the information, knowledge, experience and ways of thinking already possessed going into the research field have a relationship to other ways of thinking, other knowledges and other experiences taking place there. Thoughts have an intertextuality with other thoughts:

> Adding to the complexity ... is the notion of intertextuality defined simply as the complicated interrelationship connecting a text to other texts in the act of textual creation or interpretation. Central to the importance of intertextuality in the context of bricolage and the effort to understand complexity is the notion that all narratives obtain meaning

not merely by their relationship to material reality but from their connection to other narratives

(Kincheloe & Berry, 2004: 27)

I argue that this intertextuality not only applies to the written word but also to conversation, to interviews and to convergences of people. I concur with Kvale and Brinkman (2009: 2) when they say that 'the research interview is based on the conversations of daily life and is a professional conversation; it is an inter-view, where knowledge is constructed in the inter-action between the interviewer and the interviewee'. Therefore, it can be seen as the *interaction* creating the knowledge in those situations, especially where the researcher is aiming to contribute to the struggle. Coffey (1999: 23) adds, 'fieldwork involves the enactment of social roles and relationships, which places the self at the heart of the enterprise. A field, a people and a self are crafted through personal engagements and interactions among and between researcher and researched'. I would argue that the important point here is that *interaction* rather than patient listening produces research knowledge, particularly in this context. I found in my inter-actions that many of the people I spoke with during my research asked whether they too could record the interviews, a request which was never declined. This introduced the notion of the interview as a 'mutually useful conversation'.

> As researchers, we belong to a moral community. Doing interviews is a privilege granted us, not a right that we have. Interviews are part of the dialogic conversation that connects all of us to the larger moral community. Interviews arise out of performance events. They transform information into shared experience. They do more than move audiences to tears. They criticize the world the way it is and offer suggestions of how it could be different
>
> (Denzin 2009: 216)

> It was interesting that she got out her iPhone laid it on the table and said 'you don't mind if I record this too, do you?' It got me thinking about the nature of the interview in this context. Why should I be the only one getting something out of this? We continued to talk and I heard the hesitation, the correction of statements, the careful choosing of the right words to convey the sentiment that she tried to get across. The ever present iPhone on the table next to my voice recorder changed the interview. This conversation was not about me as researcher getting what I wanted in order to more fully understand her situation, it was about us both talking and listening and then being able to listen reflectively again in order for us both to understand the gravity of what had been said, to understand the nuances of the situation, to hear the changes that voicing an opinion has on that opinion and to change the way we saw the world ...
>
> (Fieldwork Journal, 2012)

Kvale and Brinkman (2009: 33) assert that 'we should not regard the research interview as completely open and free dialogue between egalitarian partners', and, overall, I would tend to agree. There can be many power plays throughout the course of interviews but predominantly the interviewer holds the majority of the power in the specific research situation. Kvale and Brinkman do concede, however, that 'some interviewers attempt to reduce the power asymmetry of the interview situation by collaborative interviewing where the researcher and subject approach equality in questioning, interpreting and reporting' (p. 34). And that 'an interview is literally an inter view, an interchange of views between two persons conversing about a theme of mutual interest' (Kvale & Brinkman, 2009: 2). It is this final assertion that is possibly of most interest to the notion of the mutually useful conversation. I was interested in what people participating in alternatively organised education had to say, not only about the education but also about the context of that education, the socio-political context, the aspirations for that education and the hopes and desires that that education had induced. I found that people were not only interested in talking about the things that I was interested in, but they were also interested in reflecting upon what had been said within the interview and learning from that too. I also felt that in order to lessen the inequality between us and hopefully get the interviewee to open up and not to censor what they said, I should converse rather than 'interview': we both had information, knowledge and experience that was useful to the other in our respective journeys. It was reported that the people I spoke to were willing to talk to me because they felt that they were doing something important and wanted to explore that further through our conversations. In addition, I think that a great deal of confidence can be placed in what was revealed because each of us benefitted from the exchange. All of the interviews were set up as forms of storytelling with interaction. My interaction was as honest and candid as possible and I found myself able to inform them and their thinking with interjections of how theory supported their experience, how they had reinvented forms of education that were theoretically sound as interventions and interruptions into the status quo. To reiterate Shukaitis and Graeber (2007: 37), 'these moments embody not just practices ... but are in themselves ways of understanding the world and forms of research in action'. Kincheloe and Tobin (2006: 6) put it this way, 'to be in the world is to be in relationship. People are not abstract individuals who live as fragments, in isolation from one another', the hope here is that 'in these moments borders that separate people burst open into renewed periods of social creativity and insurgencies' (Shukaitis & Graeber, 2007: 37). I wanted to create the possibility that we are no longer researcher and respondent, but human beings collaboratively finding a way to assist each other in making the world a better place through creative conversation and reflection. This view of the interview, I would argue, allows an embrace of complexity in that it 'constructs a far more active role for humans in shaping reality and creating the research processes and narratives that represent it. Such an active agency rejects deterministic views of social reality that assume the effects of particular social, political, economic, and educational processes' (Kincheloe & Berry, 2004: 2–3). There is, however, a need to maintain a sense of strangeness during fieldwork (Coffey 1999), this was achieved by merely using the politics of the movement as contextualisation and the pedagogical aspects as the central focus. I argue that this allowed me to work in solidarity politically, whilst maintaining a critical distance through a strangeness for the research subjects: enquiry about the pedagogy, thus knocking off balance the emerging 'normal responses', that the Occupiers were used to giving to political theorists and social movement scholars. A second response, however, is that, as The Invisible Committee (2009: 14) suggest, 'the past has given us far too many bad answers for us not to see the mistakes were in the questions themselves', maybe the questions were wrong before, maybe more connection, more subjective understanding, more human solidarity is what is needed to understand research knowledge as a tool of radical change. Third, Kincheloe and Berry's (2004: 74) bricolage focussed response may well be that 'bricolage is dealing with ... a double ontology of complexity: first, the complexity of objects of inquiry and their being in the world; second, the nature of the social construction of human subjectivity, the production of human "being"'. In other words, we are both being produced in some way by the interaction, our subjectivities being (de/re)constructed in the moment of interaction, in however small or significant a way.

The mutually useful conversations also create a feeling of inclusion in the research, because a dialogue has been initiated between the research and the research topic which may go beyond interviewing to engage participants in critical give and take (Howe & MacGillivary, 2009). This critical give and take is what has the potential to create the mutual usefulness of the conversation. Moreover, as Stake (2000: 19) upholds, 'we expect an inquiry to be carried out so that certain audiences will benefit – not just to swell the archives, but to help persons toward further understandings'. This idea further justifies the dialectic nature of the mutually useful conversation as it invites not only descriptive accuracy and critical give and take but helps persons to better understand their own actions as well as understanding the critical power of research, creating a more useful witness to the life worlds of the research collaborators. Again, I would argue that this recognition of the 'complex ontological importance of relationships alters the basic foundations of the research act and knowledge production process' (Kincheloe & Berry, 2004: 73–4) to a grand action research cycle through better understanding of the role of the other in the critical reflection of one's own position. Kincheloe and Berry (2004: 27) also assert that 'in this context an autopoietic process is constructed as new modes of knowledge emerge in the interaction of these multidimensional perspectives'. This allows 'the adept bricoleur to set up the bricolage in a manner that produces powerful feedback loops – constructs that in turn synergise the research process'. This notion not only reflects the interaction during the mutually useful conversation, but also the whole research project has this internally built in through the grounding of the theory and the questions in the data. Thinking of the overall process in this way has the potential to make the research report an analysis and *extension* of what happened. This would then be 'fed back' to the movements that the research was attentive to. This sits on an ontology explained here by Whitehead and McNiff (2006: 23):

> if you see yourself as part of other people's lives, and they of yours, you may adopt an insider approach, which would involve you offering descriptions and explanations for how you and they were involved in mutual relationships of influence.

This explanation potentially makes obsolete the insider/outsider tensions expressed at the ORC and involves taking a fresh look at the necessary role of the researcher as part of the activist circle in the context of radical research for social change.

In order to properly understand the chapters that follow, some words about how the stories were analysed is needed, outlining the process through which sense and meaning were made of the mutually useful conversations and other sources for the specific task of allowing a conversation to emerge between the theoretical understanding of what was possible, and what was claimed and observed. Howe and MacGillivary (2009: 569) explain this process as 'testing the claims and counter-claims of social researchers [and indeed theorist] by entering them into *critical dialogue* with those whose perspectives are informed by relevant lived experience' (my italics). I argue that it is also important to realise that 'the strategy involves an un-writing of the normal pattern of writing up research' (Schostak & Schostak, 2013: *ix*), but achieves a meaningful exploration of the relationship between theory and data making them work for, rather than in tension with, each other.

The stories from the actions were examined initially to produce the descriptions of the sites, and to get a sense of what was being said in order to mine theory to find ways of thinking about the education and pedagogy that took place that interrelated with the data. The data was selected due to its relevance to the story of pedagogy and experience running through the sites of interest, this conceptualisation of the data was chosen in line with the notion of intertextuality: 'one text relates to another in a multiplicity of ways – it is intertextual' (Schostak & Schostak, 2013: xi).

The conversations I had with the Occupiers all entailed them talking about their learning as well as their general, political and personal experience; sometimes what they saw as not being specifically about 'education' due to their understanding from prior experience, I saw as directly relating to the theories of radical, popular education and critical pedagogy. For example, one Occupier, Jane, with no theoretical knowledge of education described her experience in a way that could have been written by Freire himself. She said such things as 'I understand a lot more after talking to others that I can change how I live my life' (understanding the conditions of one's own reality and the power one has to change it: Freire, 1993a); 'I don't just read the headlines now, I go away and read the whole story from different sources because I think I should find out the facts' (overcoming sloganisation through the development of epistemological curiosity: Freire, 1993b). There were many examples of these kinds of direct connections that happened in conversations where Occupiers said phrases such as 'I'm not sure I have really learnt anything, but I have changed a lot'. Kincheloe and Berry continue on to say that a particular interpretation is chosen because it does one of several things. One of those things, that is of particular interest to this work, is that it 'grants access to new possibilities of meaning', it raises 'new questions and suggests new types of research into the phenomenon' (2004: 101). A particular interpretation also helps 'in the construction of future insights'. I would argue that there is not much use to the research if it does not help in the construction of future insights, as the commitment to research work that can be enacted attests. Other questions Kincheloe and Berry insist must be asked of the interpretation of research data are issues such as:

> Does it identify where individuals are situated within the socio-political web of reality? Does it uncover the ways ideology operates to undermine individuals' desire for both self-direction and interconnectedness? Is there coherence between the analysis and the phenomenon being researched? Does it raise questions of self-understanding, for example, the nature of the relationship of the producer of the text to the phenomenon in question? Does it indicate an awareness of the discourses, values and ideologies that have shaped it? Does it engage its subjects to better conceptualise the world so they can transform it?
> (Kincheloe & Berry, 2004: 101–2)

If one asks these types of questions whilst executing a theoretical reading, or what Schostak and Schostak (2013) call a 'symptomatic reading', a reading that might reveal the hidden, latent or repressed theorisations of the data, one should find that 'what is being heard in such readings are previously silenced discourses, or discourses that could only be heard elsewhere that bring to the fore in a newly opened space, a new agenda' (Schostak & Schostak, 2013: 15). So, once again, no strict methodological rules were followed as a theoretical/symptomatic understanding of the issues had been developed from the initial reading.

Kvale and Brinkman (2009: 236) suggest,

> a researcher may read through his or her interviews again and again, reflect theoretically on specific themes of interest, write out interpretations, and not follow any systematic method or combination of techniques.... This may perhaps suggest that recourse to specific analytical tools becomes less important with a theoretical knowledge of the subject matter of an investigation.

Christians (2000: 145) suggests that the watchword for this type of analysis is 'interpretive sufficiency' and goes on to describe this as an account that 'possess that amount of depth, detail, emotionality, nuance, and coherence that will permit a critical consciousness. Christians comes to this conclusion because of a belief that 'through conscientization the oppressed gain their own voice, and collaborate in transforming their culture' (p. 148). Therefore, the thematic and theoretical/symptomatic analysis of the data once again has a symmetry with the topic of the research, by again listening to the voices telling about their experience (Kvale & Brinkman, 2009). The pedagogy discussed in the literary theory concludes that this should happen in the specific learning environment, the work then 'compares their descriptions with claims about their work from literature' (Kvale & Brinkman, 2009: 237). Therefore, the researcher, in the practice of analysis becomes 'hitchhiker' (Schostak & Schostak, 2008) or 'traveller' (Kvale & Brinkman, 2009) in the life world of the other. And as Kvale and Brinkman (2009: 48–9) describe, 'the potentialities of meanings in the original stories are differentiated and unfolded through the traveller's interpretations of the narratives he or she brings back home to audiences. The journey may not only lead to new knowledge: the traveller might change as well'.

> Having visited the camp at St. Paul's I feel as if things – I, can never be the same. Something changed there, something changed me. I couldn't pin point what it was, I really don't know what it was, but I cannot think the same way, I cannot understand the world as I did before, there is something fundamentally challenging about this form of collective action, about this form of commons creation, about this form of prefiguration. It changes the way you see things – if you let it.
> (Fieldwork Journal, 2012)

In the next chapter, I dialogue with theorists in an attempt to understand the conditions necessary to enhance the potential of education to create social transformation. Examining the different models suggested by the initial examination of the spaces under study and how they might, hypothetically, interact and produce new ideas and constellations of resistance. Alternatively, how they might (re)create enclosures, or (re)produce sites of academic vandalism (Neary in Class War University, 2013). This will be done by attempting to identify a range of possible explanations as to how to organise education for a more just and equal pedagogy.

## Note

1 I am using the word 'data' here, although I dislike this word due to its reductionist implication of some sort of private ownership by the researcher of the personal and intimate stories related to me throughout the research. I reluctantly use it here as a word that has shared understanding amongst students and scholars of research methods.

# 3 Political? Pedagogical? Philosophical?
## Putting the theory to work in conversation

My argument throughout is that education, appropriately organised, is an essential tool for the types of social change advocated by performing a prefigurative politics. Holloway (2010: 206) says 'the flow of determination that comes from the capitalist totality of social relations is constituted by the way in which our doings relate to one another'. I tend to agree, the issue at stake is one of relations. Therefore, authors who constitute these countervailing discourses and advocate unveiling the oppressive conditions of neoliberalism through political critiques and pedagogies are now explored. Within this discussion, two specific models of education will be focussed upon in an attempt to really understand what has occurred in the pedagogical sites and what may be sustainable into the uncertain future as a model for a revolutionary, transformative pedagogy.

Society is currently manipulated by capitalist mechanisms, or the social synthesis produced by capitalism (see for example Cleaver, 2000; Holloway, 2010; Hardt & Negri, 2000, 2004, 2009, 2012; Harvey, 2011; Shantz, 2013; Žižek, 2009, 2012). This is the starting point of this discussion, the notion of a capitalist totality that we cannot control, it is argued in this work however, and by the people involved in the spaces this work examines, that even if we cannot control this totality, we can change it and create new truths of social life. Therefore, although I start this discussion from the point of view that the ideologies and systems of capitalism and of neoliberalism are totalising, with no 'outside' of their controls, there are ways to think otherwise, ways to enact other relations that escape this form of enclosure. There are also attempts to prevent the creation of another totality; instead they are attempts to allow for individual equality and forms of individual and collective freedom. The discourses that shall be heard throughout this work, from the theorists, from the Occupiers and from the purveyors of the other spaces, are an attempt to counter totalisation, as well as an attempt to support a communing, a way of being that holds our collective endeavours in common. Therefore, the countervailing discourses attempt to propose/construct an alternative reality because, it is argued, capitalism encloses, neoliberalism more so, as it gives rise to the need for more regulation of its false promise of unfettered free markets (Harvey, 2011). The individual liberty promised by neoliberalism referred only to the wealthy and their corporations whilst the individual person was enclosed into a system of, not 'trickle down' economics as capitalism had promised (Fisher, 2009; Harvey, 2011) but a form of economics that might be termed 'flood up' wealth accumulation.

This work can be seen as an attempt to understand how to build models of practice that have the potential to bring about fundamental change, to create critically engaged learners who might continue to sustain the project of the constant and ongoing democratisation of public life. An attempt not to enclose the enclosers, but to open up social life into a new common, that has revolutionary potential, through the production of new multitudes (Hardt & Negri, 2004). Therefore, I will briefly concentrate on the primary task of understanding the connection between social change and education in general. Then, I look at the reasons for analysing critical pedagogy, in particular, as a tool of social transformation before going on to examine that tool in detail. I will then subject it to a contextual reading through the data, which will dialogue with the theories and build new knowledge through the living examples of education put to work in order to attempt to overcome and delegitimise the current social order.

Holloway (2010: 255) asks

> how do we light up our eyes with amazement, how do we touch that half-awareness, that tension, that ec-static distance, how do we bring it clearly into focus, how do we magnify it, how do we open it up, how do we strengthen and expand and multiply all those rebellions in which one pole of the ec-static relation (doing) repudiates with all its force the other pole (labour)? That is the question of revolution.

This question echoes the crux of the inquiry. Perhaps then, it could be argued that now, more than ever, it is true that 'revolutionary theory is now the enemy of all revolutionary ideology *and knows it*' (Debord, 1977: para. 124). In addition, what of Gorz's (1997: 46) insistence that 'the bourgeoisie succeeded in destroying at root what consciousness the proletariat might have had of its sovereign creativeness'. How then do we tackle the idea that 'if we allow ourselves to fall for the trickery of neoliberal economic discourses, which affirm realities of homelessness and poverty as inevitable, then opportunities for change become invisible and our role in fostering change becomes absent' (Freire, 2007: 4)?

Shor (in Macrine, 2009: 121) illuminates a possible answer to inform the discussion when he says 'the values embedded in any *learning process* can shape us into people who question the status quo or into people who accommodate to the way things are or into people who celebrate the system we live in' (my italics). This sentiment is echoed by many other theorists (see, for example, Brookfield, 2001, 2005; Brookfield & Holst, 2011; Freire, 1985, 1998, 2004, 2005, 2008; Freire & Faundez, 1989; Heaney, 1993). Therefore, can we conclude that 'education' is the answer – if we just, as a state, as a society, educate people better, then we can abandon revolutionary theory and watch the miraculous transformation of society into a just and equitable future? Maybe, but there is caution to be taken – to romanticise any form of education in that way may be to run head first down a blind alley. Mostly, in the current society I have described – one that is governed by capitalist social synthesis and mediated by the commodity exchange – education, when appropriated by the state, can only mean *school*. Holloway (2010: 116) asks

> how can we think of changing the world radically in a world in which people are personifications of their social functions? If we are entrapped by roles generated by capitalism, how can we think of breaking the pattern of social relations formed by these roles? .... How can workers, as personifications of labour, constitute a revolutionary class, a class that would overthrow labour?

According to this point of view and the view of several others (Gorz, 1997; Hardt & Negri, 2004, 2009, 2012; Merrifield, 2011a; Holloway, 2010), the answer seems to be to rethink class, and raise the political consciousness of all (Freire, 1985, 1998, 2004, 2005, 2008) and to create what Holloway calls 'cracks' in capitalism:

> *a crack is the perfectly ordinary creation of a space or moment in which we assert a different type of doing.* We start from two antagonistic ways of doing: that which we reject and that which we try to create. The cracks are revolts of one type of doing against another type of doing.
> (Holloway, 2010: 84)

A focussed question then becomes: how do we begin to assert these different types of doing through raising political consciousness and rethinking class? The beginnings of a potential answer may lie in Holloway's statement that we need to start from two antagonistic ways of doing: understanding what it is that we currently create and what it is that we are trying to create instead. Without these understandings any effort to recreate social relations in other ways might be difficult, if not impossible. However, I would argue that this notion needs to be understood in real terms, in terms of what actually happens when people assert their right to the freedom of assembly and begin to attempt to help each other understand these issues. This is where, in this conversation at least (and I am sure in many others), critical pedagogy comes in. Critical pedagogy is a pedagogy of question (Freire & Faundez, 1989), a pedagogy of hope (Freire, 2004) and a pedagogy of desire (Freire, 2007). It is to this pedagogy that attention shall now be turned in the hope that critical pedagogy, enacted through public forms of popular education, mixed with the prefigurative politics that offers a crack in the fabric of capitalism may offer a way of exploring education, the 'public', and the building of countervailing forms of organisation.

## 56  Political? Pedagogical? Philosophical?

Freire himself invited those reviewing and using his work to reinvent and rethink his philosophy and thoughts for their own context. However, there are what might be called 'soft' readings of Freire; these constitute a 'community based approach which stresses group work, mutual respect, discussion and experiential learning. This approach would be essentially non-directive and operate on pluralist assumptions' (Lockhart, 1997: 19). In this work, however, I am advocating what might be considered, by contrast, a 'hard' reading of Freire, a more radical reading that allows a stress on the more political functions as primary and emphasises the necessity of transformation and confrontation, and potentially creates the processes for what Mouffe (1999, 2013) calls the constant revolutionising of democracy. I argue in this work that this transformation and confrontation should refer not only to the social world around us (the status quo, capitalist relations and so on), but also the transformation and confrontation of the way in which people think of their 'place' in this social world, how they absorb it and to what extent they question or accommodate it, transform themselves within it, and confront the extent to which they are alienated and oppressed within it. In other words, to what extent they escape their schooling. I argue that this way of reading Freire's work is essential for the purposes here as it contributes to the understanding of education as a process for revolutionary social change and social justice rather than as a tool for individual empowerment or localised community action on isolated issues.

It is generally recognised that Freire has been thought of as the 'founder' of critical pedagogy since the publication of his book *Pedagogy of the Oppressed* (1993a). I turn predominately to his work because he articulates the process of education that, I argue, is recognisable in the pedagogical processes in Occupy, his work with the Brazilian rural workers was to assist them to read the word and the world, to understand their place in the social milieu and to develop their power to change it (Freire, 1993a). This is an attempt to ensure that although this work operationalises Freire's writing in a very different context, his work allows the articulation of the pedagogical processes that were claiming to be for the same purposes in Occupy: to critically awaken and to realise the power of learners to change the world. Central to Freire's understanding is that the essence of human existence is transformation. According to many critical pedagogy scholars (Giroux, 1992, 2001, 2011; McLaren, 1998a; Macrine, 2009; Mayo, 2004; Shor, 1992, for example), Freire believed that individuals transform the world through their work and actions, and in doing so transform themselves and the world around them. This is the basis of Freirean critical pedagogy and will guide this work to understand how practicable critical pedagogy is as a tool for social change at the current socio-political juncture, as a countervailing discourse in its own right and as an attempt to create the conditions for new discourses against global capital to be heard and acted upon, especially in the light of Occupy and the other sites examined here.

Nocella *et al*'s (2010) book, *Academic Repression*, attests critical pedagogy's potential power has not gone unnoticed, certainly in North America, by supporters of a system that schools. This is partly because critical pedagogy is an attempt to find a 'language of possibility' (Cho, 2013: 69) rather than relying solely on critique to elicit action therefore opening the possibility for the production of new dialogues. One of the main notions in Freire's thinking agrees that schools cause inequality and are sites of capitalist reproduction (ibid), whereas, as explored earlier, education emancipates and creates the conditions for the imaginings of alternatives to dominant ideology. Illich (2011: 2), however, takes this idea a stage further and suggests that 'not only education but social reality itself has become schooled', suggesting not only that 'education' is becoming co-opted into the schooling machine, but also that the public pedagogy (Sandlin, *et al*, 2011) of everyday worlds is schooling people into compliance and conformity. This is an important point because it resonates with ideas around the manufacture of 'lonely crowds' (Debord, 1977; Riesman, 1969) and the destruction of the consciousness of the proletariat by the bourgeoisie (Gorz, 1997). This notion of the co-option of everyday life insists that individuals are schooled into these acts, these states of being. The question becomes, therefore; can individuals be educated out of their schooling, through this language, this countervailing discourse, of possibility contained within the philosophy of critical pedagogy, as an alternative to the inevitability and determinism of the neoliberal discourse? According to Shor (1996: 17), learners 'are constructing the subordinate self at the same time that they are resisting and undermining it, while believing that their "real selves", real lives, are somewhere else'. Shor argues that 'in such cultural conflict, there is no simple way critical-democratic pedagogy can transform the anti-intellectual stalemate of an unequal status-quo'. Thus, it can be argued, finding a language of possibility becomes paramount to begin social change, as does the awakening of the social consciousness, creating an understanding of what social relations are pushing individuals to do. Freire refers to this 'schooling' as the 'banking method' (Freire, 1993a), wherein deposits of knowledge are placed into the mind of the learner, to be drawn upon when that, apparently objective and neutral, knowledge is required. Bahruth and Steiner, (2000: 120) add, 'the basic assumption, that [people] are identical empty vessels, is not only erroneous, but punitive to [people] who have non-mainstream backgrounds', or are trying to think and do otherwise. However, Freire (1993a: 60) states that

> unfortunately, those who espouse the cause of liberation are themselves surrounded and influenced by the climate which generates the banking concept, and often do not perceive its significance or its dehumanising power. Paradoxically, they utilise this same instrument of alienation in what they consider an effort to liberate.

In other words, they continue, through their attempts at liberation, to reproduce the inequalities and social relations that alienate, by utilising the educational paradigm that is most familiar to them, the banking method of schooling. But not just that, it could be that they are not merely utilising, but that they are conditioned into this by their own experience of social relations and social life, a conditioning that may be very difficult to escape. It therefore seems that there needs to be a robust outline of an educational paradigm that supports social change, whilst taking into account the potential for damaging relations and emphasising mechanisms that inhibit these phenomena of reproduction that appear in attempts at liberation, as these damaging relations only strengthen the fatalism of the capitalist social synthesis. As Holloway (2010: 39) insists, 'if our struggle is not asymmetrical to capitalism in its forms, then it simply reproduces capitalist social relations, whatever its content'. This asymmetrical form seems to be one of the essential factors that should be present in critical pedagogy, or it perhaps should be abandoned for something new.

Heaney (1993: 19–20) states that education facilitates 'democratic reflection and action through critical identification of the issues', rather than serving to 'domesticate learners ... and adjust minds to the inevitable conformities of a mass society'. I suggest that the key phrases here are 'democratic reflection', and 'critical identification'. These phrases give hope to a search for a transformative pedagogical paradigm. Freire (1993a: 60) offers this:

> those truly committed to liberation must reject the banking concept in its entirety, adopting instead a concept of women and men as conscious beings and consciousness as consciousness intent upon the world. They must abandon the educational goal of deposit making and replace it with the posing of problems of human beings in their relations with the world.

This idea of consciousness is central to all the work in critical pedagogy and the raising of consciousness is a central task in creating the conditions for countervailing discourses to arise as Steinklammer (2012: 31) explains:

> consciousness raising and reflection are tasks for critical education because education constitutes an anti-habitual attitude, in which the human being critically decides again and again on his/her consciousness and relation to the world rather than letting it become affirmative. Education is not a habitus, but a force that objects to every kind of habitualisation of habits that chain the human being to what already exists.

I would argue that education should indeed 'constitute an anti-habitual attitude' and certainly critical pedagogy seems to. Methods such as problem posing and questioning the status quo which Shor (1996: 61) insists is an 'unpredictable adventure that interrupts routine behaviours, expectations, and relationships'; dialectics which create from a critical-democratic pedagogy, 'contact zones' (Pratt, 1991) or 'zones of proximal development' (Vygotsky, 1962) which become laboratories for the 'counter-hegemonic reconstruction of the social self' (Shor, 1996: 23). These acts from critical pedagogy can be understood as producing anti-habitual attitudes. This is arguably because one of the tasks of critical pedagogy is to engender critical thinking in people.

An important aspect of Freire's work, described here by McLaren (2000: 8), is that whereas mainstream educators often 'decapitate the social context from the self and then cauterize the dialectical movement between them, Freire stresses the dialectical motion between the subject and object, the self and the social, and social structure and human agency', thus connecting the individual with the world and visa-versa. Making these connections is not only an essential aspect of critical pedagogy as Freire insisted, but many educators and theorists would insist that the connections are also essential for a politics of social transformation which hopes to put an end to the injustices and inequalities built into the capitalist system (Bonefeld, *et al.*, 1992; Hardt & Negri, 2000, 2004, 2009, 2012; Harvey, 2003, 2011). What Freire claimed to be articulating, was a well-founded 'critical hope' that was a tool to counter the fatalism of neoliberalism (Freire, 1998: 70). Freire's attitude to education was that it was fundamentally a political act (Allman, 1987; Aronowitz, 1993; Freire, 1985, 1993a, 1998, 2004; Giroux, 2011; McLaren 2000a). According to Freire, and others, its main task was to awaken the political consciousness of subjugated and oppressed peoples in order that they more clearly see the shroud of oppression that surrounded them and clouded their judgements as agentic human beings, unfinished and in process (Apple, *et al.*, 2009; Freire, 1976, 1993a, 1996, 2004; Shor, 1992, 1996; Shor & Freire, 1987). Shor (1996: 37) asks what I would assert is a poignant question: can a critical pedagogy 'come to grips with the political fictions disguising social realities?' Freire insisted that 'it is in our seriousness as professional people *with a competence for political organisation* that our strength *as educators* resides' (Freire, 1998: 65, my Italics). This statement acknowledges that educators are political actors and it is this aspect that educators should perhaps be acutely aware of to elicit real change. Shor (1996: 54) adds to this that '[students] too must become questioners and problem-posers, not only [the educator], because questioning is the epistemic stance of critical learners and citizens'. Therefore, a robust definition of critical pedagogy is akin to the one espoused by Apple *et al.* (2009: 3) which insists that it

> involves a thorough-going reconstruction of what education is for, how it should be carried out, what we should teach and who should be empowered to engage in it. This more robust understanding ... involves the fundamental transformations of the underlying epistemological and ideological assumptions that are made about what counts as 'official' or legitimate knowledge and who holds it. It is also grounded in radical shifts in one's social commitments. This involves a commitment to social transformation and a break with the comforting illusions that the ways in which our societies and their educational apparatuses are currently organised can lead to social justice.

Apple *et al.* seem to be asserting the necessity of what the three sites explored in this work claim to be doing. Creating the conditions, at least, for the emergence of countervailing discourses through the reorganisation of education away from schooling and therefore control and conformity.

A contemporary and situated reading is now appropriate in order to attempt to place critical pedagogy in the service of the new social movements who are engaging in forms of radical pedagogy, either intentionally or not, in order to transform our world through the potential reimagining and recreation of social relations and societal organisation.

I would assert that in the case of Occupy, the educator became everyone and everything. The educator was the context, the encampment, every individual that stepped foot through that square. The educator became in that context a potential burgeoning awareness and an immanent community of learners. In the case of the other sites, which have some form of hierarchy, albeit a possibly shallow one in the case of the SSC, it is important to understand the questions asked by Apple *et al.* in context regarding who can teach, who can engage in education and for what purpose. Apple *et al.* (2009: 7) restate that 'throughout every region of the world, there are powerful movements and examples of radical pedagogic efforts both within the formal educational sector as well as in community literacy programmes, labour education, anti-racist and anti-colonialist mobilizations, women's movements and others'. Therefore, a deeper understanding is needed of the politics that make these new social movements apparently different, apparently more pedagogical. What politics are involved in the movements that have created the possible need for a re-reading and re-contextualising of critical pedagogy? Moreover, where might they take education to reorganise social lives? And, what might an alternative university as a laboratory for social organisation look like?

So now, I turn to a development of Holloway's *Crack Capitalism* thesis as a response to the emergent potential of countervailing discourses and counter-hegemonic ways of being within Occupy London.

> The sight of Tent City was a rip, a fissure in the reality of London life. The city is arranged for the ease of commerce and power wrangling, it is unexpected to find this rag-tag community of people bustling about, organising meetings, having discussions, collaborating, thinking and imagining together. Tent City is a place where all the commodified relationships seem to melt away; a place of mutual aid, of conviviality, of sharing and caring, of holding the property, the wishes, the dreams, and the desires of those involved in common, it is a crack in the everyday reality of capitalism.
> (Fieldwork Journal, 2012)

> In a cold world, we are the sun shining on the ice, creating the cracks that can move with terrifying and unpredictable speed. Or not.
> (Holloway, 2010: 79)

According to the people I spoke to during the research, there are a number of authors who have been instrumental in the thinking and practice of the new social movements and particularly Occupy (see for example The Invisible Committee, 2009; Hessel, 2011; Holloway, 2005, 2010; Sharp, 2012 among others). However, Holloway's (2010) *Crack Capitalism* thesis was often directly credited by some as inspiration for the spaces under discussion in this work as it echoed the notions of taking control of one's own position within the totality and coming together through acts dissent to create new ways of doing, seeing and thinking. Holloway (2010: 171) has this to say, which frames the ideas behind the *Crack Capitalism* thesis, especially considering the St. Paul's camp:

> [The] *other side* [of ourselves that is not made by capitalism] is not a mere potential or possibility. The *other side* is potential, it is an anticipation of the world that might exist, but to treat it as mere possibility leaves us dangerously in the air, postpones yet again the realisation of this potential to some vague and undetermined future. A potential that is not a live antagonism, a living struggle is worth nothing ... to understand abstraction as present process means that that which is abstracted exists not just as potential, but as a real force in the present.

Holloway's thesis is based on the idea, then, that people do *something* now to change the conditions of their lives that they 'fight from the particular' (83) that they move together in a 'discordant harmony' (78), that using 'trust as a central organising principle' (65) they 'stop making capitalism and do something else' (109). In effect, people create 'cracks' in the very fabric of capitalism and capitalist social relations. One of the intriguing things about Occupy and the other sites was that they seemed to be attempting to 'crack' schooling with countervailing ideas about education. This is important, as what this *something* is, remains up to the individual, as Holloway insists that there can be no homogenising, no totalising. In this work, that *something* is seen as pedagogical, the sites explored here, particularly Occupy, are the contexts. The possibility of a critical pedagogy practiced through popular education and the supplementary spaces are posited as potentially enduring *somethings*, following the temporary *something* of Occupy.

Merrifield (2011a: 129) insists, 'the factuality of the 'real world' was being afforded too much critical right. One simply lashed out in the prison-house of negativity'. Before the various dissident eruptions of 2010–2012, all Western societies seemed to be doing was concentrating on this 'factuality', the 'what was', the TINA syndrome (There Is No Alternative), through mantras of economic growth, perpetual war, measures of austerity and the essentialism of schooling as a means to create an acceptability of these 'facts'. As has been said (unknown[1] quoted in Holloway, 2010) said, 'it is easier to imagine the end of the world than the end of capitalism'. Holloway (2010: 50) insists that by creating a crucial shift in emphasis, 'instead of focussing our attention on the destruction of capitalism, we concentrate on building something else', he purposely does not say what that something else might be and instead allows for the possibility of a politics of the first person (Katsiaficas, 2006), the potential of a multitude (Hardt & Negri, 2004). He also adds,

> the idea of a future revolution has become the enemy of emancipation. We can however create now free enclaves or temporary autonomous zones, moments of uprising (Bey, 1985): an uprising is like a 'peak experience' as opposed to the standard of 'ordinary'.
>
> (Holloway, 2010: 33)

This notion of the peak experience speaks to my impression of Occupy and of the elation of the Occupiers whilst the camp was still in situ. These autonomous zones, in spaces such as the SSC, moments of uprising and peak experiences, such as Occupy, are what potentially constitute the 'cracks' in Holloway's thesis. In Holloway's words then, 'revolution is simply … the assuming of our responsibility as the creators of social reality, the social assuming of our power-to-do' (2010: 249), an idea that follows on from the Spinozan (2006) notions of the powers of individuals: thinking, imagining, desiring, running, making, and so on: the stuff of education itself. But can these 'powers' be 'educated' in order to crack the enclosure of schooling? Can they be 'educated' in a free and egalitarian manner to form an internal democracy of the individual, an internal set of agonisms that ensure our individual powers are reflecting the external democracy that is desired, an aggregation of individual and collective powers that resist enclosure and domination?

According to Holloway, experiences of cracks can come in many shapes and sizes, and should all have their own character, some might be collective and some might be individual, but Holloway insists that they are all important, without exception, if society is to change at a fundamental level. Therefore, as a revolutionary theory, 'revolution, then, is the return of the repressed. Not just of the repressed sections of the population (proletarians, women, indigenous, blacks, and so on), but of that which is repressed within us' (2010: 224): in other words, the desire to stop conforming to the 'factuality' of the present, our schooled selves; our repressed desires to not conform are therefore revolutionary desires.

> It is the revolt of that which exists against and pushes beyond. It is the revolt of creative doing that exists against alien determination and pushes beyond, towards self-determination. But creative doing is not just creation of that which exists outside us, but self-creation, creation of our own sexuality, our own culture, our own thinking and feeling,
>
> (Holloway, 2010: 224–5)

a re-education project that begins from within. It is my argument here that an appropriately organised critical education could, indeed, have the potential to 'crack' schooling and release these revolutionary desires and go some way to this self- (re)creation.

The question now becomes that of if revolutionary theory now consists of our desire to not conform to the 'social synthesis' created by capitalism, what positive desires do we have? What, according to Holloway might we desire to do? Holloway (2010: 45) considers that 'the idea is gaining ground that the only way to change the world is to do it ourselves and do it here and now', an example, then, of the prefigurative political behaviour of Occupy? The sentiment is also echoed by Gorz (1997: 3) when he stated, some time ago, that 'the outline of a society based on the free use of time are only beginning to appear in the interstices of, and in opposition to, the present social order'. A society based on the free use of time, even a micro-society, such as Occupy, or the spaces in the margins such as the SSC claimed to inhabit, can be counted as potential cracks in Holloway's terms. This can be argued due to Holloway's thought that 'capitalism, ever since its beginning, has been a movement of enclosure, a movement of converting that which is enjoyed in common into private property' (2010: 29), that which is enjoyed in the sites explored here to some extent, such as free time and the assertion of the right to free association. Therefore, if capitalist enclosure is to be resisted, these societies based on the free use of time, which are beginning to appear, according to Gorz, may hold the key. Creating these societies may mean a (re)education, creating commons, open source sharing, and a democratic, effective multitude, such as the one attempted in Occupy's temporary autonomous zone, where the countervailing discourses allow potential resistance to the manipulation from ruling elites, but now on a more permanent basis.

Holloway (2010: 45) asserts that these varying forms of cracks 'can be seen as examples of pre-figurative politics, the idea that the struggle for a different society must create that society through its forms of struggle'. I argue that when people practice a prefigurative politics, they also learn by doing, or as Horton and Freire (1990) might say, 'we make the road by walking'. Prefiguration also describes the idea that 'if you can embody the change you struggle for, you have already won – not by fighting but by becoming' (Holloway, 2010: 45). This, in essence, was what Occupy claimed to be trying to achieve; they attempted to 'become' the society they wanted to live in and create cracks in their schooled selves and others. According to Horton and Freire (1990) we will discover what can be done by actually doing, despite believing that little can get done at a certain moment, and despite our theories about what should happen compared to what actually does.

According to Holloway (2010: 94–5), our lives are not woven together by the state producing schemes to improve social cohesion, as is often assumed. It is through the abstraction of labour, the synthesis of these relations is formed through the abstraction of 'doing' (Marx's concrete labour) into 'labour' (Marx's abstract labour). This is the problem that the cracks face, our lived abstraction from our 'doing', our *socially* necessary labour, which is why as Merrifield (2011a: 112) says, many rebellions are founded on acts of negation:

> on resisting and resistance, on refusal, on saying NO, on fighting against a force with which one disagrees, sometimes putting one's life on the line.

It's an act of fending off, of fighting *against* job cuts, *against* neoliberalism, *against* a fascist state, *against* the government, *against* bourgeois policies, *against* the WTO. Negation is quite rightly the stuff of radical politics; but it isn't the stuff dreams are made of.

'A crack' according to Holloway (2010: 84) 'is the perfectly ordinary creation of a space or moment in which we assert a different type of doing'. Here the revolt of education against schooling might be considered – the capitalist way of doing that commodifies and encloses all our social relations and the rebellious way of doing, the reassertion of ourselves as agentic beings into social relations of our choosing and our imagining. That this agentic doing comes from negation is possibly not as problematic as one might think; as Freire (1998: 45) insists, 'anger should be a right as long as it is appropriate and is not allowed to degenerate into rage or even hatred'. Nevertheless, the reassertion of our agentic selves should, supposedly, compensate for any possible degenerate rage or hatred and create those countervailing discourses, because in Occupy's prefigurative context, they are apparently living their imaginings, their desires and they are, temporally, attempting to not make the capitalism that is creating their rage, which consumes people to produce their hatred. This 'subversion of politics' (Katsiaficas, 2006: 6) – the reinvention of revolution by ignoring the state and capitalist relations instead of fighting them head on, in this case by creating that space for new discourses to arise – should mean, according to Katsiaficas, that we need 'a complete reorientation of our understanding of the role of nation states and individual obedience to their laws'. This obedience is currently censored by the application of force; from the violence of both militarisation and of precarity, disobedience involves a personal risk, mediated by the type of violence that can be inflicted for the types of disobedience enacted, it is not an easy choice. However, the problems are probably inevitable, and it is 'important not to romanticise the cracks, or give them a positive force that they do not possess' (Holloway, 2010: 20). Holloway emphasises that 'the purpose of the cracks is not to produce a community of saints but to establish a different form of relations between people. They cannot be based on purity, or on puritanism' (2010: 64). 'And yet, this is where we start: from the cracks, the fissures, the rents, the spaces of rebellious negation-and-creation' (2010: 20). This notion is pertinent because the argument is that the master should not be toppled only to be replaced by a new master, ochlocracy should not abound (Thrasher, 1927), nor populist leaders installed (Arditi, 2008) only to school us otherwise. However, if this can be avoided, these hoped-for and worked-for possibilities which seek unexpected openings despite the limits of an age have been called 'untested feasibility' by Freire (1994).

Shor (1996: 61) wonders 'how much alternative thought is possible in lives crowded with distractions and work but not with critical learning or dissident culture?' For both Holloway and Freire, it is this crowding of our lives that needs to be addressed. Holloway refers to this phenomenon as alienation, whereas it can be seen in Freire's work as 'cultural invasion' (1993a: 162).

Cultural invasion, for Freire, is a form of alienation in which a culture outside of the individuals' human 'doing' 'kills the creative enthusiasm' of those individuals, groups and whole cultures who are invaded, 'leaving them hopeless and fearful of risking experimentation, without which there is no true creativity'. This notion of cultural invasion makes the act of creating the 'cracks' seem very difficult indeed. It also gives rise to the problem that the cracks themselves might practice some form of cultural invasion upon each other in order to fight the totality of capitalist relations and form a totalising form of counter-culture. Whilst, on the surface, this may seem the answer to the problem of cracking capitalism, it must be remembered that the cracks are ways in which to assert individual and collective will to reinvigorate human doing, this may be different for each individual group or community. Therefore, any attempt at creating a counter-totality could be seen as just another form of oppressive cultural invasion, hence Holloway's insistence that difference is not to be seen as a barrier or as gaps between the cracks, but as a radical democratic way of life where there can always be space for countervailing discourse and debate. Holloway argues that

> The central issue is not consciousness but sensitivity: the ability to recognise insubordinations that are not obvious and the capacity to touch those insubordinations. Consciousness or understanding certainly plays a role, but it cannot be a question of bringing consciousness from the outside but of drawing out that which is already present in undeveloped form, of bringing different experiences into resonance with one another. This takes us to a politics not of talking but of listening, or of listening-and-talking, a politics of dialogue rather than monologue.
> 
> (Holloway, 2010: 77)

The question then becomes twofold: how do we create critical awareness and space for emergent discourse in our crowded, capitalist social synthesis, and how do we create within ourselves and others the sensitivity to recognise the cracks created by others?

Holloway insists that we should walk, and walk with our eyes open, because as he says 'the revolt of doing creates a new constellation of struggles that often do not recognise themselves as part of the same constellation' (2010: 198). This is because there is possibly no one way to enact the revolt of doing; but instead a myriad of resistances, of dissenting actions, a constellation of struggles as he puts it. Here it is argued that Occupy is one, the SSC another and even the SaP initiative, and so, in its way, is this book. However, although they are connected, they are not the same. Therefore, an understanding is needed of the mechanisms that create solidarity between the 'constellation of struggles' whilst not inducing a 'cultural invasion' as Freire insists. One of the reasons for avoiding a homogenising of the individual struggles through even a well-intentioned form of cultural invasion is because, as Freire (1993a: 66) says, 'any situation in which some individuals prevent others from engaging in the process of inquiry is one of violence'. It is also pertinent to remember Holloway's warning:

> however much we try to do something different, the contradictions of capitalism reproduce themselves within our revolt. We are not pure subjects; however rebellious we might be. The cracks, both as spaces of liberation and as painful ruptures, run inside of us too.
> 
> (2010: 64)

Hence I argue that we are not only fighting capitalism on the outside, we are fighting it on the inside too:

> [D]omination itself is objectively divisive. It maintains the oppressed I in a position of 'adhesion' to a reality which seems all powerful and overwhelming, and then alienates by presenting mysterious forces which are regarded as responsible for a reality about which nothing can be done. The individual is divided between identical past and present, and a future without hope. He or she is a person who does not perceive him/herself as becoming; hence cannot have a future built in unity with others. But as she or he breaks this 'adhesion' and objectifies the reality from which he or she starts to emerge, the person begins to integrate as a Subject (an I) confronting an object (reality). At this moment, sundering the false unity of the divided self, one becomes a true individual.
> 
> (Freire, 1993a: 154)

There is the need perhaps to understand how the process of sundering the false unity of the divided self comes about. If individuals are to resolve this tension of the divided self – the self that adheres to 'reality' as Freire put it – then maybe the question should be whether we understand our situation as complete and permanent, whether we feel we know the 'truth' or whether our knowledge about 'reality' is partial and temporally situated. McLaren (1995: 15) states that this is the 'task of the ... critical educator – to live with courage and conviction with the understanding that knowledge is always partial and incomplete'. This is why critical pedagogy seems to 'fit the bill' as a mechanism to develop sensitivity to the struggles and critical awareness of the situation that they evolve within, giving space for new countervailing discourses to emerge.

However, as McLaren (2000: 15) warns, *Pedagogy of the Oppressed* cannot be taken as a 'rule book' and implanted in our own time and space. McLaren insists that

> the globalisation of capital ... and the consolidation of neoliberal education policies demand not only a vigorous and on-going engagement with Freire's work, but also a reinvention of Freire in the context of debates ... global economic restructuring, and the effort to develop new modes of revolutionary struggle.

Following this notion, this work seeks to explore whether this is happening in Occupy and the other sites. One of vital conditions of exploring this 'vigorous and on-going engagement' and beginning a 'reinvention of Freire' is advocated by Freire himself (1993a: 42), when he asserts that 'trusting the people is the indispensable precondition for revolutionary change'. Was this trust being attempted in Occupy, the SSC and SaP to varying extents? This brings the argument back once again to Holloway's notion of using trust as an organising principle. The question becomes, how should this trust be created in a world where competition and envy have become a way of life, where in both schools and the workplace individuals are kept in positions of precarity (Hardt & Negri, 2000, 2004, 2009, 2012; Harvey, 2011; The Invisible Committee, 2009) which engender mistrust, even when people appear to be working toward the same goal; this is the capitalist co-option of cooperation at work (Marx, 1867/1990). The answer, perhaps, is to start once again from the particular, to show commitment to each other's cognitive health, to engender critical thinking in all people. This starting from the particular seemed to be obvious from my experience of Occupy and somewhat so in the SSC and SaP. Each person is a particular, a unit of change, if you like, the actions in these sites attempted to create the politics of the first person heard about earlier. The idea at least, of the pedagogy in these sites, whether explicitly expressed or not, is to create critical thinkers.

Brookfield (2001: 5) tells us this about critical thinking, 'critical thinkers are actively engaged in life.... They appreciate creativity, they are innovators, and they exude a sense that life is full of possibilities'. However, this still does not create the trust apparently needed, but goes a long way to creating the conditions for individuals to create 'cracks' in their relationships with capitalism through the expression of countervailing discourses as the sense of imminent possibility might encourage individuals to enact those possibilities. However, Brookfield (2001: 7) goes on to add that 'emotions are central to the critical thinking process' and Ollis (2012: 216) attests, 'humans are emotional beings and the emotions are central to any learning process'. Polletta (2006) further confirms that emotions take a central place in protest and politics. We also feel, according to Brookfield (2001: 7) 'joy, release, relief and exhilaration' as we find new ways of thinking about and viewing our personal and political worlds. This emotionality was evident in the aspects of Occupy that I observed and the Occupiers I spoke to, but in no simple way and the discussion is here primarily to underscore that sundering the false unity of the divided self and becoming a true individual as Freire insisted earlier is no simple or logical act.

However, as several thinkers agree (see, for example, Holloway, 2010; Brookfield, 2001; Freire, 1993a; among others) finding the right time and motivation to encourage critical thinking is essential in the context of the political juncture in which this enquiry sat; Castells (2012: 15) offers this:

> if any individuals feel humiliated, exploited, ignored or misrepresented, they are ready to transform their anger into action, as soon as they

overcome their fear. And they overcome their fear by the extreme expression of anger, in the form of outrage.... The faster and more interactive the process of communication is, the more likely the formation of a process of collective action becomes, rooted in outrage, propelled by enthusiasm and motivated by hope.

Groups and organisations that already exist and new ones in formation as a result of this 'outrage' might be well served by rising to the opportunity and creating this fast and interactive communication by way of displaying and encouraging critical thinking. I argue this because of the following notions proposed by Brookfield: first, 'critical thinkers see the future as open and malleable, not as closed and fixed. They are self-confident about their potential for changing aspects of their worlds, both as individuals and through collective action' (2001: 5); and second 'critical thinkers become immediately suspicious of those who say they have all the answers to all of life's problems' (2001: 9). If these notions are correct, then the people within these groups should be well placed to create the cracks in capitalism. In addition, under this assumption the pedagogy of the popular education of Occupy and the attempts at change from the other sites become essential elements of the overall political project, as once again, starting from the particular, the individual, change may occur.

According to Shor (1996: 163), these notions also fit Freire's (1993a) definition of critical consciousness as 'subjective intervention into history, as consciousness of, for, and against something, as "intentionality" vis-à-vis social experience, a reaching out to rethink reality and to act purposefully in it'. If critical thinking, leading to a critical consciousness, which engenders acting purposefully through subjective intervention into history, takes place in collectives and groups, then, I argue, trust would have to become the centrally organising principle; it would, if the argument were to be followed, be a definite precondition of any social change. This trust would therefore, as Holloway (2010: 261) proposes it must, 'break the walls around our thinking, the rigidification of our thought'. With this newly developed critical consciousness individuals should then have the potential to 'break the walls by refusing to build them' (Holloway, 2010: 261). What is more, the conditions seem to have the potential at the present historical moment as Katsiaficas (2006: 244) reminds us, 'under post-Fordist conditions, the locus and content of social movements assume new forms'. Therefore, if social movements are the groups and collectives spoken about here, then they could have the potential to become the mechanisms for building sensitivity and critical awareness.

However, in the past, and indeed in the literature, critical thinking, critical consciousness and revolutionary change have usually had a teacher, a leader, a vanguard. Next we need a discussion of what the possible conditions are for disposing of these old roles in creating revolutionary subjects from the people who are angry and outraged. Merrifield (2011a: 133) says that we need more zone[s] of indistinguishability, another space of slippage, a space in which there's a lot of spontaneous energy as well as a few signs indicating where to go and what time the action begins. We need a new space of slippage in which we can organise and strategize, act without self-consciously performing, encounter others without walls, and hatch en masse a daring Great Escape from capitalism.

These zones of indistinguishability, spaces of slippage, can be seen as education, as learning, as personal development, whatever name one wishes to place on the human activity that increases knowledge, the capacity to understand and act, and the exercise of the collective imagination. However, it is important to fully understand this romantic notion – a zone indistinguishable from what, slipping to and from where? The indistinguishability comes from the notion of the boundary police spoken of by Foust (2010), a space which is not too far from normative practice to be noticed by the boundary policing authorities, but slipping enough from hegemonic control to be of some revolutionary worth. These sites that are not yet so alternative that they are crushed, co-opted or disintegrate from the disappointment of unrealistic expectations, but have the ethos of creation, of spontaneity, of sociality reborn. Occupy was seen to be more than a space of slippage; it certainly did not escape the boundary policing authorities of public life, of the mass media and of the state. Perhaps, however, the SSC was a site of slippage, indistinguishable from other community projects that do not threaten the status quo, but with the potential to slip incrementally further from the control of elites to the point where the Great Escape can be hatched.

Contemporary forms of Open Marxism (see Bonefeld, *et al.*, 1992; Della Costa, 1995; Fine, 1995; Gerstenberger, 1992; Gunn, 1992; Negri, 1992) call for the abandonment of revolutionary leaders promising us a future revolution, leaving revolution as a perpetual possibility and never a present reality. In these ideas, it is argued variously that there is no longer the need for Trade Unions, for example, negotiating what Holloway calls the 'new terms of our enslavement' (also see Gorz, 1997; The Invisible Committee, 2009; Lotringer & Marazzi, 2007, among others). Therefore, working in this context, further exploration with the express purpose of understanding the relevance and necessity of the pedagogue, the educational vanguard, if you like, in education needs to take place.

Here, then, is an exploration of the work of Ira Shor and Jacques Rancière. Setting Shor and Rancière into 'debate' provides a way of drawing out what is at stake because in Rancière's book *The Ignorant Schoolmaster*, he posits an interesting argument which connects with Occupy's refrain 'anyone can teach, everyone can learn' (Tent City University, 2012), and therefore may give some theoretical insight into the pedagogy of Occupy. Whereas in Shor's work, a democratic, power sharing pedagogy is defined wherein the 'teacher' is still the 'teacher' but invites a shared power in the pedagogical space. Therefore, putting them into debate potentially allows for the development of an

## 70  Political? Pedagogical? Philosophical?

understanding of the (un)necessity of the teacher in an emancipating pedagogy, in addition to a possible understanding of what is it that emancipates people from passive reception of learning, and therefore the logic of capitalism that pervades their lives. First, some general thoughts from various educators and educational theorists before, second, concentrating on these two particular schools of thought, in order to attempt to understand 'people'- as *producers of knowledge* (Roggero, 2011; Neary, 2012; Neary & Amsler, 2012) and then move onto the detailed debate. So, how does one become a producer of knowledge?

Dewey (1997: 67) has this to offer as a starting point:

> there is, I think, no point in the philosophy of progressive education which is sounder than its emphasis upon the importance of the participation of the learner in the formation of the purposes which direct his activities in the learning process.

The starting notion, then, is that any learner must be involved in the *formation of the purposes* of education. The learner must be in charge of, not only the content of their learning, but also the purpose for which they are learning it. This notion rules out the 'banking' of officially sanctioned knowledge into learners (Freire, 1993a) of 'truth'. This may at first glance suggest merely a critical education, however, Holloway's warning that 'teachers who take their schools to create a critical education may possibly reproduce authoritarian practices as bad as those which they are rejecting' (2010: 19) is pertinent, especially in the contexts being explored here. Care must be taken, therefore, not to allow a radical concept of education and social change to be subsumed into the liberal discourse of individual empowerment and emancipation, which, according to some leads only to producing better consumers, and a better army of workers for the purposes of capital (Allman, 2010; Au & Apple, 2009; Reitz, 2000). The critical pedagogy that this work proposes, is *at the very least* what Freire (1993a: 36) espouses:

> the pedagogy of the oppressed ... has two distinct stages. In the first, the oppressed unveil the world of oppression and through praxis commit themselves to its transformation. In the second stage, in which the reality of oppression has already been transformed, this pedagogy ceases to belong to the oppressed and becomes a pedagogy for all people in the process of permanent liberation. In both stages, it is always through action in depth that the culture of domination is culturally confronted.

Thus, creating a conscientised oppressed people that will transform the conditions of their lives rendering oppression defunct, this is because the more people who become conscientised and committed to transformational praxis, the less oppressors' tactics will be successful in seducing the people into conditions of consensual oppression (Herman & Chomsky, 1994; La Boétie, 1548/2002). I use the term consensual oppression, for as long as people do not want to acknowledge the oppressive conditions of their lives, or do not see their condition as oppressed, then they are consenting to oppressive practices. As Freire says above, the pedagogy becomes a *process* of *permanent liberation*, through deep cultural confrontation with any culture of domination. The question therefore, is how do we prevent emerging cultures of domination, especially when even in Freire's work, there is a pedagogical vanguardism that could, in itself become a dominating force, as Holloway suggested.

A detailed examination of two models or theories of pedagogy now seems appropriate – first Rancière's work and then, later, Shor's, in order to utilise their arguments as a framework for the analysis of the stories from the actions in the next chapter.

In his book *The Ignorant Schoolmaster* (1991: 4), Rancière examines the work of Joseph Jacotot, whose explorations in teaching led him to wonder, 'were the schoolmaster's explications ... superfluous? Or, if they weren't, to whom and for what were they useful?' In other words, did learning need an 'expert teacher'? The point of Jacotot's, and therefore Rancière's, argument is that no one who considers themselves a learner needs a teacher to *explain* their learning – neither the content, nor the reason for learning – to them. Additional ideas on this notion could also be gleaned from The School of Barbiana (1969) in Italy, where the children taught themselves, but for this discussion I shall limit the ideas to those posited by Rancière. The issues explored in Rancière's book also illuminate the notion that no one person knows everything and that all individuals are ignorant in some sense or other. This notion ties in, also, to the idea expressed earlier that knowledge is always partial and temporary. The title of the book, *The Ignorant Schoolmaster*, also sheds some light on the dichotomy of 'Master' and 'the ignorant', in that it posits the Master *as* the ignorant and thus allows for the intelligence of the student, the multitude, the democratic subject to be announced, thus *potentially* providing a way of thinking about the removal of the Master without having to replace the figure with another. In light of the pedagogical and political arguments under examination in this work, this is an important argument for the kind of autonomous prefigurative politics I have already discussed.

Creating the conditions and possibilities for the production and sharing of knowledge is, for many critical educators, the most essential role of the teacher or pedagogue (see, for example, Giroux, 1988, 2001, 2011; Macrine, 2009; Mayo, 2004; Shor, 1992, 1996; Shor & Freire, 1987). At the heart of what Rancière calls 'universal teaching' – that is teaching what one does not know – in order to create emancipated subjects, however, is the idea of equality of intelligence. It is this foundation that, he insists, is missing from other educational projects, even ones that claim to be emancipatory:

> explication is the myth of pedagogy, the parable of a world divided into knowing minds and ignorant ones, ripe minds and immature ones, the capable and the incapable, the intelligent and the stupid.
>
> (1991: 6)

In other words, the foundational belief underpinning traditional explicative pedagogy is that intelligence is nurtured through teaching; one begins education stupid and finishes it intelligent, through the efforts of the knowing and capable minds of the pedagogues. These are argued to be attractive myths for those who wish to subjugate the production of lived knowledge and oppress those whom society does not deem worthy of entering their grand institutions of learning. Rancière argues, however, that a 'peasant, an artisan, will be intellectually emancipated if he thinks about what he is and what he does in the social order' (33). This can be accomplished with 'a minimum of instruction, drawn from the principles of reason, science and the general interest' (34). This intellectual emancipation constituted by the learner thinking about what they are in the social order resonates with Freire's (1993, 1998, 2008) arguments about conscientization. In Freire's view, people are conscientised when they become aware of their place in society, locally, nationally and globally, their political awareness is heightened by this understanding and therefore their capacity to act upon the conditions of their own existence is extended. In the view of critical pedagogy, this is how the unveiling of oppression to the oppressed is achieved, or perhaps, as Rancière puts it: 'to put sane notions into the heads that would otherwise form faulty ones' (1991: 34).

Rancière's justification for universal teaching, or what a Freirean might term teaching through a questioning pedagogy, what one does not know oneself, is simple:

> there is no one on earth who hasn't learnt something by himself and without a master explicator ... universal teaching ... has existed since the beginning of the world, alongside all of the explicative methods.
> (1991: 16)

It becomes apparent from this that the main argument as to why universal teaching would work is that it is a human trait, hard wired since birth, to learn, by observing, by questioning and by trial and error. One might ask at this point why are we not all using this method of universal teaching? This is however, where we return to the earlier discussion about mechanisms of sensitivity to the cracks in capitalism: how do we recognise the cracks and how do we prevent them from being consumed by the logic of capital. Rancière offers this:

> how can the learned master ever understand that he can teach what he [sic] doesn't know as successfully as what he does know? He cannot but take that increase in intellectual power as a devaluation of his science. And the ignorant one, on his side, doesn't believe himself capable of learning by himself, still less of being able to teach another ignorant person. Those excluded from the world of intelligence themselves subscribe to the verdict of their exclusion. In short, the circle of emancipation must be begun.
> (1991: 15–16)

Herein lies the problem. Everyone in this social relation of learning must *believe* certain fundamental things about themselves and others in order for universal teaching to become commonplace, workable and accepted. This is, again, where the debate returns to the tenets of critical pedagogy and of Holloway's thesis. Freire insisted that the levels, modes and logic of oppression must firstly be unveiled to the oppressed in order for them to become emancipated. Holloway (2010: 212–13), on the other hand, talks in terms of 'character masks', wherein the character masks that we don in our forced social roles hide a deeper conflict within ourselves, where there is no pure human being waiting to be emancipated but a disfigured, shadowy figure (2010: 222). He argues that what is needed is a dialogue that tries to 'see and hear and touch the shadowy figure behind the character masks' (225), which would 'give voice to and stir the passions and dignities that lie below' (226). Only then can the emancipation that Rancière's ignorant schoolmaster hopes to engender be accomplished, because as Rancière maintains,

> to emancipate an ignorant person, one must be, and one need only be, emancipated oneself, that is to say, conscious of the true power of the human mind. The ignorant person will learn by himself what the master doesn't know if the master believes he can and obliges him to realise his capacity.
>
> (1991: 15)

Therefore, it seems that a tension exists in this argument about how to begin. Rancière's argument is most persuasive and indeed seems to be in keeping with a radical reading of critical pedagogy in certain ways; both its insistence in the equality of intelligence, as a foundational starting point for any emancipatory learning, and with the notion that the project has to be begun by an emancipated pedagogue in order to start the cycle; in Rancière's words:

> we know that it is this that defines the stultifying vision of the world: to believe in the reality of inequality, to imagine that the superiors in society are truly superior, and that society would be in danger if the idea should spread, especially among the lower classes, that this superiority is only a conventional fiction. In fact, only an emancipated person is untroubled by the idea that the social order is entirely conventional.
>
> (1991: 109)

As Rancière points out, in effect the project of universal teaching cannot be begun in mainstream educational establishments as

> how, without opening up an abyss under their own feet, can they [those that are tasked with the governance of our education systems] say to working people that they don't need them in order to be free men [sic], in order to be educated in everything suitable to their dignity as men?
>
> (1991: 129)

Therefore, I would argue that we need to return to subversive cracks in order to *begin* this project, sites of slippage and radical, emancipated pedagogues, as those with a vested interest in the status quo cannot be trusted to begin the project, as Rancière has pointed out above. Where then to begin the project as the 'vanguard' of this method, whilst avoiding the traps of a permanent vanguardism and potential slide into oppressive regression?

It is here we turn to the work of Ira Shor, and in particular his reflexive book *When Students Have Power* (1996) which examines democratic pedagogy. Because the politics of Occupy were apparently democratic and horizontal, then maybe a pedagogy that reflects these values has the potential to lead to a greater understanding and uncover untested feasibilities for the sites explored here. Shor insists that in educational settings, before teaching any disciplinary content and conflicts among scholars in our chosen fields teachers must first 'face the always already existing conflicts between students and the teacher, between students and the institution, between students and the economic system and between students and themselves' (Shor, 1996: 17). This conflict was evident from several of the Occupiers who told me they had no education and no jobs and therefore would be of no interest to my study, indicating that this conflict was debilitating in terms of self-esteem. Shor insists that one of the ways that these conflicts can be addressed is by what he calls the 'withering away of the teacher' (1996). Shor stresses that this withering away is not to suggest that the teacher is to be got rid of all together, but merely in a symbolic sense and in the specific sense of the ultimate power of the teacher being shared with all of the pedagogical participants. Shor warns thusly: 'years of socialisation have led us to internalise the unilateral authority of the teacher as the normal 'common sense' way to do education' (27) and reflects that 'without formal participation in decision making, students develop as authority-dependent subordinates, not as independent citizens' (31). The Occupiers I met were participating in decision-making, but as we shall see in the next chapter, their participation was not formal and therefore sometimes ended up feeling disempowering. However, it is this dynamic that is the crux of the issue for Shor, the participation in formal decision making, not, as for Rancière, the teacher's explication. However, where Shor and Rancière do seem to agree, if one reads an unspoken assumption into Shor's work, is that education should be founded upon a belief in the equality of intelligence: one cannot insist that students can fully participate in formal decision making without being equally as intelligent as the teacher. What Shor does say, however, is that 'it is risky to hand over authority to the students all at once. That could be bewildering and unproductive, even arrogant' (18). Later in the book, Shor elaborates on the reasons why this is so:

> the students don't see themselves constructed intellectually and emotionally by the 'system' and its machinery. It sometimes feels to me like we are living in two different worlds, their blithely ignoring hegemony and mine ferociously foregrounding it, theirs a place of autonomous individuality

and self-creation while my world is a place of the socially constructed self. They focus on individualism and self-reliance, two hegemonic values deeply embedded in corporate society, but which they experience contradictorily as values through which to resist the 'system'.

(1996: 103)

Therefore, for Shor, one might assume it is this socialisation that has led to the students seeing themselves as autonomous individuals, self-constructed rather than seeing themselves in relation to hegemony – resisting the system with the very values it itself instils in them – that is the problem, not the explications of the 'master', as in Rancière's view. However, on further examination, Shor comes back to the idea espoused by Freire: it is through his power sharing methods that the pedagogue creates the conditions for learning, not merely transmits what is to be learned. One of the questions for Occupy particularly, but also the other sites, is that of whether these conditions for learning were being created without the assistance of a skilled pedagogue. Shor describes how students become empowered by sharing power with the teacher, by participating in the 'formation of the purposes which direct his activities in the learning process' as Dewey insisted earlier. Shor's students very much direct the process in the classroom. However, Shor is not attempting to teach what he does not know. Shor's students are not autonomous learners in this sense; Shor insists that he is not attempting to produce autonomous, but *collective* learners. He asserts that he is attempting to engender a classroom culture of criticality, through a democratic critical pedagogy:

the borders of critical culture appear when a discourse questions existing knowledge and unequal power relations, when it imagines democratic alternatives departing from authoritarian business-as-usual, when it connects subjectivity to history while relating personal contexts to social contexts and academic texts, when it situates the theme of 'social justice' at the centre of knowledge-making enterprise.

(1996: 180)

One of the emergent questions, then, becomes whether a critical culture can appear through a *popular education*, such as Occupy seemed to be, that is apparently doing the very things that Shor refers to in the quote above. Shor describes in the book how he used his expertise, his assumed authority as a white male professor in a community college to create the conditions for reaching, at least the borders of, a critical culture if not creating a micro-culture in his classroom. However, could this be achieved on the streets in Occupy, the SSC or even SaP, as well as the social centres and public spaces, enclosed by capitalist social relations? Holloway (2010: 95) insists that 'going to the root of things and understanding that root as our own activity is crucial'. This, I argue, can be read in both Shor and Rancière as an agreed fundamental; that the education we practice has to be a 'root' of society and therefore has to be *our own activity*. In all the sites explored here, creating an educative practice that is the learner's own activity was attempted, but with how much success? What more could be asked of these sites? Rancière argues that 'government doesn't owe the people an education, for the simple reason that one doesn't owe people what they can take for themselves. And education is like liberty: it isn't given, it's taken' (1991: 107). Perhaps if education is understood in this way, as like liberty, something that cannot be given or even provided for us, then the idea, declared by Occupy, that 'anyone can teach, everyone can learn' becomes crucial to the understanding of how an emancipatory pedagogy, with the specific aim of escaping from capitalist enclosure and creating a new form of commonism (Neary & Winn, 2012; Shantz, 2013), can be constituted. However, further to this, the notion of 'taking' education rather than it being granted also speaks of the *demand* to do things differently, it becomes therefore, not about promoting interests as with schooling, but about having a voice; demand requires constituting the multitude's voice, creating countervailing discourses, as do radical forms of democracy. Is it so then, that the multitude demands, in its multiplicity, that radical education provides us with the necessary know how to produce a commons that becomes a shared symbolic place for creative responses (Mouffe, 2013) to social problems, responded to by the strength of our differences (Hardt & Negri, 2004), rather than our consensus?

Shor says that his classroom was 'very busy, intense, and often difficult as well as conflicted, but it was also ... convivial and enchanting' (1996: 126). This is surely an attribute of radical democratic culture in general, and particularly deliberative democracy, as can be seen in the works of Mouffe (2005, 2013), Rancière (1998, 2004, 2011), Merrifield (2011a), among others. Rose (1990: 238) has this to say on the subject; 'democratic culture is, by definition, vibrant and dynamic, discomforting and unpredictable. It gives rise to apprehension; freedom is not always calming'. Holloway adds, 'we light a match: that gives light and heat, but if a spark flies, the whole forest catches fire, then the flame acquires a different meaning' (2010: 73). I argue that this idea can be read as relating to either the spreading cracks in capitalism, as was intended, or as the disquieting effects of democracy, even pedagogical democracy, or even as the power sharing methods espoused by Shor.

In his practice, Shor insists that he attempts to

> search for the untested and unpredictable openings at the margins and in the cracks of the group I was approaching, where I might find territory less captured by the status quo, where some critical thought, civic ideals, and democratic relations were possible even in conservative times.
> (1996: 3)

He admits that if the power-sharing, critical and democratic lessons were at the behest of the students 'an entirely different counterhegemonic politics would be represented' (1996: 75) and as a result his efforts are 'a cultural exercise or laboratory, not a social movement of broad change in school and society' (74). However, this recognition, although important, need not take away from the discussion underway here, nor the references to Occupy. What Shor found during his cultural exercise or laboratory teaching was what he describes as becoming

> repositioned in the process as a special participant, not exactly equal to the students and not exactly separate from them either. Affectively, in power sharing, I experience a changing role which feels like moving with instead of pushing, a lightness of being part of instead of the weightiness of being solely in charge of. Shared authority is thus a transformative 'apparatus of power' ... a means to overcome unilateral authority by democratising power relations and a means to critically study subject matter.
>
> (1996: 154)

This feeling that Shor describes is important for understanding how a vanguard of educators might be created, who can then *relinquish that power*, ensuring that the teacher vanguard does not become a dominant authority who can then exercise unilateral power over learners. The implications of this are many: instead of officially sanctioned knowledge being 'banked' into learners, a carefully orchestrated production of living knowledge, garnered from the sometimes antagonistic democratic relations of a classroom in which the power is shared may be possible. A new relationship between learners and teachers could be brought to bear on the pedagogical process, one in which the learners would have an active and collective role in productively policing the authority of the teacher. This would ensure that the learners' voice was heard not only in the production of knowledge but also in the way that knowledge was handled and transmitted from subject to subject, thus potentially ensuring that there could be no real *hidden* ideologies in the education being practiced. In this context, the teacher need not relinquish his or her position as 'expert' in a particular field, as Rancière feels is imperative for emancipation to ensue, but would have that expertise examined by learners for signs of ideological positioning and manipulation. The pedagogical relationship would become one of mutual respect and collective self-monitoring. The learners would then be able to collectively manage their own learning independent of the teacher. The teacher and their expertise would become a 'springboard' from which the learners, autonomously of the teacher, continue their learning though collective discussion and dialogue, switching to a form of universal teaching. I argue that this is where this particular reading of the theory progresses to, these logical assumptions. As Freire says throughout his work, critical pedagogy creates the conditions for learning to take place: it does not emancipate on its own, it cannot unveil a single truth. However, what he claims it does – and I would argue this is evidenced in the reflective writings of Shor and others (see, for example, Bahruth & Steiner, 2000; Kincheloe & Steinberg, 1988) – is create a problematisation of the everyday lives of oppressed peoples and reflect those conditions back to them as objective problems to be collectively solved (Freire, 1993a). In turn, this allows for objective distance from the issues, conflicts and woes of lived experience. Placed in a modern context, this technique of problem posing has the potential to allow individuals and groups to think and imagine differently. It can allow people to step outside the subjective view of their own lives and to relate their worries to the larger social milieu and view them as connected to the whole and socially constructed through dominant and oppressive practices. The expertise of the teacher, both in subject content and in delivery of the pedagogy, then creates the conditions for oppressed peoples to emancipate themselves. Simply put, critical pedagogy asks learners to think of the personal as political, thus enabling a connection to others and hopefully creations of common goals against domination, oppression, and exploitation.

Having situated the case studies in Chapter 2, and examined the theory that is indicative of the thinking of those involved in the groups, movements and initiatives, pertaining to the pedagogical and educational aspects in this chapter, the theory needs to be engaged in conversation with the data in what comes next.

## Note

1 This quote has been attributed to many people, for example Slavoj Žižek, Holloway quotes it from Turbulence (http://turbulence.org.uk/turbulence-4/present-tense-future-conditional/) whose article states the difficulty tracking down the original source for the quote.

# 4 Organic education from the ground up
## Stories from Occupy

Here, I explore whether the forms of pedagogy practiced within Occupy were transformative, or whether they merely (re)produced forms of schooling. Asking, is it possible to dispense with current educational organisational forms? Can we introduce new forms containing, and developed by, countervailing discourses? Would these forms of organic pedagogy challenge conditioned behaviours? I now explore Occupy in detail.

> Rick: *I love it here, in the camp. It's so free, we can talk about anything, imagine anything and people are so respectful of other people's views. It's been a great experiment in creating a new society, where, even though there are rules, because we need to make sure everyone is safe and no one feels threatened or dismissed, even though there are rules we are really free and pretty much anything goes ... unless of course you criticise direct democracy, some of us don't think it's working as most people don't get their say and one person can block everyone else because we have to reach consensus ... you can't criticise it though, you'd be, well I don't know, I don't really want to find out what might happen, nobody is talking about it, but I bet there are a few of us who think it ... anyway, it's still great here, we really are imagining a different way to do things.*

These words illuminate the problematic nature of the organic pedagogy unfolding in the movement – we are here to dream, to imagine, but what we imagined has to be seen to work and should not be criticised.

To understand this problematic, the discussion here concentrates on the interactions I had with Occupiers to give preference to the *voices* of the *individuals* involved, and to supplement these voices where necessary from stories and experiences collected elsewhere; from the internet and scholarly works. These interactions will be in italics in what follows, so as not to crowd the text.

The theory explored in the last chapter gave rise to some fundamental questions to assist with the exploration that follows, these are used to guide discussion. There were some 'indications' as to what to look for to identify whether the pedagogy was transformative and equitable. So, what follows puts the theory and the stories into dialogue.

I want to attempt to generate a picture of the learning and question whether it engaged the Occupiers with new social relations, replacing those synthesised by capitalism. Did it engender relations that allowed countervailing discourses to emerge from the assertion of the right to public assembly. Understanding the political as not merely party business, but as the moment when a radical change becomes possible (Rancière, 1995, 1998, 2011), where social and political organisation fall into each other to create the conditions for transformative change. Therefore, the questions firstly attend to concerns such as whether the education produced a collective experience (Holloway, 2010)? Did the education unveil how individuals view their place in the world and connect the self with the social (Freire, 1993a)? And did the education use the notion of free use of time through the right to public assembly (Holloway, 2010)?

The Occupiers told me that they felt that they needed to reimagine social relations in order for Society to move beyond corporate greed and bank bailouts. They understood the hegemony of neoliberal economic theory as having an alternative, and often asserted that that alternative lay in the way individuals connected themselves to each other, to the modes of production, and to the sociality of the human experience:

Lisa: *We can't change things if we carry on with capitalism. If we try to stick to this system, then they're right, there is no alternative. But if we change the way we think about each other, the way we think about the relationships we have, the idea of sharing rather than owning, if we cooperate instead of competing, then maybe we can get things done. If we just learn to trust each other and think creatively about what things could be like, then I reckon we can change things, yeah.*

This begs the question, were people were learning to change these relations, or if not, what prevented them from doing so? Although this quote seems to affirm that they were at least trying, does the previous one indicate that this was a façade of a more deeply embedded necessity to be *seen to be* doing something, rather than letting the unfettered imagination and prefiguration play its course? This creates a complex picture.

Occupiers I spoke to stressed the importance of *making connections* with others, connections that were emotional and productive. Meeting and working with new people that one might otherwise never have met was mentioned repeatedly. The eclectic mix of people in and around the camps meant that individuals were encountering many different people. There were homeless, middle class, and unemployed people, ex-soldiers, full time activists, graduate students, academics, and others who were interacting, sitting around discussing politics; helping each other cope with the cold; making banners; telling stories; providing nourishment; and sharing resources. In addition, there were those who wandered in, attempting to understand what Occupy were doing, something that often entailed quite intense discussions. One Occupier, Sarah, told me, '*now I value friendships more and I value the people that I meet and their* views more. *At work, it was all about who you met and why you met them and what they could do for you and now I feel I always have as much to offer as to gain'*. Shor (1996: 61) pertinently asks, 'how much alternative thought is possible in lives crowded with distractions and work but not with critical learning or dissident culture?' The apparent inclusivity and space in people's lives, allowing them to make connections with a variety of others, they insisted, gave rise to new experiences including the understanding of different epistemologies and worldviews.

> Wendy: *I know so much more about other cultures and nationalities since coming here, usually you're afraid to ask what it's like being someone else, but here, for the most part, no one minds.*

Understanding different world views is important in the theorisation of transformative pedagogy, these experiences and connections between otherwise unacquainted lives can lead to a newly developed sensitivity to the Other; their needs and desires. As Brookfield (2001: 17) argues, when we think critically about new experiences, 'we come to realise that the assumptions governing the way we behave ... are, at least partly, the result of cultural factors'. If Brookfield is correct, the culture of the movement was of particular significance. I was told that the culture they were attempting was a collective one:

> Julie: *We want to create a new type of community, where everything is shared and everyone is equal.*
> Peter: *Everyone is an individual, but we are all in this together, as a sort of collective, we want everyone to have their voice heard, to be involved in everything in some way. Of course, everyone has different passions and interests and they are able to do things that particularly interest them, but we all have a say on the big issues, through the GAs and direct democracy.*
> John: *This is a collective, everyone has their own story, their own reason for being here, but we are all together, we share everything, including our stories.*

Identifying activities that engendered a collective culture was important to the people there, as was ensuring that this collective ethos and commons was not mere rhetoric, but was a prevailing lived experience. The General Assembly (GA) seemed to be a galvanising point for this:

> Donny: *On a weekend afternoon, when it was still quite warm [2011], there were hundreds of people, and there were bankers coming to check [the GA] out, and everybody was there and it was very exciting, fantastic and that's how the whole thing is.*

That there were also bankers at the GAs suggests that the movement was attempting to be inclusive and more about producing collective knowledge than about protesting or confronting power head on. The dynamics of power were being changed through the GA, from a power that excludes – that of normative capitalist relations – to a power that allows encompassment of all (Mouffe, 1999), if that power was felt by all involved. An educative experience can arise from such a power structure as Shor (in Macrine, 2009: 121) acknowledges when he says that

> Given that education is a social experience, that all social experience is formative, and that all formative experiences embed one value system or another it is impossible, then, to form or shape humans in any manner without implicating norms and orientations for thought and action.... Education is politics, then, simply because it develops students and teachers this way or that way depending on the values underlying the learning process.

These values of inclusiveness, on one hand, should serve to open the movement to those who might not normally become involved in collective action, or to those who merely want to know what discourses are taking place. On the other hand, this inclusiveness disrupts Shor's view that all social, formative experiences embed one value system or another, as the process of Occupy was claimed to be to prefigure new, sometimes unexplored, value systems. The ideology was reportedly 'post-ideological', which is, of course, an ideological stance in itself. So, what values were underlying the learning process? Several possibly competing values surface, those of the reported adherence to the ideal of consensus democracy as an autocratic value, and those of collectivism, commons creations, and the use of the political and sociological imagination. However, inclusiveness guards against another potential problematic: Freire (1993a: 38) warns that the oppressed must not become the oppressor, but must work with the oppressor to transform relations of power:

> it is only the oppressed, by freeing themselves, can free their oppressors. The latter, as an oppressive class, can free neither others nor themselves. It is therefore essential that the oppressed wage the struggle to resolve the contradiction in which they are caught; and the contradiction will be resolved by the appearance of the new man; neither oppressor nor oppressed, but man in the process of liberation.

The values underlying the learning process at the GAs seemed very much to be collectivist, inclusive and open to everyone. Nevertheless, as the dissent toward the ideal of consensus democracy became greater, the oppression seemed to be turned toward the dissenting Occupiers as was illustrated earlier. However, as Holloway (2010: 248) points out 'the more we join with others, the greater our creative power'. For instance, Paul told me that

> *that's how I got involved, because I popped along with my partner on the Saturday [to the GA], and we just kind of stood at the back and the next*

Saturday I ended up standing up and saying something and then I just kind of volunteered to kind of help put on the general assemblies and stuff, and that's how I got into it.

The GAs were quite commonly how people became involved in Occupy, there was a general feeling that the GA, and therefore the movement, was inclusive enough for them to become active within it. I was told by Sharon that

> sitting there on the steps of St. Paul's felt like there was now a community, a community of people who believed things could be different, who believed we should all be involved in the escape from greed and competition. Who believed that we should do this together, I didn't feel so alone, so desperate.

Without this inclusivity and feeling of common, shared experience, the enclosure of capitalist social relations may well, as Merrifield (2011: 129) suggests, have allowed 'the factuality of the "real world" [to be] afforded too much critical right. One simply lashed out in the prison-house of negativity'. These experiences of the GAs and the feeling of what Mary, called '*communing and collaborating with others*', challenges, if not undoes, this factuality and circumvents the need to 'lash out'.

These accounts suggest that Occupy did foster alternative social relationships in order to prefigure new commons, if not new societies, in what was claimed as public space. However, this collective gathering in the first months of the Occupation was fuelled by an elation that '*something really different was happening*' (John), '*there was something really exciting going on and so many people were getting involved*' (Kate) and '*it was like being in a fast-flowing river, you thought that things could and would really change, that we could make the whole world a better place, there was such a feeling of joy and optimism*' (Gerry). This elation of a different way of doing, being, creating, and feeling was described by some as '*addictive*', '*intoxicating*' and '*the most exciting thing I'd ever felt*'. These are strong emotions and are an important part of the practice of transformative politics (Ollis, 2012; Polletta, 2006), but, there was also a necessity for reason, reflection and a critical outlook on the organisational processes that are creating the ecstatic experience. Otherwise nuances and examples of conditioned repressive behaviours may be missed when experiencing strong emotions, especially, I would argue, the emotion of hope in a collective setting when that experience replaces loneliness:

> Peter: *After the financial crash, I lost my job, I almost lost my house and my relationship, it felt like I was totally alone. But going to GAs I realised that there were loads of people effected and that they wanted to do something about it. It felt so great to be around other people with similar stories all talking about what we could do about it, about different ways to change the situation. I didn't care that some of the suggestions were a bit out there, it all sounded so good, like we could do anything.*

It is pertinent to remember that what Occupy did achieve, for a few months, was a commons interrupting that which was private, exposing a rupture in individualism, which in itself was a countervailing discourse. The subsequent defence of this rupture was a learning curve as I shall explore later.

Occupy extended beyond the encampment and into virtual spaces, which allowed for the extension of the collective experience and collaborative learning practices, however messy this was in reality. Social media was used to connect Occupiers around the world, therefore connecting the self with the social through a collective identity, whether users were physically active in the movement or not as Jenny explained:

> *We use Facebook or Twitter, you have to be quite up on all the feeds and know what's going on. When you're sitting at home thinking this is really unfair and I can't believe what's going on, then you can see that in London they're doing something, or in New York they're doing something. I used to watch the GAs at London Stock Exchange, and I just kind of found it really inspiring, so I started to email people or on the live talk when the GAs were on saying I'm watching you in [city] keep up the good work, and stuff like that. I've joined a lot of the global occupy, feeds and email and every now and then I will just like send a message saying sending best wishes. I come to London regularly now though, because of that.*

The connections across the different Occupy sites and groups were important, as many Occupiers told me. The feeling of solidarity gave individuals and groups the chance to learn new tactics, new ways of thinking about things, and most importantly to them the feeling that they were not alone, that there were other people attempting to prefigure new cultures around the globe. Occupiers told me that the national and international movements have been inspired by each other, movements such as the so-called 'Arab Spring', the student occupations against cuts and fees and other uprisings, such as in Greece, Hong Kong, and the Ukraine (Byrne, 2012; Chomsky, 2012; Hensby, 2014; Mowbray, 2010; Panayotakis, 2009). The feeling of solidarity provided by these connections created a collective cultural politics that was being learnt as it unfolded. The virtual connectedness seemed to work well as Occupiers, rebels and protesters felt that they had found solidarity and learnt from each other's tactics and triumphs. Stories were shared about how to resist arrest, how to build barricades and how to keep up morale. The learning from these virtual interactions was specific: knowledge that others were supporting you from around the globe and specific 'training' information on practical matters. Here the 'teachers' were experts, through a lived learning and the students needed their specific expertise, although, no 'learned' pedagogue was required, just the lived knowledge of those in opposition to the repression they experienced as a galvanising mechanism.

The networks of people were able to share that collective space in a very different way to the camps, there was no real, physical commitment to each other online. The camps had specific problems as people readily explained:

*Organic education from the ground up* 85

> Danny: *Sometimes it feels like we are just surviving here, we can become so inward looking, there is so much to organise, beds, blankets, warm clothes, when we don't get the donations we need, politics goes out the window, we just need to keep going, sometimes, it's easy to forget why we're here.*

The LSX camp was in occupation throughout a bitterly cold winter, and there were conflicts within the camps:

> Paul: *It's really difficult when you don't agree with people here, you quite often find people shifting alliances, we live so close to each other, even if you don't sleep here it's still hard cos everyone knows everyone else and we all try to get along, but there are always some people you'll never get on with, no one has figured out what to do about that, so we have lost some people.*

These tensions are difficult to resolve and it seemed that no one felt that it was their responsibility to try. The question came up in my mind of was the learning about new social relationships at a disadvantage from having no leaders? Or at least from having no recognisable form of democratic or perhaps cooperative principles or procedures for finding resolutions? There was no one to stop the action and pick up the tensions and begin a dialogue about them.

These problems arose whilst people worked out how to best respond to the crisis that had led them there in the first place, making the learning more difficult in many ways. Peter, told me *'we are trying to make sense of what is happening, it has had to be somewhat inward looking'*. These issues illuminate the notions of both power sharing pedagogy of the expert 'teacher' who may be able to negotiate ways to deal with both the inward and the outward contexts, and the non-expert pedagogue who may be able to shed light on some self-learning based on the already existing knowledges. In both cases, the shared experiences of the multi-various encampments, protest camps, and uprisings become the pedagogical-political moment, where no external 'power', influence or leadership is required for survival, but may, perhaps, have been welcomed for guidance.

These notions of enacting learning suggest that a form of praxis was being developed, although not a true Freirean form as this would have included theory and action, rather than just the acquiring of knowledge and implementation of action, although it is true that many Occupiers were reading a great deal of political theory. However, it seemed that the Occupiers may have started learning about their place in the world through the solidarity networks, connecting themselves to the wider social milieu through a combination of new and diverse experiences, and involving themselves in dialogue and debate. An example of this was uncovered here: *'we were learning about concepts such as white privilege and even though you knew the term, you learnt what it meant to you'* (Jade). Another added, *'I guess I evaluate things still in relation to my* view of the world but I think that the way I live my life has changed a hell of a lot' (Sarah). This suggests that praxis was being produced, because new theories, as well as learning about action, were being added to the experience of everyday life through the discourses taking place. The theory was then being converted into actions that were not present before the experience of Occupy's unique form of educational commons. The diversity of the learning was mentioned time and again, for example it was said that

> Sam: *It has been a hugely educational experience both formally, through initiatives like TCU but also informally in that, the camps have been alive with discourse related to ways to find a more sustainable, just and democratic economic system. People of all backgrounds have been engaging in this discourse. By no means has this been the preserve of the educated few.*

This notion that the camps were '*alive with discourse*', that they were collectively trying to '*make sense of what was happening*', and learning skills from '*communing and collaborating with others*', suggests that they were indeed concentrating on the use of free time, (Holloway, 2010). The camp occupied that space and attempted to find a formative way to make use of free time in a political way, indeed, one Occupier told me that '*Occupy has shown that collective action is good for the human condition*' (Jade). This was also suggested in this extract from my own reflective fieldwork journal:

> an older, scruffy man in a wheelchair enthusiastically attempted to organise my visit for maximum effect. Telling me who was who and where and when I might find them. In that way and in that context, he mattered. He was important, he could influence and assist. He was someone, yet again I was never offered a name. He did however tell me of his struggle with the cold and of the difference it had made when some other unnamed person had found him a hot water bottle; what a comfort it was when battling elitism and corporatocracy out there on the streets of London, sleeping in a tent on the pavement in sub-zero temperatures. I think I would have gone home, but I wasn't entirely sure whether he had a home to go to, I don't think it really matters. Whoever these people are outside of tent city, outside the movement that has brought them together, they are someone whilst they are there: there, they matter a great deal
> 
> (Fieldwork Journal, 2012).

This was the power of the collective experience for many: that everyone in the collective struggle was important, and felt it. However, conversely, Kate told me '*activists are driven by personal opinions and are reluctant to listen to others. They sometimes have a small knowledge of critical theory, but often manipulate that knowledge to support their own opinions, therefore cliques arise*'. Unfortunately, this is probably to be expected in any burgeoning community of committed and passionate people, and again points to the need for a system of shared principles for democratic or cooperative decision making and mediation. There were, of course groups within groups and despite the insistence on leaderlessness, there were issues where 'ownership' of work became a problematic issue of guilt, rather than of pride or celebration, for example:

> Sarah: *people feel they don't want to start TCU again, but we have people coming at us wanting to reinstate TCU, and interestingly, because sometimes you don't know how you feel about something until you're faced with the choice, interestingly we've all sort of made that decision that we don't need to do that. So there's loads of people who really enjoyed TCU while it was in full swing, and would like to reinstate it and join the working group and the few of us that are left are really reluctant to let that happen and that's really interesting to me because that's the very thing that we argued against in the beginning was that ownership, yeah? So I've sort of fallen foul of my own.*

The 'ownership' that is described here, wherein those who worked to establish TCU in the first place felt an affection for, and a responsibility to, the project, could be read as acceptable in this context, as it cannot be exchanged for any sort of profit. However, it restricts others from taking on that project and carrying it forward, therefore the endeavour stops being held in common. Although these are two different notions of *ownership*, one notion cannot help but feel like the other as Sarah explained. Nonetheless, as Holloway (2010: 256) says, 'knowing is a process constructed collectively, a dialogue rather than a monologue, an asking-we-walk: not necessarily polite, at times a provocation, but a provocation that opens, not one that lays down the law', the idea that Sarah could have fallen foul of her own ... what? Conditioned behaviour, maybe? I would argue that this knowledge of 'ownership', remains here a provocation, the painful exposure of what could be a conditioned, culturally constructed notion, in the sense that no one else can access the (re)production, or an emotional bond to an achievement that creates a reluctance to see it changed by new 'owners'? Here, one might acknowledge this advice from Shor (1996: 122) that 'democratic culture, is, by definition, vibrant and dynamic, discomforting and unpredictable. It gives rise to apprehension; freedom is not always calming'. This perhaps needed to be more recognised within Occupy, perhaps this painful exposure could have been seen more as exposing the vibrant and dynamic, discomforting and unpredictable feeling that comes when one realises that freedom is not always calming. Occupy included, it seems, not only finding out what could be done by doing, but how we might feel about it by feeling.

So, did the pedagogy produce hope for change? Was there promotion of critical awareness and raising consciousness? And importantly, did Occupy's organic pedagogy produce a language of possibility going beyond critique? Moreover, was trust a centrally organising principle, a revolutionary necessity?

> John: *It is about an idea, but the idea is, what would the word be, well, the way I like to put it is that it's not about people going here's what we think, you should think it too, it's about people thinking and finding out together, and this is kind of a razor sharp way of loads of people doing that together.*
> Paul: *We have awakened and not just to complain, we aim to pinpoint the true causes of the crisis and to propose alternatives.*

Here we can see the importance of connections to others again, reiterated and extended:

> Sally: *I have learnt a lot more about how the system works and why it works, just through talking to people, and like talking to homeless people that have come to GAs, finding out their situation and thinking, this person needs help, you know, I've come in to contact with a whole other world out there and a new kind of experience and different people, different people and different backgrounds.*

The interaction between people from different backgrounds not only had the potential to teach them about each other, but also to elicit a deeper educative experience of 'how the system works and why it works', this was because the Occupiers had begun using various political and critical theories to deconstruct the social and political systems that they found themselves in. People who had very little formal education in matters of political economy were reading and critiquing the system through Marx, Kropotkin, Chomsky, Harvey and many others. The interaction and personal connections with what Sally called 'different people and different backgrounds' seemed to be allowing other epistemologies to enter their knowledges and utilising critical theories to understand 'how the system works and why it works'. Occupy seemed indeed, like another world, existing within the norms and everyday world of the City of London:

> The physical and virtual spaces broke the ordinary and disquieted the mind. Groups of people sat in the freezing cold, discussing their imagined futures, arguing about the way things could and should change. The steps of the Cathedral often over spilled with individuals from all walks of life, all there to change the future, all there to make the decisions themselves, instead of leaving them to the elite classes. Direct, participatory democracy was seen to be played out here, everyone mattered, every voice potentially had equal weight. Despite the cold, despite the effort, there was a freeform of noise: drums; voices; music; pots and pans; and lively debate. All in mixed with the hubbub of the business as usual taking place all around.
> (Fieldwork Journal, 2011)

Sally's words above suggested that the connections between people were thought about not only in terms of their humanity, but also in the wider context, indicating the birth of what Freire (1993a) calls an epistemological curiosity: a curiosity that goes beyond what he terms ingenuous curiosity, to one that wishes and seeks to know more, to connect self to systems. This ethos was illustrated by one Occupier's many Freedom of Information requests on a host of topics; by the lively debate and well used library; and by the plethora of independent media that was set up by various Occupy actions around the world. I argue that the development of an epistemological curiosity is an essential component of any revolutionary education project if the multitude (Hardt & Negri, 2004) are to escape what Freire (1993a) calls the sloganisation of the people. That is, the manipulation through slogans and propaganda, epistemological curiosity defies this because individuals have genuine curiosity to find out for themselves, raising their own awareness of issues affecting their lives and the lives of others and thus promoting and utilising a critical consciousness. This critical consciousness, acting upon the life world, interrupts patterns of capitalist social relations and nurtures the side of us that is not controlled by capitalism (Holloway, 2010), but only if the conscientised person does not feel isolated and alone. Freire (1993a: 38) insists, however, that 'it is precisely because ingenuous curiosity does not automatically become critical that one of the tasks of educational praxis is the promotion of a curiosity that is critical, bold and adventurous'. Freire acknowledges the importance of connections and their knowledge production capabilities – their ability to transcend the mere potential of the critical conscience – beyond the critical educator as he insists that 'knowledge emerges only through invention and re-invention, through the relentless, impatient, continuing, hopeful inquiry human beings pursue in the world, with the world and with each other' (53). Sometimes the impatient, hopeful inquiry seemed to be ongoing *during* the conversations I had with Occupiers:

> Jane: *[Occupy] put me into contact with lots of different people that think different things and by talking to people that think different things you kind of go you know, 'hmmm, actually what do I think about that' and has that changed how I, sometimes it hasn't because I've always thought, I've always felt, I've never been a revolutionary, I never thought that we could overthrow the government I always thought work within the system to change it so I don't think there's going to be a revolution, but now working with occupy its small steps, chip away at it, chip away at it and I'm quite amazed how quickly things have been put on the agenda, you know?*

This shows the usefulness of reflection and the potential of the mutually useful conversations for reflection and consolidation of thoughts and ideas. Thinking through the potential of their own subjectivity in process could be argued to be an important aspect of the process of solidarity and becoming. The notion of 'small steps' expressed here is also reminiscent of Holloway

(2010) and of the bricolage notion of knowledge in process, temporal and context bound. Jane went on to critically assess the effect that Occupy's actions had had more broadly:

> Jane: *But then there's other things, like the government are getting wise, like no camping allowed in any area of the Olympic site they've rushed some laws through that you're not allowed to put a tent near an Olympic site, you know so there's things like that, that are kind of the government fighting back.*

This reflection and connection expresses the development of the epistemological curiosity, the personal experiences and the wider effects are recognised as being a continuum of the struggle. Castells (2012: 5) argues that 'the fundamental power struggle is the battle for the construction of meaning in the minds of people', I tend to agree, especially from a pedagogical point of view. Critical thinking, epistemological curiosity and finally conscientization (Freire, 1993a, 1998) have the potential to ensure this power struggle is not easy, if possible at all, for any current dominant ideology to win, or a new totalising one be instigated. This is reached when as Davis (2011: 49) says, 'slogans of dominance and subjugation should no longer be accepted at face value by the critically thinking person and therefore lose their grip'. The pedagogy practiced within Occupy indicated a realisation of this notion. However, authors such as Crouch (2011) have argued that neoliberalism has 'shrugged off' the challenges of these protests, uprisings and occupations. Does this mean then that there is something missing from the emergent theory? I think that there is not too much missing, *per se*, but ensuring a critical mass, a counter-hegemonic block is surely part of the key to fundamental change.

This notion of critical mass, then, begins to make the pedagogical nature, the symbolism of TCU, the emphasis on teach outs, workshops and debates with 'experts', look like a genuine and purposeful strategy: the more public the pedagogy, the more individuals you reach, the more likely you are to create that critical mass to form the Multitude that ensures a counter-hegemonic block, creating loud countervailing discourses. However, this was not indicated in the conversations as strongly as one might expect. Nonetheless, the beginnings of a critical awareness that may have the potential to interrupt and encourage the critical faculties not controlled by capitalism, can be seen emerging from the conversations.

TCU seemed to go much further than learning about the subject of economic justice:

> CE: *[A Professor] came down to do a workshop at TCU, he said, 'I got there and what I thought I was there to do was to talk about my ideas' and 'it was about two minutes in when I realised that that is not what I was there to do'.*
> Sally: *And that's exactly what happened every time it was wonderful.*

CE: *He said it was so much better than anything he had envisaged, he's a good person, but I can imagine some people being quite shocked by that different form of social relations.*
Sally: *Yeah, but you know, even John Snow came in and sat down one day, from ITV, he ended up being in a big debate with somebody who was worried about his social housing, and John came in to say something and didn't say it at all and in the end he [John Snow] thanked us profusely and said that that was probably the most amazing afternoon he'd ever had.*
CE: *So was that your experience of people who came in thinking they were experts.*
Sally: *Over and over again.*
CE: *That they were actually grateful.*
Sally: *Over and over again.*

Holloway (2010: 39) says, 'if our struggle is not asymmetrical to capitalism in its forms, then it simply reproduces capitalist social relations, whatever its content'. A real and practical insistence on the subversion of the positioning of the 'expert' can be seen as quite asymmetrical to normative capitalist relations and has the possibility of creating a public usefulness of the expertise of one for others, but goes further than public intellectualism. That TCU were thanked by the visiting 'expert' so many times, and that this way of connecting people in an equitable and unpretentious way was appreciated, indicates that relations were being subverted; those who interacted with Occupy on an ad hoc basis seemed to enjoy nurturing that side of them not controlled by capitalism and its hierarchical constructs. This resonates with the democratic power-sharing critical pedagogy advocated by Shor (1996) with a touch of Rancière's (1991) *Ignorant Schoolmaster*, in that the power sharing was instigated by the 'students', but the 'expert' sometimes ended up debating and discussing issues they were not 'expert' in.

One of the problematic elements of Occupy for many was that it had no set political position. Again, this political positioning, of choosing one political ideology over another, could be argued to be a trapping of the oppositional politics of late capitalist realism (Fisher, 2009). The lack of ideological restrictions was one of the elements that made Occupy so interesting and enigmatic to many: *'no one knew what Occupy was, Occupy or the political elites, this made Occupiers free and the elites fearful, everyone was learning!'* (Peter). This ties in to what Marx (1844/1975: 276–7) said, although referring to estranged labour, concerning the very humanity of human beings: 'free, conscious activity is man's species character'. He argues that estranged labour estranges the person from his 'species character', that it takes away 'his real objectivity as a member of the species, and transforms his advantage over the animals into the disadvantage that his organic body, nature, is taken away from him'. This echoes in some respects what Holloway (2010: 113) insisted, 'identification or reification is an enormously destructive force in everyday

92  *Organic education from the ground up*

struggle. We give our protests a name, a label, a limit'. If prefiguration and critical, utopian thinking are abandoned for the relative safety of a set ideological standpoint, then a limit is set.

Holloway (2010: 4) insists that people 'dedicate ourselves to what we consider necessary or desirable. Either way, we live the world we want to create'. This was seen, on the surface at least, within the Tent City. There is a temptation to over romanticise this open and free prefiguration. Recalling Holloway's character masks, add to this Freire's insistence that the oppressed house the oppressor within them, one began to wonder whether the freedom and openness could be a surface façade that does not run as deep as one might think on initial contact:

> Jane: *I think part of the problem with Occupy is it's so different that people can't relate to it, I think part of that too is that we've never had a statement of who we are and what we stand for. All political movements say this is what we stand for, this is what we're against, and we've still not really got that together and it has been a big criticism. But in a discussion [with a man who had lived without money] I started off thinking this guy's too far, you're too utopian, too far away from anything that makes any sense to the people that I hang out with, but then I started to think well ok can we not see that as the ultimate goal of a fairer world? So, he is over there and that's fine we need to move towards there, but within our structure and within our society you know?*

This is surprising as surely, the 'new social relations' they thought they were producing were outside those structures: a social world differently organised. However:

> CE: *There have been some quite savage critiques of Occupy on a gender basis.*
> Judy: *Well, there's more, some very serious stuff (Long pause – it became obvious she was not going to elaborate).*
> CE: *Yeah? So .... in that respect, the social relations within the space of Occupy were reproducing some of the relations outside?*
> Judy: *Yes and no ...*
> CE: *Or perhaps not effectively breaking them down, is that it?*
> Judy: *They were different and they were better, but it's hard not to confuse two different things here because the big camp and the big GAs, yes, I would say you're right, that is reproducing a pretty close model to all that might be wrong gender-wise, but in the smaller situations, there was a really funny dynamic going on there. There are many women still involved in Occupy, some very strong voiced women, and so appearances are one thing but its, (pause) sorry I hesitate because there's paranoia all around us. Anyway I just found myself in a situation where I was the female in the room, (pause) I've got a voice and I've*

> got respect, but despite the fact that I can do tactical planning and strategic, and I do all those things, I'm the one in the kitchen washing all their filthy dishes because they won't do it. And then they make all these gender jokes, like 'oh the little woman's in the kitchen' and they think they're hilarious ... So those strong women that you see at the face of it, they come forward and they're doing the interviews and all that stuff, but actually in that nitty gritty bit where its hard and you have to sleep rough, they're not doing that, (pause) the women that will come into those spaces, are probably what I would say the most vulnerable, who shouldn't possibly be there, and so I'd say there are some real gender issues and I will say that there is some abuse of those people, which makes me sick.

There are several things at play here, one is the obvious gender issues that were experienced which ranged from sexist jokes to more serious issues such as abuse and the other is the mention of paranoia. Both these were serious issues in Occupy and have received, further discussion elsewhere (for example see Anonymous, 2012; Bella, 2011; Ng & Toupin, 2013). Although I am not going to go into detail about the issues relating to gender, they are extremely pertinent to the overall issue of creating alternate social relations and indeed learning about how we implement and sustain popular education initiatives. I will return to this issue later.

The issue of paranoia was difficult to avoid as Tracy told me: *'paranoia is awful, just the other day someone I didn't know phoned me to say the guy I was seeing is an undercover cop, I had to end the relationship just in case'*. This paranoia was heightened by the behaviour of the police force's undercover officers at various other protests, most famously their infiltration of environmental movements. The paranoia on the one hand made it impossible for trust to be used as a central organising principle, and on the other may have made it very difficult for outsiders to understand what was going on in the movement:

> Sarah: *I was told not to come today.*
> CE: *Why?*
> Sarah: *Some people reckon that most of the people who want to talk to us are undercover cops, trying to find ways to prosecute us.*
> CE: *But I've written to you from a university address, so you know who I am.*
> Sarah: *Well, there are some who think that the police are setting up .ac.uk addresses, so we think they're researchers, I'm not so sure.... I told them I'd met you before, but they reckoned that the police are going to those kinds of lengths.*
> CE: *That's why I'm finding it so hard to get people to talk to me ...*
> Sarah: *Yeah, I said to a couple of people that I knew you, but they still said no, just in case and told me I shouldn't come either.*

The paranoia, wherever it originated, is serious for any movement attempting to change social relations and create a society which should be based on trust. However, changes were experienced by some Occupiers as quite fundamental, because as Robin said, '*I think everybody has their own unique experience, but I think it would be impossible not take something from the experience of being here*'. Sarah offers this opinion on the issue:

> Sarah: *I think that the whole of society has become so protective of what it's got, you put a big wall up around your house to protect you from your neighbours and you have a burglar alarm and you don't share anything, everybody is just looking after themselves and I think we have got used to living like that, I'm going to be a bit more me now and I'm not going to protect myself and I'm loving sharing and realising that you can share your views or share a cup of tea or whatever, actually you get a lot more back, your part of a community.*

Here again the issue of paranoia is prevalent, however, I think that this was one of the triumphs of Occupy, that the people involved could reflect not only on their own lives but on the conditions of life that they felt instituted the relations between people constituted by mistrust and fear of Others, this became the past, and the reappropriation of themselves and their relationships to wider society. This created for some a language of possibility that often did go beyond critique, a new experience for many:

> Peter: *Whenever I've been involved in politics before, it's just been a load of people sat round, shouting each other down about what is the most important thing that's wrong in the world, nobody ever seemed to have any suggestions about what to do about it. Just a whinge fest really, that's why I thought I didn't like politics.*

So, is there a moment when the politics of critique ceases to be useful and a new politics of possibility emerges? Perhaps finding the language of possibility constitutes the political moment (Rancière, 2010) for some, when the oppressive conditions of everyday life cease to be inevitable: there is an alternative. Jane, who had been involved in politics before, said '*Occupy is the first time that I came to self-identify as an activist*'. When I asked why, she answered '*I don't know, I suppose it's because Occupy looks forward and tries to build the future rather than just complaining about what's wrong, we do that too, but it's not the focus*'. Moving toward this language of possibility and enacting this new lexicon, should interrupt capitalist social relations, as Holloway (2010: 171) predicted.

> Sarah: *Expectations and hope is very high, you come into that environment as an individual and you do begin forming social and working relationships, and through those you sort of learn how to channel that hope*

*and it's very empowering in the beginning because suddenly you find yourself in a group of people who didn't necessarily agree on how to do things but agreed basically on political aims and thoughts with which I identified. So that was a magical time, you know, anything was possible, you could move mountains and you knew it, and we felt we did particularly well. And for me, the experience is intrinsically linked to what we had during the camp and how these social relationships, due to having actual space, unfold without that space, and what new spaces are created, and how the social relationships and learning occur around those new contexts?*

This was recorded after the eviction of the LSX camp and shows that the learning that took place within the space created by the camp was quite fundamental, at least to Sarah, and the reflection regarding how the new relationships were growing and changing indicates an increased awareness of how relationships work in the context of utility and focus. Many people involved in Occupy might now have a heightened awareness of potential solidarity relations, more sensitivity to finding other groups and individuals making 'cracks' in capitalism (Holloway, 2010) as a result.

As Griffiths (2003: 63) insists, 'valuing oneself and others is central to recognising, getting, and struggling for justice'. These values are illustrated strongly in many of the conversations I had, despite the rising distrust:

Peter: *I think [Occupy] raised issues, and its provided a voice that says 'this is wrong', I don't think it's only Occupy that's done it, in the UK, UK Uncut have done it, as well, because it's put certain things on the agenda amazingly quickly. Like the whole tax thing, that started with UK Uncut, how quickly that became part of the agenda and became part of the national consciousness.*

Thoughts like these were evident in the conversations and seemed to constitute the beginnings of discourses countervailing to normative ones of individualism and competition. Here, another extract from my journal after visiting the 'Tech Tent' and talking to a group of people inside:

They explained things to me as if they would be revelations. It was as if they had thought so many new thoughts there, in that camp, that they couldn't believe they were saying anything that had been thought before. They were exploring and discovering things that they found exciting and extraordinary. They were learning about themselves as learners, listeners. Midwifing themselves and each other from states of ingenuous curiosity into states where their curiosity had become genuine and epistemological, where the act of 'knowing' no longer seemed to be good enough, they needed to understand and that understanding needed to be shared, to be given freely to others who could then experience this critical birthing

process as they had. They were eager to create new ways of thinking, of doing, of being in anyone who came across them with an open ear. They had discovered a new way of constituting society, there was no hesitation that what had to be done next was to extend their new knowledge to wider society. These people, some with low levels of education, some with high, all thinking alike in a way that anyone can think – curiously and with a desire for the passion of learning and self-improvement. I believe that there in the freezing temperatures an intellectual public is being created
(Fieldwork Journal, 2012)

Sharing this extract reminds me how infectious hope becomes. Concentration on what could be done, the possibilities of a new world, a new way of being, set the camp ablaze with positive possibility. This was obviously important, as Holloway elucidates:

building a new world does of course mean changing the existing one, but the shift in emphasis is crucial: instead of focussing our attention on the destruction of capitalism, we concentrate on building something else. This is an inversion of the traditional revolutionary perspective that puts the destruction of capitalism first and the construction of the new society second.
(2010: 50)

Katsiaficas (2006: 187) discusses that this exploration of new worlds through both prefiguration and a theoretical language of possibility can also be explained by 'the absence of any central organisation (or even primary organisations)'. According to Katsiaficas this is because this absence 'helps keep theory and practice in continual interplay'. The argument continues that 'the sheer volume of decentralised happenings generated by small groups acting on their own initiative prohibits systematic understanding of the totality of the movement, a first step in the dismantling of any system', a hint of the anarchist principles that seemed almost incidental in the camp. This prohibition of systematic understanding seems to have been part of the goal of Occupy, creating a specific kind of revolutionary potential that very few other movements have been able to create. However, as Judy told me,

*one of the dangers of pure, theoretical academic thought is not putting things into practice, and pressing, and seeing what happens. Here, you can't gloss over things, the things that you gloss over become apparent, you have to face them and you realise that for example with the direct democracy thing, you see what the challenges are and you see on paper it looks great but in practice might need a bit more nuance to it.*

Glossing over the obvious criticism of academic practice, it also seems that the critique might have extended to their own practices of such things as

*Organic education from the ground up* 97

direct democracy, or consensus decision making. This, however, was problematic as discussed earlier. There are indications that the movement were, at the very least, reticent about criticism of them, which seemed to include by their own activists. As this conversation extract shows:

> CE: *I did an interview in TCU and one of the things that was said was that they weren't sure that consensus decision making was working or could work.*
> Harry: *And that's a very brave thing for somebody to say, especially at that point, because that's been a real bone of contention to this day that, if you say, I don't think consensus decision making is working for us – oh my god! Shit would fly!*

Considering this, one has to ask, despite the apparent nurturing of collective experience, despite the reported solidarisitic connections between people, whether trust may well not have been *the*, or indeed *an*, organising principle, as Holloway (2010) says it must for real revolutionary potential to emerge. There is, however, the usual mixed message on this issue, as Jane, told me that *'networks of trust were very important'*. This is to be expected due to the complexity of what was being attempted and the notion that everyone had their own unique experience of the movement, in addition to the decentralised happenings. Also, Castells (2012: 6) states, 'each individual human mind constructs its own meaning by interpreting the communicated materials on its own terms, this mental processing is conditioned by the communication environment'. In other words, the experience of 'trust' may well be different depending on what working group you were in, or how fully you were involved in the movement and which camp you participated in, among many other aspects and experiences. Pertinent here, however, Castells goes on to say, 'the transformation of the communication environment directly affects the forms of meaning construction, and therefore the production of power relations'. This notion, coupled with the concrete examples of how different communication environments were variously experienced, challenges the understanding of the potential differences between Rancière's Universal Teaching and Shor's democratic power sharing. This is because if 'the transformation of the communication environment directly affects the forms of meaning construction, and therefore the production of power relations', then the necessarily different styles of pedagogy in these two philosophies will have a fundamental effect on power relations and meaning construction. It was said that *'the camps allowed people to speak, they nurtured individual agency through a culture of sharing. They became beacons for discussion'* (Sam), which echoes the notion of universal teaching, that everyone was learning without explication, the inception of the movement having been the 'teacher' that prompted them to learn. However, did that free ranging educative activity leave them satisfied and fundamentally transformed? One Occupier told me, a while after all the encampments had gone, that

> Fran: *I'm so frustrated with Occupy London because all that hope and all that wonderfulness at the beginning, it's not beaten out of me, I just don't know where the shit to put it. I'm walking around and the engine's revving but there's no road.*

However, there were many examples of how trust was at least a *guiding* principle, if not an organising one, but to create countervailing discourses, trust must be apparent, otherwise voices become silenced. This will probably come as no surprise:

> Heather: *We have failed to provide safe space on every front. That's where we've failed and without it people have left because they couldn't tolerate a situation that wasn't going to successfully make the change.*

Questions that still arise however, concern whether the education practiced did perceive the dehumanising power that education and indeed wider society can have? Whether people uncovered conditions of oppression disguised as social realities? Did they prevent the crowding out of people's lives and see people as intelligent and agentic beings? Did they develop and build the sensitivity and critical awareness that might allow them to see other potential cracks, to work in solidarity but not to culturally invade (Freire, 1993a)?

One political fiction, discussed earlier, that of 'acceptable' sexism, was uncovered by those oppressed by it and not as an issue to be discussed, but as a complaint after the fact. Freire (1993a: 154) describes this is a problem:

> Domination itself is objectively divisive. It maintains the oppressed I in a position of 'adhesion' to a reality which seems all powerful and overwhelming, and then alienates by presenting mysterious forces which are regarded as responsible for reality about which nothing can be done. The individual is divided between identical past and present, and a future without hope. He or she is a person who does not perceive him/herself as becoming; hence cannot have a future built in unity with others.

The sexist 'jokes', mentioned earlier, had the potential to create a reality where the women are, as Freire insists, unable to think of themselves as becoming alongside the men in these (re)organised social relations. In conversations with several of the women from Occupy, this barrier to thinking of themselves as becoming alongside the men was apparent, not as explicit statement, but as a feeling, an attitude toward what had transpired. This is possibly because although the relations were generally different, for them things seem to have changed very little, they were not entirely productive subjects in the formation of a new way of being. However, because all social relations should be under the microscope in this context, women may be able to tackle this form of sexism and not understand themselves in its terms:

But as she or he breaks this 'adhesion' and objectifies the reality from which he or she starts to emerge, the person begins to integrate as a Subject (an I) confronting an object (reality). At this moment, sundering the false unity of the divided self, one becomes a true individual
(Freire, 1993a: 154)

The problem with this sexism, was that very few people during my conversations wanted to acknowledge that it was an issue, despite it being apparent in many interactions that I witnessed or was a part of. However, the issue of conscientization in this context was brought up by one Occupier who told me that

> Jane: *I think that everybody is conditioned to live within the safety of his or her individualism. And that's the problem with Occupy, its reaching out to those people, but not in a patronising way, not in a way that's saying you're wrong, but just sort of saying.... I don't know how we do it because the whole world's sort of got protectionist of their own little corner haven't they? And just saying there's a better way there's a different way of doing it, what I've seen happen just from other little things I've been involved in as well, people only get involved when it affects them.*

That people only get involved when it affects them was interesting because Occupy were there initially to protest a banking crisis and consequent austerity measures that would affect everyone. It should be considered, that Occupy were not successful in uncovering political fictions and oppressive conditions disguised as social realities, either inside the movement or as an action of public pedagogy. Had these conditioned behaviours, these political fictions, been brought up sensitively as 'teaching points', which takes skilled pedagogues, they may have been able to move beyond the fiction of the sexism being acceptable. However, these shifts in perception can be thought of as an essential stage in developing criticity, and as Brookfield (2001: 17) says, 'making the attitudinal shift to reinterpret as culturally induced what were initially held to be personally devised value systems, beliefs, and moral codes can be highly intimidating. To realise that the moral and behavioural codes we regard as our personal creations are, in fact, culturally induced is threatening to our sense of self'. This is echoed in these words from Judy:

> *People come along and they say 'I want change', but then you create a fluid rupture in which there's a fluid situation and you find that people are really reluctant to change anything, so you find there is a lot of resistance and a lot of defensiveness and we do fight amongst ourselves, and so much of it is that individuals aren't able to trust others and they've got a defensiveness and the walls will not come down, and so within that any change they want to see is very much through a regulatory framework, they can only work through the idea if its passed through that. But then, they are so*

*defensive that they will personally attack somebody that they feel is not in their class and well there can't be a change if that's how you are. If everything is like this and that's the way it is, well then where is that change going to come from if you're not actually going to allow it to happen and you're not going to welcome it when it comes at you? Because this is what I believe, if you want change you've got to accept fluidity. And your concepts and your theories must be responsive to what you see around you, you need to be able to learn something else.*

This reluctance to let go of certain ways of doing things was sometimes quite potent in the conversations, I reflected upon the issue in my own fieldwork journal after the Occupy Research Collective (ORC) Convergence:

It seems that the conditioning in people at the ORC from their previous experience is still prevalent, they haven't shaken it, or, alternatively, they are not ready to replace it. There is still a very 'us and them' attitude to education (i.e., us, the people and them, the educators) although they are starting to come around to the idea that they themselves could practice peer education, but only technical skills. They seemed to feel that one had to be trained to teach anyone. I'm not sure they understand the power of what they are already doing and how it is working.

(Fieldwork Journal, 2013)

These two extracts suggest that not only were they failing to uncover political (and indeed, educational) fictions disguised as social realities, but it seemed that they were also either unable or unwilling to perceive the dehumanising power of education and society at large (Freire, 1993a). This division in the attitudes, behaviours and viewpoints of Occupiers, all going through roughly the same experience, at the same socio-political juncture, challenges the notion that this form of organic, critical, politically awakening education will allow the conditions of one's own oppression to be unveiled, thus enabling a challenge to that oppression. Individuals were apparently not becoming aware of *their part* in the oppression of others. This is a political fiction that is often (dis)missed, that if you fight for social justice, you cannot be a part of the oppressive class. The oppressive conditions of capitalism were unveiling themselves for many at such a rate during this highly critically educative experience, but with no one objective enough to pick up on the oppressive conditioned behaviours in Occupy itself, except the victims, they apparently went unnoticed. Can oppression and the formation of counter-oppressive relationships be addressed one oppression at a time by creating what might be thought of as incrementally countervailing discourses? Or does that leave some sections of the newly emerging multitude less realised than others? According to Hardt and Negri (2004, 2012) the multitude can only become a revolutionary subject when diversity is recognised as strength, not, as it seems in the case of Occupy, when it divides people through 'acceptable' subjugation.

The inability to perceive dehumanizing aspects of their practice, did seem to have a split between those who had worked in formal and institutionalised education before the encampment and those who had never initiated group learning before:

> The more 'intellectual' the individuals saw themselves as being, the more they wanted to rely on existing mechanisms to understand how things work, the less 'intellectual' they saw themselves as, the more they seemed to have the freedom to imagine what could be and interpret what was happening.
>
> (Fieldwork Notes, 2013)

Perhaps then, Gorz (1997: 46) was correct in saying that 'the bourgeoisie succeeded in destroying at root what consciousness the proletariat might have had of its sovereign creativeness'. The question then is how do we *collectively* get it back?

Holloway (2010) brings up another difficult issue pertinent here: were they actually creating social relations that would allow for the emergence of a countervailing discourse or merely building a community of saints? This is a difficult question as the answer is complex and open to individual interpretation. However, the danger is that the issue could become masked, as it was very easy to romanticise what was happening, for me and other visitors and for the Occupiers themselves:

> Jess: *I've seen lots of people come down and there's the meeting of minds and people with lots of very interesting ideas, discussing them, exchanging ideas, seeing how they can develop them, so, there's an interesting social experiment, you could say.*
>
> The occupy camp has been an education. It has posed many questions and answered some.... The tent city at St. Paul's provides space for visitors from around Britain and the world to reflect on what we are doing and consenting to. For the first time, we've had an opportunity to speak plainly to those who have a disproportionate amount of power; we only gained this by camping on their doorstep. It is in the public interest that we are learning about conditions worldwide and starting to identify with people around the globe. What I am really grateful for is the communal exploration of imagination and creativity. The unexpected interactions and enlightening conversations.
>
> (Ashman, 2012)

These accounts may be dismissed as romanticising the movement and at this point caution should be taken, as many scholars had a tendency to want to see only the best of Occupy. I was with them. I wanted to work in solidarity; I wanted to believe that Occupy was what it seemed to be, and more. However, researchers, as critical friend, have to assist social movements to gain a criticity that extends to their behaviours and their shortcomings.

This notion however is not always as easy as it sounds; for example, Jess told me that she was *'glad that academics are interested and taking some notice of us'*, the ORC Convergence told a different story:

> Someone said that it was impossible to research social movements unless you were 'wholeheartedly involved in the activism of the movement', refusing to accept that perhaps the criticity that comes from not being a full participant was beneficial to both research and to the movement itself. There was a great deal of divisive language and dichotomy forming; insider/outsider, researcher/activist and for some it was a case of never the twain shall meet.
> (Fieldwork Journal, 2013)

That day, some of the Occupiers went out of their way to make delegates who were researchers, not Occupiers, feel guilty about their presence there; we were an unwelcome intrusion into their private lives. Perhaps, as Schmitt (1996) suggests, they had to have an enemy, there were only friends and foes. There were some Occupiers who were obviously uncomfortable with the discussion; however, they never ventured an opinion. After all the debate, all the discussions, had Occupy never got over a fear of conflict? I wondered if the notion of agonisms, of multitude and even of truly radical democratic politics had escaped them because they did not want to seem to have internal conflict. If so, Occupy was reproducing some debilitating capitalist values: conformity, compliance and placidity. So, had this form of organic, critical pedagogy defied theory so much that it was actually merely reproducing those values under a different guise?

A further example of reproducing capitalist values was the wide usage of the expression 'sheeple', which came to mean people that blindly followed the status quo, but was often extended to anyone outside the movement. The use of such terms is what Freire (1993b) calls sloganisation that in itself masks political fictions and obscures 'reality' from the gaze of critical consciousness. This is extended in Debord's (1977) *Society of the Spectacle*: reality is masked, creating the role of the subject as object spectator rather than subject actor. Freire's argument goes on to propose that if the oppressed use sloganisation, it is with the intention to entice the people to blindly follow them and not to think critically about what the oppressed vanguard is doing, but to dazzle the oppressed people into accepting a sloganized version of reality.

> In their political activities the dominant elites ... encourage passivity in the oppressed ... and take advantage of that passivity to 'fill' that [submerged] consciousness with slogans which create even more fear of freedom. This practice is incompatible with a truly liberating course of action, which, by presenting the oppressor's slogans as a problem helps the oppressed to 'eject' those slogans from within themselves.
> (Freire, 1993a: 76)

In the case of the 'sheeple', the slogan works paradoxically to its supposed intension; the use of this sort of term correlates to support of the oppressors by continuing to dehumanise the people through sloganisation, an Othering of those not involved in the struggle. The oppressed cannot 'eject' the slogans of the oppressors if they are fed dehumanising slogans from those who see themselves as their potential emancipators. The term therefore creates a singular 'us' and a plural 'them', a friend or foe dichotomy that disavows the oppressed and undermines inclusivity. It separates the 'us' – the vanguard fighting on behalf of the wretched 'sheeple' – a 'them', the 'sheeple' who are too blind, or too stupid, or too fooled by the system to realise what oppressive conditions they are living under, and the final 'them' of the '1%'. Caution is to be taken about any form of sloganisation, however, this particular sloganized 'us' the '99%' and 'them' the 1% dichotomy had some basis: the (mal)distribution of global wealth (however (in)accurate the 1% figure was), as the basis for the Othering of the wealthy minority as 'foe' to illuminate the real problem.

Other divisions in allegiance and membership surfaced in Occupy, indicating that the movement was not perhaps as inclusive and critical as it seemed; there was expressed unease:

> Paul: *There's people who I would describe as professional activists, there's people who work for all sorts of NGOs and charities. And it's interesting, it's this whole thing of how can you ever be unbiased, because of disclosing things, because if you're involved in Greenpeace and you come down here then what's the difference between that and being heavily involved in Liberal Democrats and coming here? The answer is that technically there is no difference, but practically the vast majority of conscious people think, you have a social conscience, you're from Greenpeace so of course you can be part of this, even though you might be influencing the agenda from an outside, or I don't know, whatever.... Whereas the liberal Democrats, some people might believe that the Liberal Democrats offer us the best vision for the future, etc., so they might have exactly the same intensions but if they walked around with a Liberal Democrat badge on, they wouldn't be told to go away, but you know they would be, I don't know what it would be.... I don't know what it would be, but you're allowed to walk around with a Greenpeace hoodie ... and nobody would bat an eyelid, I'm not saying that's a bad thing, but it's an interesting thing.*

Paul's hesitation and discomfort was obvious, which could suggest that questioning these things was not encouraged and therefore individuals were not seen as wholly agentic within the movement. This was apparent when one connects these issues: the frowned upon questioning of the consensus democracy model; the lack of sensitivity concerning overt sexism; the failure to provide what was termed 'safe space'; and the use of sloganisation. There was a hegemony of sorts at work here that made some uncomfortable.

104  *Organic education from the ground up*

Freire (1993a: 72) contends that

> founding itself upon love, humility and faith, dialogue becomes a horizontal relationship of which mutual trust between the dialoguers.... It would be a contradiction in terms if dialogue – loving, humble and full of faith – did not produce this climate of trust, which leads the dialoguers into ever closer partnership ... to glorify democracy and to silence the people is a farce; to discourse ... and to negate the people is a lie.

Was trust the missing element that made the use of words like 'sheeple' acceptable to some, or the notion that you were more welcome to join the discussion in a Greenpeace hoodie than a Liberal Democrats badge, or that women were to be accepted as equals but teased for their becoming that? Certainly, there were problems with trust generally.

bell hooks (1994: 12) contends 'the classroom remains the most radical space of possibility... for years it has been undermined by teachers and students alike who seek to use it as a platform for opportunistic concerns rather than a place to learn'. The classroom on the streets of London seemed to be no different. During the encampment, Occupy did seem to be an emergent space of radical possibility, however, some of the prejudices seemed ever present as this extract from my journal shows:

> Another young man told me he was from the 'estates'. He told me education has to be the point of what they were doing, he said 'we have to teach the kids because my generation is fucked, messed up by a fucked up education system'. He was not as articulate as most of the people I had met so far, he spoke with passion, not intellect, but he got it and he obviously felt that his voice was as valid as the next persons, the others let him speak, but the attitude was noticeably different to him because of his vernacular, they looked a little embarrassed by his articulation – are they equal?
>
> (Fieldwork Journal, 2011)

The theories insisted that the learners should be trusted and treated as intelligent, agentic beings, the conversations suggest they were not *to certain degrees*. The TCU slogan 'Anyone can Teach, Everyone can Learn' was respected and enacted, *but perhaps not equally*. Rancière's (1991) Universal Teaching insists that education must start from a belief in the equality of intelligence and, although I can only speculate as to whether that was a fundamental belief or a mere slogan from TCU, what was evident was that class, among other things, was still playing a role in who got to speak, and for how long, and how they were listened too. One Occupier spoke of these tensions:

> Wendy: *There is no kind of defined leadership or goal. It's all very, I dunno, I wouldn't say vague because everybody knows what they want,*

> but it's just freeform you could say, and it's interesting to see how conversations like that can develop themselves. Because there's a number of people who try to make sure it doesn't become one-upmanship or, he who speaks the loudest gets in. It's very much a vibe in the meetings that the decisions and the discussions of specific issues, which does involve a lot of educating each other, that we're trying to place equal weight on whatever anyone says regardless of how able they are to put it across.

Another Occupier articulated this particular aspect as needing to *desire* tension in our relations: '*something also we're not used to desiring is conflict and tension because we're used to things being modelled, laid-out, but those things do change and those things do involve negation*' (Jane). Another Occupier put it this way:

> Sally: *I think we need to figure out how to be ok with not knowing, tension is hugely important to me, if everything is in place in your life, you have no tension and what are you going to do? You're going to look around for more stuff to need, to create that tension, so physically, emotionally and spiritually there's got to be some kind of inherent tension between things otherwise you won't figure anything out or learn anything if you don't need it. You need to search, but you need to know that you need to search.*

Of course, desiring, dealing with, and maintaining these tensions takes trust and constant reinvention so as not to stagnate. This is because, according to some, tensions happen when individuals co-operate and dialogue, especially about politics. These tensions are also thought of as a healthy part of a functioning radical democracy (Mouffe, 2005, 2013; Rancière, 1998); if a radical democracy is functioning as it should, then tensions will, and should, arise. However, as von Kotze (2012: 105) asks, when there are obvious signs that tension is uncomfortable or mishandled the question becomes, 'how do we get the imagination "unstuck" when it has succumbed to hegemony – when it struggles to break out of normalised values and structures, relations and oppressions?' As has been evident 'even hope and imagination are not inevitably democratic and progressive' (von Kotze, 2012: 105).

Occupy did attempt to fight against constructed desires on behalf of repressed desires as we have heard many times from their testimony here, and as Holloway (2010: 64) says, 'the problems are probably inevitable'. As this Occupier states in an anonymously written article;

> what the Occupy movement COULD do was to start conversations. We, the people, could just ignore the 1% for a minute, get together for a chat and say, 'This isn't really working out for us, is it? What kind of world do we want to live in? And how do we get there?' And that is what seemed to

be happening quite naturally. People wanted to come and tell us their stories, and we listened (some of us) … they talked about their hopes for the future. We felt the mood was growing, and it was with us.

(Anonymous, 2012: 442)

These kinds of conversations have the potential to be constitutive of a new form of 'public', a multitude whose strength lies in their ability to voice differences, sensitively and with conviction. However, what seemed instead to happen in Occupy, despite the obvious hope, was that the voices that were dissenting against what clear ideology Occupy did have were drowned out, halted, as they uncovered the problems in the movement, they showed it to be flawed. What seemed to be missing was an acceptance of the flawed nature of all democratic systems, the need for the constant revolutionising of any democracy and its basis in agonism (Mouffe, 1999, 2013). Without these acceptances and recognitions, a truly democratic and diverse revolutionary subject cannot be constituted.

These recognitions were difficult from within Occupy because of the complexity of the experience for the people involved. There always seemed to be an intoxicating sense of something different happening, and I got the impression that there was a duality at play, that people wanted to believe the movement was one thing even though they knew it was not: a constant hope. As Giroux (1983: 67) notes, 'as a distortion ideology becomes hegemonic; as an illumination, it contains elements of reflexivity and the grounds for social action' and I felt that there were elements of both evident in the camp and in the testimonies of the Occupiers:

CE: *I wondered whether it wasn't what it looked like… that it wasn't a kind of deliberative society, which it looks like from outside, but it sounds from what you're saying, that it is.*

Peter: *Well, no, I didn't say it is, I said that's the idea … but all this is, is a bunch of individuals who self-select to be here and get involved, so people are involved for many different reasons, and there are a lot of people here who are completely committed to the deliberative process, and see that as the way forward, and there are some people who are not so committed to the deliberative process, for whatever reason, be it they feel passionate about a single issue, and they have a single issue they feel so passionately about, they're not really willing to compromise on it and all they want is for that to be excelled and pushed forward, and also I think there are certain people who appreciate the theory of it but, do not appreciate or understand the nuance of deliberation. Therefore, that tension is very often in the general assemblies because having a discussion requires patience, listening, trying to understand, being empathetic, and it's very easy to cut down an argument with an attack or an over simplification or misrepresenting, it's an interesting forum in which people try their best to non-confrontationally notice*

*Organic education from the ground up* 107

*when those sorts of short circuits of logic take place and to kind of bring things back to deliberation.*

These issues not only illustrate that hegemonic ideology about spaces and relationships had not been fully shaken off by some in the camp, but also that they were not fully avoiding the vanguardism of Holloway's 'community of saints', and thus may have been reproducing the dehumanising power of society and therefore education. If dehumanisation is being (re)produced in the practice, then the educative activities cannot treat all the learners as intelligent, agentic beings. Occupy succeeded and failed to varying degrees, as a movement it gave hope for other ways of being and doing education, but did not live up to its full potential. It failed to internally produce a *fundamentally* counter-hegemonic politics and countervailing discourse through its pedagogies. Perhaps this was due to differing ideas about what constitutes the political: whether the political should be calming or disturbing, confrontational, fluid or set. This account shows the effect on the individual of this failure:

> CE: *What do you think will happen now?*
> Pamela: *I don't know, I'm frustrated and upset and I'm stuck, I've learned so much and I can do so much, but I can't fix the world by myself, I don't know, from where I sit now how I'm going to channel everything I've got.... I'm sure something will happen at some point, but right now I'm just sitting in a void.*
> CE: *It will be interesting to see what happens over the next few years ...*
> Pamela: *It will, because at the moment every day there is another bloody hit and another hit, and another hit, and I used to have escapism fantasies ... there is no way to get off this bloody Earth and it is really difficult right now not to lose hope. I refuse to lose hope but when you get right down, it's just pure despair, you're like, there's nothing, there's nothing, the world's going to hell ... so yeah, it will be interesting to see what happens because I'm not in despair, I still have hope, but I'm just so flipping angry that I have so much potential and I'm just sitting here on my arse, and you know you have to have boundaries as well and you must refuse to work at something you don't see is going to work, you must step back, even if it means you must sit on your hands for years, because if you don't know how are you going to bring about the changes, you must always trust yourself.*
> CE: *I agree, do you think the experience that people have had with the learning, the experience people have had with occupy, with TCU and with the whole thing has changed them fundamentally and permanently?*
> Pamela: *Absolutely it has, absolutely without a doubt, yes. And it's amusing, we joke about it amongst ourselves, that we're broken, but breaking is a good thing, that's the thing, it's like losing the distractions of life around you, and taking it on the chin because it's real, it's painful, it is*

108  *Organic education from the ground up*

> *so painful to be open to the real, because you see the humanity and you see how people are hurting, and you know it doesn't have to be like that yet people outside of your circles just continue to reproduce that, and it hurts, it hurts so much and that's why we joke about being broken because it's a very melancholy place, to maintain your sense of humour, and you walk around and you carry the world on your back sometimes.*

This all brings up Ira Shor's (1996) notion that education can, or should, be at the same time convivial and confronting and the question how do a group, a community, a society, sustain a sense of togetherness, of sociality, producing this conviviality, whilst navigating the necessary divisions of an agonistic democracy. Therefore, there is a need to understand such issues as the emotional responses to learning, whether it was accepted that knowledge is always partial and incomplete. Lastly, does the education generate a new revolutionary theory through the countervailing discourses?

With these questions in mind, an exploration of the moments of pedagogy is needed. Such as this one:

> Wendy: *There's one guy that I can just hang out with and have a laugh with and talk for two hours with who's very different but in the end it's fine because we've had a good old political argument, and we can argue about anything and that's fine, you know, whereas in your job you kind of can't do that you worry about losing your job, don't you?*

Telling this tale of conviviality alongside learning acceptance, which was initially confronting, Wendy was realising how much she had changed through her interaction. This realisation was a constant theme throughout, which made the conversations I had convivial too. von Kotze (2012: 111) insists that 'we must open that imaginary window and throw our imaginations beyond what is, towards what could be' and this was often illustrated through the stories and their retelling. It also seemed that the learning was greater in some ways for those taking an active role in organising learning activities under changing contexts:

> Pamela: *[After the camp] we in TCU had to shift our focus from this experiment, this place of learning to the teach-out concept, the idea was to come into this space and have a general consciousness awakening, not only within the group but, you know, when you start focussing on teach-outs, you had to play out externally what was happening internally, in our spaces, so in the spring actions you'd land in a spot somewhere in the city. One day in particular, we were on the steps of the Bank of England, and then several invited speakers will speak, interestingly, those groups that would come to us for direct action, were the kind of groups that were used to organising break out groups*

*and people were really reluctant to do that and you end up standing there talking at them and that was extraordinary because to be forced to recalibrate the whole thing because people want to just sit and listen, it was quite disheartening, actually, because what you're doing then is that you're curating the information, and there's no two way thing at all.*

The changing context here was quite confronting as there was a realisation that what they had achieved was contextualised by the space; it was a contextual and temporal achievement rather than a new set of social relations that could be perpetuated after the encampment. The 'two-way street' should create the possibilities for the (co)production of knowledge; however, context is important and this forced teach-out context necessitated a lecture style format. According to Freire (Shor & Freire, 1987: 40), however, the lecture format does not necessarily create unequal power relations. In addition, 'unequal power relations should not be equated with oppression. Rather it is the (deliberate) abuse or (unwitting) misuse of power that should be recognised as the basis of oppression' (Thompson 2007: 10). Therefore, the changing context may not need have been so confrontational if there had been more theoretical knowledge about pedagogy.

Several others found that learning to live without the usual structures was both confronting and convivial as expressed here:

> Paul: *I really didn't get a lot of what occupy was about at the start, the flat structure of it, an organisation where there's no hierarchy, I went in there thinking, right who do I speak to? Who's the person in charge of this and who's in charge of that and we need to do this, I went in with my sort of old fashioned or mainstream view of we need a hierarchy and this person needs to organise that and actually, I understand why it's got no leaders, but I do find that very frustrating, because it means that some things don't get done or that it takes ages for things to get done and I'm still fight with that internally, like if someone says they're going to do something, you do it, but I don't know maybe that's me thinking that's the old way of doing things, like you set up a committee and take a bit of responsibility and you do it. Whereas in Occupy it's fluid.*

The Occupiers' stories do suggest that the educative activities, including the experience of being involved, encouraged an emotional response. The frustration and learning to accept was an educational experience that allows an imagining that a non-hierarchical organisational structure could be possible, with time, energy, belief and political will. TCU encouraged this way of thinking but missed some forms of oppression that could have been used as teaching points for the exploration of oppressive behaviours. However, Occupy opened up the possibilities and Occupiers thought about and confronted ideas that they previously had no space to experiment with. The experience was embodied and performative because of the context, therefore emotionality could hardly have been avoided. Occupy gave its activists an outlet for their anger, whether we concede that it worked or are disappointed by its failure, it attempted to do something positive, whilst trying to avoid cynicism or unbalanced fury, and attempted it with a generous heart (Freire, 1993a).

However, as Steinklammer (2012: 33) adds

> in social conflicts, such informal learning processes are much more likely to take place. However, there is a danger that these learning experiences remain covert and unconscious and, without conscious educational processes in which those resistant and empowering experiences of practice can be taken up and used as a point of departure, they cannot fulfil their full empowering potential.

And there was a disillusionment that was felt by some:

> Pamela: *There was a final straw incident for me. Consensus is about agreement, and what continues to happen if you are going to doggedly stick to the consensus model, and this is really controversial and, well, you can't leave occupy because it's part of you, but I don't feel I can for instance do press work and stuff anymore as I had been doing, because I don't believe that the consensus model works, at all. And over time it wears you down, it's about agreement, but what happens to me, whenever I'm faced with something I would really like to get through, is, there's almost a sort of lowest common denominator factor in play, so to achieve what is seen as agreement, what you've got is a series of people voting ... for or against the proposal, but now somebody's got the right to block, now if there's a block then no consensus can be achieved. The block is where the abuse of the system lies because it goes both ways, the block can be used abusively by an individual for personal vendetta reasons or whatever their thing is, he or she can use the block so that nothing can happen, and the consensus model says that you write in the minutes consensus not reached, but that's not the end of it, in reality there's all kinds of fallout from that so that's the one direction of abuse, the other direction is how it abuses people who are reticent to use the block because they recognise that people would like this proposal to happen, if they blocked it, it wouldn't happen so they have to either stand down, or decide that they agree so then you've got a situation where somebody, whatever their personal thing is, is not prepared to make a block. Therefore, they're constantly frustrated and not in agreement but going along with what is seen as the majority, now it would be great, if the majority were actually in attendance, but they're not, so consensus might be reached on something with only seven people in the room. But the ripple effect is*

*massive so yeah, over time it wears you down, I won't block something until I did and I really meant it. But it resulted in my walking away.*

This seemed a serious part of the disillusionment in Occupy and part of the 'learning' that seemed the most uncritical. However, as an experimental community this is possibly where Occupy achieved the most, the apparent failure of the consensus model. Occupy arguably showed that this model is unworkable at that time and that participatory democracy may need to be reined in from the all-out consensus model. One of the missed potentials, it seems, was moving on and learning from this failure of their ideological organisation. The problem, Holloway (2010: 71) insists is that 'this walking on the edge of disillusionment is what dignity means in a society of negation', but is it dignified, then, to 'doggedly stick to a principle', even in the face of it being abused and not working? This is a big area where Occupy did not create new knowledge by encouraging the view that knowledge is partial and incomplete. The mistake was made that there was a system of democracy that 'must' work because it is fair, equal and allows everyone a voice, but once that mistake was realised their disillusionment in their ideal meant that they could not move on from the failure.

This insistence of sticking doggedly to a principle can have the effect of producing vanguards within the movement as it effectively says to the majority that this movement was founded on these principles, we are not changing them and therefore you are either with us or you are not. As seen, this issue resulted in people walking away. Concerns surfaced, that were ignored:

> Judy: *Even during the camp even when it was going quite well the problem with consensus is the extent to which the voices, the louder voices, are going to be heard and there was never any question as to who wasn't speaking and why they weren't speaking. There were many situations in which things would happen and things would be pushed through that I know for a fact that there were people who just didn't feel that given the atmosphere, given the conversation, they could have a voice.*

This issue of rethinking democracy, was the main place where vanguards could coalesce. By not questioning who was not speaking, or why, vanguards arose. This seemed doubly damaging to the movement, as this sort of elitism, manipulating the direction of the movement, amounts to what Freire (1993a: 162) calls 'cultural invasion, which through alienation kills the creative enthusiasm of those who are invaded, leaving them hopeless and fearful of risking experimentation, without which there is no true creativity'. Therefore, Occupy is once again damaged by creating hopelessness and fearfulness of risking experimentation, the very thing that it was set up to do.

Occupy did not release new revolutionary theory as many hoped it would. What it did do, however, was make people think differently, imaginatively, critically about what is and what could be. It uncovered some political fictions disguised as social realities yet it (re)produced others. A great deal was learnt, social relations were produced otherwise, sometimes not in the ways they were intended, but this still has the potential to produce heightened critical awareness of the issues as they relate to transformative change. Occupy also produced a warning about repression, about the new responses of the state to dissent, it produced those globally.

It seems that what Occupy did was to make connections between people that may not otherwise have ever connected:

> Pamela: *They are suddenly exposed to the utter humanity of the very things that they're talking about theoretically. And it's very ... levelling is the wrong word because it lifts you up ... because not only are you like oh my god not only is this theory one thing, you are met with human relations in their rawest form. Which you do not have in your everyday life and that to me was the magic.*

It created the conditions for learning to take place:

> Peter: *I've definitely got more critical because at the GAs sometimes we would discuss ideologies and politics for hours.*

The biggest apparent failure, which may point to some conditions upon which new revolutionary theory could be built, was that Occupy seemed to reproduce, or at least fail to recognise and confront, one of the main issues that exists in our society today. That of patriarchy:

> Sally: *I personally am generally very outspoken, people who know me generally think we'll have to make sure that Sally is satisfied before anything happens, (laughs), I never spoke at a GA, I would just sit there and watch it, why would I bother even trying? I'd be shouted down, and then it would create such a hassle for me afterwards if I disagreed with something. We occupied the women's library at London Metropolitan ... and that was a self-declared feminist space, and we had a big GA and it was very interesting to me that you couldn't stop me and I'm just watching myself there and thinking ah, that felt safe, that's when my extreme dissatisfaction with my own particular Occupy situation began, and I realised that it became normalised to me that I wasn't able to articulate myself in a GA. And I thought wow, how did that happen?*

New revolutionary theory cannot be produced until there is a safe space within the revolutionary activities for everyone, which means uncontested equality. With these forms of patriarchal behaviour present, there was a definite failing where not all people felt that they could articulate, experiment and experience the prefiguration of a new form of social relations as a whole person, defined by their individual creativity and commitment to social justice. It is important to recognise what lies deeply embedded inside of everyone and recognise that as a revolutionary problematic and not as a deceit perpetuated by others, as this is destructive. Holloway (2010: 224–5) asserts,

> revolution, then, is the return of the repressed..... It is the revolt of that which exists against and pushes beyond. It is the revolt of creative doing that exists against alien determination and pushes beyond, towards self-determination. But creative doing is not just creation of that which exists outside us, but self-creation, creation of our own sexuality, our own culture, our own thinking and feeling.

If new social relations are to be developed, individuals must reinvent themselves too. Thus, as Steinklammer (2012: 33) suggests, a task for critical education is to provide the space to bring 'informal learning processes to consciousness, to reflect on them and to develop further strategies for action in exchange with others'.

The key issues that can be learnt from Occupy, pedagogically, are that there is the need for some form of pedagogical self-monitoring, a critical friend, or even a pedagogue to pick up those behaviours and conditioned responses that infected Occupy. In the heat of experimentation, it is easy to see failures where there might be learning, despair where there might be a lesson in understanding, oppression and subjugation where there could be opportunities to understand the Other's point of view. The leaderlessness of Occupy might have been a real ideal, but in practice they created vanguards and their own repressive policing systems. Perhaps some sense of where to go when things were not as equal as they were intended to be, some arbitrator of disputes could have been productive. It may have been useful for other epistemologies to be introduced, adapted and experimented with: the Zapatistas mantra of ruling we obey (Ross, 2006); the Rwandan 'justice on the grass' model (Temple-Raston, 2005); there may even be lessons from the world's truth commissions (Grandin, 2005), the world is full of both failed and successful political projects to be learnt from.

In concluding this discussion, these stories will always be brought, as Schostak and Schostak (2008) would say, into other imaginaries in other contexts and will forever inform thinking. What strikes me as important in the accounts, was the essentiality of democracy – not the general consensus decision-making process, but the feeling of democratic relations, the essence of shared power. This speaks to Shor's model of power sharing pedagogy, guided by classroom democracy. The insistence in TCU of bringing in 'experts' but then asking them to work in a way where their expertise was not elevated above being part of the conversation creates equality, wherein power can easily be shared. A dialogue with the people, as Freire might call it, but one where the dialogue is set by no one and is allowed free range for discovery.

The big question, then, is what are the essential elements of creating the space for this power-sharing, democratic, popular education that allows for an emergent countervailing discourse? The evidence from Occupy suggests that the *priority* is creating a truly safe space: safe from oppression, discrimination, domination and abuse. Once this space is created, Occupy's experience suggests that fundamental equality of intelligence must be respected for the learning to have transformative effects and that 'experts' should value the knowledge, experience and expertise that all learners bring to the pedagogical space in order to create a truly shared, democratic power relationship.

# 5 Becoming organised

Co-operatively organised education: stories from the Social Science Centre and higher education against neoliberalised consumerism: stories from Student as Producer

In this chapter, the outcomes of the examination of Occupy are utilised to understand whether there were structures that already existed, or could be collectively constructed, that could support popular education initiatives, in this case the Social Science Centre (SSC) and Student as Producer (SaP), in snapshot during the period of 2011–2013. These two examples were chosen for several reasons; first, they were already linked together and indeed have linked themselves to Occupy and consequently had the potential to form part of a learning feedback loop and second, the University of Lincoln was an unusual example of a university doing things differently in neoliberal times. This exploration was attempted by garnering an understanding of these organisations and what insight they might offer that would lead to less hierarchical forms of pedagogy being able to rid themselves of oppressive behaviours and attitudes.

The task, now, is to turn to these two sites of potential slippage to understand which of these conditions, and their associated nuances, were met in other spaces purporting to be doing things differently. Then, if they were not met, or go far enough, how much (re)organisation might it have taken to bring a more popular education to these spaces of learning? How best could these types of spaces be utilised in order to bring about a practical theory of action to support these new social movements and popular education initiatives? What forms of organisations could this education move towards, adopt and deploy, to create the necessary conditions for transformative change to a more socially just and radically democratic society? These questions are asked of the two supplementary sites: were they any more successful in creating forms of organisation that can include voice, support action and create a countervailing discourse?

It is pertinent to mention at this point for a full picture of what occurred within the research that Mike Neary, who is often quoted in this chapter, is one of a group of academics from the University of Lincoln who have been instrumental in setting up the SSC. He was (at the time of the original research) instrumental in realising the Student as Producer (SaP) Project at the University and very much saw the two projects as one in process. A great deal of the data in this section will contain Neary's words, as he was the most accessible person regarding the project. This gives a dominant view of what happened in these two projects and it is wise to exercise scepticism, and recognise that what here is predominantly rhetoric as contact with the projects has been limited by time and access.

## The Social Science Centre

When I spoke to the members of the SSC, there was a sense that they were doing something important, something politically different and that it mattered. There was also a sense that they felt that they were part of a vanguard movement of radical teaching and learning spaces. I couldn't help thinking that this was not entirely true, there was a history to what they were doing, their ideas were borrowed from others and they were only really having small success. However, I admired them for doing it, for experimenting with form and content. They were committed, that was obvious, to doing education otherwise, to creating the conditions necessary to ensure fundamental learning about the place they occupied in the world was understood, to create the conditions for understanding better the connections between the personal, the political and the global structures that need to change. Were they actually doing this? I remain unsure, I felt very much an outsider when I was there, some of the members were very welcoming, but they seemed to feel they were a special group, as if no one else could have been as radical as they.

(Fieldwork Journal 2013)

Clearly education cannot be a social movement unto itself. Rather, education is an instrument of power which shapes knowledge within social movements

(Zacharakis-Jutz, 1991: 9)

The 'scholars' at the SSC might have tended to disagree with the above statement by Zacharakis-Jutz. In fact, when I spoke to Neary, he told me that education had become the social movement of our time (conversation with Neary, 2013), a seductive idea, however, difficult to substantiate and not (so far) obvious of any educational project. Occupy tried to integrate education into their protests, with varying success, as has been seen, but it was merely part of the whole event, happening, movement and was often obfuscated by the will to be seen to be doing something. The pedagogy was not a, or the, movement in itself. So, what does happen if the event, the protest, the banners and slogans are left behind? Can education become the social movement? Can it create a large enough site of slippage (Merrifield, 2011), a significant enough crack to be considered a movement? Giroux (2001: xxvii) concurs with the *possibility* of education as a movement: 'at the very least, radical education proposes that education is a form of political intervention in the world and is capable of creating the possibilities for social transformation'. In addition, Castells (2012: 11) describes social movements thus, 'by constructing a free community in a symbolic place, social movements create a public space, a space for deliberation, which ultimately becomes a political space', which is essentially what the SSC attempted to do, somewhat supporting Neary's claim that education may, indeed, *possibly* be considered a social movement as long as it meets the criteria of being a political, public space for deliberation.

At the time of my original research there was a 'wall' of positivity around the SSC and particularly around Neary himself; he is a charismatic educator who is vocal at a time when most academics fear for their jobs (Bailey & Freedman, 2011; Collini, 2012; Williams, 2013). There is a great deal of support for both Neary and the projects he runs and it is difficult to find anyone saying anything negative about either. It is therefore with caution that I proceed into this exploration.

If one listened to those taking part in the SSC and to the rhetoric of the literature, one heard a group of people claiming to be determined to do things differently, to create a social movement of higher education that organises things otherwise, utilising what they assume is a more equitable and just organisational structure. Darder (2002: 30) asserts

> there is no question that, in today's world, no authentic form of democratic life is possible for the future without a revolutionary praxis of hope that works for both the transformation of social consciousness on the one hand and the reconstruction of social structures on the other.

This is apparently what the members of the SSC aim for – creating this revolutionary praxis, this transformation of the social consciousness that develops sensitivity to any form of despotism and unequal power relations, coupled with the reconstruction of social structures. This was one of the failings of Occupy, to recognise the unequal relations that were perpetuated within the camps and beyond, therefore their revolutionary praxis was not complete. The SSC needed to be able to fulfil this criterion of a revolutionary praxis to be assumed a mechanism or new social structure that could support initiatives, events or movements such as Occupy and other organically grown popular education projects. The task then is to try to understand if the SSC had the potential to fulfil this role as the next step in a trajectory from the streets to the academy. Therefore, if the SSC is examined as a differently organised popular education project that attempts to bridge the gap between the community and the University the following questions become central to this understanding:

- Did it use democratic power sharing as a central principle?
- Did the SSC resolve the tension between student and teacher?
- Did the SSC create a 'safe space' in which the possibilities for learning flourish?

The question of whether the SSC 'used democratic power sharing as a central principle' was answered with a cautiously simple 'yes'; it did, to varying extents, as I will further explain shortly. The question of resolving the tensions between teacher and student is slightly more complex, in that the answer is that it seemed to try very hard to do just that. As for the question of safe space, the answer seems to be that potentially, if they resolved the tensions contained within the first two questions, an affirmative on the third should be the result. As Goodlad (1984: 249) explains, however, 'we will only begin to get evidence of the potential power of pedagogy when we dare to risk and support markedly deviant classroom procedures'; is it possible to make the argument that the SSC was one of those spaces of 'deviant classroom procedures' that could illuminate the potential power of pedagogy?

This is from the original proposal for the SSC:

> Courses will run in existing public spaces, with a view to buying or renting a city-centre property further down the line. Attached to this (preferably on the premises) would be some kind of cooperatively run business, which would bring in an income to help cover running costs and act as a way to connect with local residents apart from and beyond the educational provision of the Centre
>
> (Winn, 2010)

This idea of attaching a business to the Centre carries with it the monetary relations of capitalist organisation (Marx, 1867/1976), however, it would subvert the flow of capital into the educational endeavour to enable it to be sustainable (Winn, 2010). The co-operatively run business could potentially make the centre accessible to those with low or no income and, as Winn mentions, connect it with the community in a variety of ways. Katsiaficas (2006: 6) explains this as movements 'subverting politics', because they are 'transforming public participation into something completely different from what is normally understood as political'.

We return now to the first criteria: did it use democratic power sharing as a central principle? The condition of democratic power sharing here is essential, because if the SSC did not create new social relations from its pedagogical initiative, the experience may not lead to social transformation and therefore it could not support other initiatives that do. The SSCs education should make explicit that the formation of conducive social relations is the key to the 'circle of power' (Rancière, 1991) which will enable learners to understand the conditions of their oppression and act upon them (Freire, 1993a).

The Constitution of the SSC (Social Science Centre, 2012) states, 'the purpose of the co-operative is to pursue its objects as an autonomous association of persons united ... through a jointly-owned and democratically controlled enterprise'. This indicates that democracy, co-operation and shared ownership (if not power) were a main aim of what the SSC was attempting to do. The web site states, 'the SSC is organised on the basis of democratic, non-hierarchical principles, with all members having equal involvement in the life and work of the SSC' (Social Science Centre, 2012). This statement expresses principles that have been discussed as essential and although Neary (in conversation 2013) told me that the reality is clearly messier than the ideal; they insist that they attempt to resolve any tensions that arise from trying to enact this ideal, although there is still a way to go. Day (2005: 8) argues that the character of today's resistance undermines the standard ways of doing, and thinking about, political action:

> what is more interesting about contemporary radical activism is that some groups are ... operating non-hegemonically rather than counter-hegemonically. They seek radical change, but not through taking or influencing state power, and in doing so they challenge the logic of hegemony at its very core.

This changing the logic of hegemony, speaks to the treatment of the 'expert' as was seen in the discussion of Occupy. The hegemony of the 'expert knowledge' no longer exists in the power-sharing classroom as it can be questioned and problematized. If the SSC was truly sharing power between the academics and the students then that suggests that there was potentially some sensitivity to the needs and desires of others in the SSC. In addition, what seemed to unite the members of the SSC was their belief in co-operative, critical and autonomous education (conversations at the SSC, 2013). Of course, I cannot include 'free' education there as some of them did pay to be members of the SSC:

> We do ask people to pay, but only if they can afford it. We ask for one hour's salary per month, so that's worked out on how much they earn. If they earn below a certain level, or they don't work, then they don't pay. That's how we make it both accessible and sustainable, hopefully! We have some members who pay, but have never actually come to a session; they're just supporting the work we do
> (Neary: conversations at the SSC, 2013)

The SSC was well supported with around ninety members in their first year, only nine of which were active student scholars (conversations at the SSC AGM, 2013; conversations at the SSC, 2013). This suggests a good level of support for the idea and indeed their web site states; 'we think that our work in co-operative higher learning has the potential to transform the way in which higher education is being imagined, designed and undertaken' (Social Science Centre, 2012), suggesting that they had big ambitions. This sentiment is qualified here by Neary (Neary in Class War University, 2013), when he insists that

> the SSC is not a demand for the state to provide higher education, but a recognition that revolutionary education cannot be provided by the

capitalist state; and, therefore, we have no other option but to establish our own necessary revolutionary alternative form of higher education.

This perhaps positions the SSC as a possible site of slippage between initiatives such as Occupy and the academy. As Bonnett (2013) suggests, 'there is an interesting and potentially creative tension here. The centre offers a structured and supportive educational experience, but the nature and politics of this experience is of its own devising'. There does seem to be an interesting tension and as Shor (1996: 180) points out, 'producing critical thought in an anti-critical culture is about as challenging as producing democratic relations in an unequal school system'; the SSC seemed to be effectively attempting to do both. I think it could be argued that the SSC was attempting to produce a democratic, power sharing curriculum, as their web site states, 'we are working to create alternative spaces of higher education whose purpose, societal value and existence do not depend on the decisions of the powerful' (Social Science Centre, 2012). Whether that works in practice remains to be seen.

I now turn to the question of the resolution of the tension between teacher and student. Neary (Neary in Class War University, 2013) explains that he 'was interested in how teaching could be used as a way of radically transforming academic labour and student life', believing that 'at the very most, teaching politically can be used to reinvent higher education as a revolutionary political project' (Neary, 2012: 234). This is not a new idea, as has been discussed already, but this project was, at least, something concrete in a world of political flux. Neary and Winn (2012: 14) have this to say about the teaching practices at the SSC:

> The co-operative practices on which the management of the SSC is based extend to the ways in which courses are taught. All classes will be participative and collaborative, so as to include the experience and knowledge of the student as an intrinsic part of the teaching and learning programmes. Students will have the chance to design courses as well as to deliver some of the teaching themselves with support from other members of the project. Students will be able to work with other academics on research projects as well as publish their own writings. A core principle of the centre is that teachers and students and the supporting members learn from each other.

Certainly, at face value, this sounds very much like an attempt to resolve any tension between teachers and students.

The SSC did however have a pre-planned curriculum, or syllabus, but that was perhaps flexible enough and open enough to change. Bahruth and Steiner (2000: 120) insist that

> to engender student engagement, in which students are involving their very beings and human conditions in the meaning making of academic

subjects, one must recognise that learner backgrounds and life experiences, including their academic experiences, are the only tools they have in order to engage in current learning.

The SSC seemed to have attempted to recognise this, the first, entry-level course, 'The Sociological Imagination' contained the ideas taken from Mills' (1957/2000) book of the same name. This course is described by Members of the Social Science Centre (2013: 66) as,

> an open class run by and for people who want to develop a critical understanding of the social world through social-scientific inquiry. The class proceeds from scholars' everyday problematics to theoretical critique. Through this emerging curriculum, we take up Mill's key challenge: how can individuals who appear powerless change and transform wider social structures in ways that are progressive and humanizing. Why does it matter that we learn to make links between our own private troubles and our more collective public issues?

The group goes on to say that

> underpinning 'The Sociological Imagination' is the SSC's pedagogical approach, which attempts to fix the dysfunctional relationship between teaching and research that constitutes the core of higher education. We want to find ways to reconnect research and teaching, whilst at the same time removing the distinction between students and academics, seeing them both instead as scholars in pursuit of creating new knowledge.
> (Members of the Social Science Centre, 2013: 66)

However, this grand premise can be distorted as Shor (1996: 51) explains from his experience, 'my authority can create an unauthentic discourse, what I call faux learning, a kind of theatre of manipulative discourse where students play at postures they think will help them get by'. This faux learning did not seem to be evident in Occupy as there were no 'teachers' for the learners to please and the experts were treated as equals in the learning process, as was seen, however, it did take place on some levels mainly as positioning for different viewpoints and groups. The SSC members asserted that they are committed to resolving what Neary calls this 'dysfunction', and it seems that this commitment was somewhat enacted. Neary (Neary in Class War University, 2013) also insists that this essential aspect is monitored from within

> [a] sense of imagination and the imaginary extends to the way in which the centre is managed and run, with time set aside to consider the meaning and purpose of the Centre, using the critical concepts developed in the SSC sessions: gender, ethics and power, to build our own sense of collective activity. These critical reflections can lead us to challenge our

own working practices, including, and in particular, how power is distributed across the collective and whose knowledge within the group is privileged.

This reflection is something that Occupy lacked and may have contributed to its downfall, as discussed.

This stated reflection on relationships would have the potential to allow for the challenges to power relations that were absent in Occupy, but only if sufficient time were set apart and if a sufficiently skilled pedagogue were present to challenge unequal power relations in a sensitive way until the relationship grew, as Freire insists it would,

> through dialogue, the teacher-of-students and the students-of-the-teacher cease to exist and a new term emerges: teacher-student with students-teachers. The teacher is no longer merely the-one-who-teaches, but the one who is himself taught in dialogue with the students, who in turn, while being taught also teach. They become jointly responsible for a process in which they all grow.
>
> (Freire, 1993a: 61)

This aspect of the SSC model could be a crucial aspect for the trajectory that this work explores, however, my observations of the interactions between the various members of the SSC indicate that they may have some way to go before all of the tensions are resolved; there did indeed seem to still be a hierarchy between the 'academics' and the 'students' at the SSC and there did seem to be some divisions along gender lines. However, these types of examinations of the working relationships, if taken further and acted upon, could assist movements and other popular education initiatives to come to terms with their conditioned behaviours that threaten their existence, as the gender and other relations did in Occupy. More generally, they could allow any form of education, organised with this reflection as central, to ensure that it was actually creating useful knowledge about our own subjectivities and therefore midwifing real transformation in our relations and social selves. However, this takes skill, sensitivity and courage in a time when these attributes need to be (re)developed in our relations.

This brings us on to the last condition in our trio, that of creating a safe space. This is the crux of the learning that would be needed to assist initiatives such as Occupy, as this is where it was reported that they mostly failed. As has already been mentioned, it does seem that the SSC was potentially beginning to create a safe space in the act of attempting to resolve the tension between teachers and students and in internal and collective monitoring of their own actions and behaviours. It is possible to assert this because of the all-important emphasis on the reflective practices described, how that works in reality is difficult to say as I have not been privy to these sessions.

Neary (2011) and the Members of the SSC (2013) agree that the SSC has its roots in the 'history of how those excluded from higher education have organized their own intellectual lives and learning in collaboration with university academics', another hint at the site of slippage, this time from the university to the SSC. Consequently, the pedagogy starts with forms of subjugated knowledges, albeit from mostly white and middle-class scholars, and student experience, placing it within the realm of popular education as defined in the introduction to this book. This does have the potential to create a safe space for expression in that 'building pedagogy and knowledge on experience (student's experiences) is regarded as one way to counter the claims of hegemonic truth' (Cho, 2013: 78), therefore making the pedagogy of the SSC explicitly political as it was in Occupy, but with the added time for reflection. In addition, as Castells (2012: 15) adds, 'the more interactive and self-configurable communication is, the less hierarchical is the organisation and the more participatory is the movement'. This again, in principle, produces a safe space, because the communication in the SSC was characterised by democratic, non-hierarchical and power-sharing principles as discussed.

The curriculum of the SSC, described earlier, also leaned itself to the creation of a safe, experimental and expressive space, as Shor (1996: 61) expounds from his experience, 'questioning the status quo is an unpredictable adventure that interrupts routine behaviours, expectations, and relationships'. As this was a collaborative and personalised activity in the SSC, it brings us back to Castells' (2012) assertion that togetherness is a fundamental psychological mechanism to overcome fear. In addition, as the curriculum asked learners the questions from Mills' (1957/2000) book, whilst they were potentially 'interrupting the routine behaviours, expectations, and relationships', they may also have been connecting these interruptions to the larger questions concerning social change.

Castells (2012: 10) also remarks that social actors 'need to build public space by creating free communities in the urban space', as Occupy did; 'since the institutional public space, the constitutionally designated space for deliberation, is occupied by the interests of dominant elites and their networks, social movements need to carve out a new public space [that] makes itself visible in social life' (Castells, 2012: 10). The SSC did do this to an extent; there was very little pedagogy behind closed doors. The SSC not only attempts to resolve the tension between the hierarchies of student and teacher, it also attempt to foreclose on the hierarchy between private and public space by conducting its activities in public spaces.

As Neary (2011) states, 'the SSC is grounded in forms of organisation that have arisen out of the development of the Social Centre network in the UK and around the world.' According to Pusey (2010: 176) social centres are 'managed autonomous spaces.... They have their roots in the Italian *autonomia* and German *autonome* movements of the late 1970s and early 1980s, and the associated politics of autonomy and social struggle'. This description fits with the SSC as they were reportedly attempting to be politically autonomous and engaged in social struggle. As we heard from Winn (2010) at the beginning of this section, 'courses run in existing public spaces'; Neary (2011) adds that 'autonomous education is a critical response to the crisis of the university, involving an alliance between faculty and students in co-operative learning, forming an experimental space for an academic commons against the pedagogy of debt and enclosure'. This is supported by Pusey (2010: 177) as he insists that 'many city centres are becoming increasingly dedicated to the further reproduction and circulation of capital through endless consumption.... Social centres represent an attempt to open up pockets of space that are dedicated to "people rather than profit"'. A founder member of the SSC explained, in an article in the *Times Higher Education Supplement*, that the centre needs to be 'understood as "an active part of the city" rather than a "discrete entity"' (Bonnett, 2013). Neary even goes as far as to say that the SSC could be seen as 'reclaiming our 'right to the city', or 'occupying' the city as 'a new pedagogy of space and time" (Neary in Class War University, 2013), a large claim indeed. However, Hardt and Negri (2012: 6) might agree in classifying the SSC as a struggle for the common in the sense that they 'contest the injustices of neoliberalism and, ultimately, the rule of private property' even if only in a small way. The Invisible Committee (2009: 58) state that 'urban space is more than just the theatre of confrontation, it is also the means'; the SSC may have the potential to become such a confrontation with the mechanisms of power, should it grow and spread.

The self-monitoring and discussion on the weighty social issues of society's malaise, coupled with their insistence on 'reclaiming the right to the city' as a learning agora potentially create from the SSC a crack in the capitalist infrastructure of enclosure and surveillance and, moreover, a potentially effective form of educational organisation for social transformation. Carrigan (2011) concurs with his description; 'it's a radical, optimistic and most of all practical attempt to discover alternative ways of teaching and learning within the present climate' and Bonnett (2013) explains, 'as fun as the centre sounds, there is also a sense of urgency and anger that motivates these scholars and students. Resistance to government changes requires more than protest'.

Neary and Winn (2012: 13) describe the SSC as 'being a new "institution of the common" or "autonomous institutionality"'. Moreover, they did appear to be intent on enacting what Rancière (1991: 39) insisted emancipated educators should do: 'to give, not the key to knowledge, but the consciousness of what an intelligence can do when it considers itself equal to any other and considers any other equal to itself'. Of course, this notion has massive implications for the notional roles in education: student; under/postgraduate; lecturer; professor. These roles are boundaries that currently imply that one intelligence is not equal to another and are perhaps the boundaries that need to be cracked in this context the most. But how, in what Schostak (personal communication) calls the 'contemporary compliance machines known as universities' is this to be done? In the final analysis of the SSC, whilst accepting the complexity and messiness of the reality of enacting the principles upon which the SSC is based, it does present a convincing argument, on paper at least, that it is indeed a crack in capitalism and resolves much of the tension it needs to, to become a revolutionary pedagogical space and an effective form of educational organisation that could, perhaps be mobile enough to set up in situations such as Occupy. This space also seemed to have the potential to become useful in other ways to social movements, such as Occupy, alongside other popular education initiatives. These initiatives seem to require the assistance of those who have spent their lives becoming experts in fields that are essential to the understanding of how to elicit social change: sociologists, psychologists, linguists, political theorists and many others including the educational theorist, all of whom reside for the most part within academe, which is where the attention is now directed.

So now we take a trip into corporatized territory: the University of Lincoln and Student as Producer.

Although the Student as Producer (SaP) initiative has now come to an end and the University that was its base has continued the work inspired by it in what some might call a watered down and depoliticised way, it is still worth examining here as, whilst in full swing, the initiative not only put the University in question 'on the map' in terms of a very successful initiative and a way to organise higher education otherwise, but it also garnered much support from the students who interacted with the University at the time and from academics who experienced the initiative first hand and heard about it from others. It has to be understood that the SaP was a funded project with finite funding, but it taught a great number of people what is ultimately possible in HE, and what the costs of implementing such a political project in tense times for the sector might be. In addition, this particular model of higher education organisation serves the purposes here of illustrating a possible model that could complete the trajectory explored here and be the turning place for the loop of learning from the streets to the academy – and back. However, the main difference to the other sites is that it enacts its oppositional politics within the confines of the university structure. Therefore, different questions have to be asked of this project, in other words, the interrogation is not on the grounds of it being a grass roots or popular pedagogical movement, but as a 'crack from above'. In that respect, Student as Producer (SaP) reorganises its resistance from within and against, rather than beyond.

The authors of the Student as Producer project asserted that the project was in political opposition to the dominant culture in English higher education (HE) – that of students as consuming subjects (Neary in Class War University, 2013; Williams, 2013). As a site of potential slippage, the project slipped out of the control of the dominant culture in HE – for a while and to a point – but what is essential is that it did so in a somewhat, but maybe not enough, indistinguishable way when viewed from above, from the realm of policy (University of Lincoln, 2011–2012) and may have been subversive enough to create a new form of organisation if given enough time to bed in and grow. It did not use an overtly popular education, in this book's understanding of the term, and it did not call itself critical pedagogy, at least not aloud. The main premise was that the student should become the (co-)producer of knowledge, not its consumer (Student as Producer, 2010), an uncomfortable premise in the literature which was still couched in market discourses. This, hypothetically, turned the culture of the student as consuming subject on its head and expected that students are agentic beings, that knowledge they co-produce alongside academic staff throughout their time at the University would form within them a different, counter-hegemonic relationship to issues surrounding knowledge, power and agency (In conversation with Neary, 2013). A noble sentiment, but imagine if the notion of 'co-produce' was to become co-think, co-imagine, co-create, co-critique – where could those terms lead? Perhaps the corporatized world of UK higher education is not ready for that, so there is a need, perhaps, to think of SaP as a place to start?

So, what needs asking of Student as Producer in order for it to become relevant to the task here, of creating sites to support social change and countervailing discourses? If we are to understand ways in which we can garner forms of more popular education within academe, SaP could indeed be a good place to start. Therefore, an understanding of how SaP attempted to encourage and nurture a counter culture with new social relations, if it did do this, is essential.

There are traits of popular education (University of Lincoln, 2011–2012) within SaP, but can the learning from Occupy and the SSC provide an insight, not only of how to create a deeper form of popular education within academe, but also to support popular education initiatives and social movements from within the university using this research-engaged teaching initiative? In addition, what can be learnt from the organising principles of SaP to allow a new form of educational organisation, perhaps even in existing HE institutions (HEIs), to be realised?

Crowther *et al.* (2005: 6) stress, 'there is both the need and the potential to create opportunities and spaces for popular education in all aspects of academic work'. So, did the SaP initiative exploit this need and potential?

Much of their literature at least *suggests* it did, through the main aspect of the initiative: research-engaged teaching:

> As well as being academically led, research engaged teaching suggests that the process of teaching and learning can be considered in an intellectual manner. This means designing teaching and learning activities that connect knowledge and human interests through a theoretical engagement with research, in a culture based on augmentation and critique (McLean, 2006). In this way, it is possible to, 'deepen understanding of where problems might lie and what to do about them', in a series of professional academic conversations grounded in the principles of 'solidarity and reflection' (McLean, 2006: 109 and 125).
>
> (University of Lincoln, 2011–2012: 4)

These principles, 'solidarity and reflection' and the teaching and learning activities that 'connect knowledge and human interests', certainly seem to be a sound basis for creating a popular education, or a popular education support, within a university. There also seemed to be a valid attempt at nurturing the creative imagination with the abandonment of learning outcomes, taking away the limiting effects of outcomes and replacing them with learning outputs (University of Lincoln, 2011–2012: 14). Learning outcomes were seen by SaP as overly prescriptive and limiting to the creative potential of the students:

> Learning outputs build on learning outcomes by recognising the importance of creativity and originality of student work. Learning outputs encourage students to develop their own critical insights and understandings through interactions with teachers. Learning outputs recognise the tensions and complexities ... of the learning environment.... Learning outputs might include research reports, published papers, designed objects for exhibition, organisation of academic event, public performances, etc. a key aspect of learning outputs is that the nature of the output cannot be identified at the outset of the programme, introducing a degree of creativity, originality and uncertainty into the learning process.

This notion of introducing uncertainty, creativity and originality contains the possibility of enabling the learning subject to explore and examine the depths of their potential. It also should allow for that all-important aspect of critical pedagogy and bricolage: not knowing, not being sure, and accepting revision of knowledge.

> The admission that we do not know is both a principle of knowledge and a principle of organisation that aims at the participation of all in the process of determining our individual and collective doing.
> (Holloway, 2010: 256)

But perhaps more than that, they have the potential to form different social structures as creativity flourishes when we do not know in a safe place.

> Knowing would lead to a different organisational structure, a structure of monologue with established leaders and institutions to hold them in place.
> (Holloway, 2010: 256)

Holloway's words here suggest that the element of uncertainty, the not knowing the predetermined outcome, may have the effect of fostering more collective, collaborative and inclusive organisations in the future. The SaP notion that learning outputs cannot be identified at the beginning of the programme and are designed by the students, facilitated by the teachers, connects the notion that 'the world must be approached as an object to be understood and known by the efforts of the learners themselves. Moreover, their acts of knowing are to be stimulated and grounded in their own being, experiences, needs, circumstances, and destinies' (McLaren, 2000a: 11) with the HE curriculum. It may, of course, be easy, from this stance, to introduce a more explicitly political engagement with the students in order to foster an overtly counter-hegemonic ethos to the institution as Bahruth and Steiner (2000: 121) describe:

> teacher-scholars would have to explore and understand social, political and historical contexts of hegemony (Chomsky 1995) to be effective in counter-hegemonic pedagogy. Teachers are no longer the dominant voice in the classroom. Students are asked to become active learners, critical thinkers, non-passive and their voices are respected as constructive contributors. We collectively work to become a community of learners.

Most of the suggestions from Bahruth and Steiner were claimed to be contained within the organisational ethos of SaP, active learning, critical thinking and constructive contributing to the learning process. Nevertheless, as Neary (in conversation, 2013) told me they did not engage the students in an explicitly political way, rather through the curriculum. This engagement through the curriculum could be construed as a 'gentler' way for students to come to their own decisions about change and hegemony: 'The passion for learning must be kindled and nurtured in subtle ways so as not to drive students further from the intended purposes of education' (Bahruth & Steiner, 2000: 131). Cho (2013: 99) adds this:

> students do not change just because they are told to change. Similarly, teachers do not change just because they encounter the 'truth'. Individuals change their moralities, values and behaviours when social structures are conducive to and can support such changes. The real task of critical pedagogy is to create the social structures that allow individuals to change and grow. Rather than focussing on reforming individuals per se, critical pedagogy should explore alternative visions of social structures and conditions, so that ordinary teachers and students can practice and experience a pedagogy of hope, love, equality and social justice.

It should also be remembered that the students that experienced SaP did not enrol into a social movement for change, they wanted a university degree. Therefore, this nurturing of a counter-hegemonic pedagogy, *within an alternative structure*, should encourage at least thinking otherwise, and the SaP project, asked students to go out and engage with real world problems through the research-engaged ethos. This gentle curriculum engagement is perhaps what is needed to create the safe space that was missing in Occupy on a much larger scale if adopted throughout HE, or to extend the co-operative, collaborative and democratic values of the SSC. However, when as Couldry (2011: 37) states, 'the UK coalition government's funding reforms are a sustained attack on the idea of the university in England. Unless defended, that idea will die', it is difficult to be patient and to understand on a practical level, that institutional and cultural change take time, if they can be achieved at all.

What was perhaps most interesting about SaP was that as Neary (University of Lincoln, 2011–2012: 3) attested, the 'initiative has received enthusiastic support from staff and students across the university, as well as some critical responses'. He adds,

> the point is not that everyone agrees with the principle of research-engaged teaching, but that the university engages in an intellectual discussion about the nature of teaching and learning and its relationship to research ... in a progressive and collegiate manner.

This should have had the effect of ensuring that the SaP initiative became 'not a template on which academics are being asked to base their pedagogical activities, but a starting point to generate a fundamental debate about how we teach'. The authors of SaP (University of Lincoln, 2011–2012: 6) accepted that research engaged teaching and learning was 'becoming increasingly prevalent in universities'; however, what apparently made this University different was that 'no one university has sought to implement it across the whole of its teaching and learning provision'. According to them 'it is this ambition to adopt research engaged teaching and learning as the organising principle for linking research and teaching across the University that is the really significant aspect of this initiative'. I feel that it is not only making this way of teaching and learning the organising principle that was really significant, but also that it was posited as 'a starting point to generate a fundamental debate about how we teach'. This seems indeed to be what Cho (2013: 122) might call 'Utopian pedagogy' which she describes as 'a broad idea to help us pursue alternative thinking and models, beyond what seems common and feasible'. For a whole university to attempt to disengage with the dominant culture at a time when UK universities were under attack at their very foundations from an ideological government (Bailey, 2011; Couldry, 2011; Roggero, 2011; Neary, 2012; Walton, 2011; Williams, 2013) is indeed beyond what most people would consider 'common and feasible'. However, it is important to remember, 'marginalised alternatives remain virtually unknown and are rarely debated' (Milojevic, 2006: 26), and it is therefore the job of politically motivated researchers in HE to examine these alternatives. SaP looked like an exercise in subversive prefiguration because, as Neary (in conversation, 2013) told me,

> we are doing what we can under the current hegemony, but the important thing is that we are just doing it, and so far, it's going well, it's a messy reality, but we have a great deal of buy-in from all over the university – including, most importantly, the students.

The notion that the students are expressing this 'buy-in' is vital for the understanding of SaP as part of the trajectory for popular education, because without the 'buy-in' from the students the trajectory would not work.

The SaP project carried with it the notion of choice, Newman (2005: 30) argues that 'popular education is about teaching choice, about helping ourselves and others understand that we do have choices, and about helping ourselves and others develop the necessary capabilities to make those choices'. The way the teaching and learning was organised, according to SaP's 'key aspects' document suggests that choice making was built in as students were in

> an environment in which learning is driven by a process of enquiry owned by the student.... Starting with a 'scenario' and with the guidance of a facilitator, students identify their own issues and questions.... Students examine the resources they need to research the topic, provided as part of Learning Development@Lincoln, thereby acquiring the requisite knowledge.
>
> (Student as Producer, 2010).

It is this connection with 'real problems' of their own identification, investigated with the 'guidance of a facilitator' that suggests that SaP could have been of great assistance not only to movements such as Occupy, but also to creating social change in general, should students' attention be engaged in specific, politically orientated ways. Bailey (2011: 98) asserts that what is needed is

> striking a judicious balance between education as the acquisition of objective knowledge and education as helping students realise their full potential for the greater good. Conceived in this way, education is of crucial importance for the fostering of a social consciousness, socio-cultural exchange and the gradual strengthening of the democratic process.

SaP seemed to strike this balance when judged on its literary output,

> the essential aspects of research-engaged teaching and learning is that it involves a more research orientated style of teaching, where students learn about research processes, and where the curriculum emphasises the ways by which knowledge is produced, rather than learning knowledge that has already been discovered.
>
> (University of Lincoln, 2011–2012: 5)

Understanding the way in which knowledge is produced is of crucial importance for fostering social consciousness, for as Brookfield (2001: 5) once again corroborates, 'critical thinkers are actively engaged in life. They see themselves as creating and re-creating aspects of their personal, workplace and political lives. They appreciate creativity, they are innovators, and they exude a sense that life is full of possibilities'. The argument here is that this attitude cannot but help strengthen a just and democratic society exponentially. In addition, this research-orientated style of teaching not only has the potential to allow the students agency in their own knowledge production activities but also assumes an equality of intelligence, if not skills and knowledge, that Rancière posited was essential for 'universal teaching'. Moreover, Illich (2011: 39) contends, 'learning is the human activity which needs the least manipulation by others.... [Learning is] the result of unhampered participation in a meaningful setting. Most people learn best by being "with it"'; this seemed to be the aim of SaP – to create, through research engaged teaching and learning, a form of experiential learning reminiscent of Dewey's laboratory school (Dewey, 1965). Whilst Tent City University did a great deal for raising the critical awareness of the people involved in Occupy London, SaP had the potential to allow learners to rework social relationships more generally through this form of research engaged teaching and learning whilst reaching a mass audience. To be involved in research is to be involved in critically analysing social relationships, from whatever disciplinary lens you use to look, as all involve a literature review, examining the thinking about the world around us through a critical lens. This suggests that education, especially when connected to real world research problems, is an appropriate organisational form to prefigure, intellectually and practically, what is needed to re-make social relations.

This form of prefigurative intellectual work is particularly pertinent when the research engagement takes the form of action research, creating living knowledges that in the arena of the HE classroom and the collaborating organisation, can be worked, analysed and reworked. This could have been the potential of the SaP pedagogical methodology. As Borg and Mayo (2007: x) insist, 'it is through multi-levelled, dialogical encounters, firmly rooted in the day to day struggles, and communicated in accessible languages, that oppressions can be named, shamed and eventually, tackled'. Suppose, then, that the collaborating groups or organisations were social movements, or popular education initiatives. Learners, through the pedagogical methods of the SaP, would now be able to be instrumental to creating research action cycles with these groups, thus having the potential to improve their efficacy by creating a praxis of theory and action that allows the action to be done by those on the ground and the theory to be injected into that action by the learners and academics practicing the SaP ethos.

What then, was the philosophy behind SaP, why was this initiative implemented at that time? Neary felt that

> knowledge had now become a key commodity in the process of valorisation, and the university a key site of production of commodified knowledge. Any sense of knowledge being produced for common good, or that academic work requires open networks of collaboration was now being enclosed behind intellectual property laws, student debt, budget cuts, knowledge transfers, marketization and privatisation. The valorisation of knowledge had produced a new regime of accumulation; cognitive capitalism.
> (Neary, 2012: 241)

This view suggests that academe has at least one of the same problems as those experienced by Occupy, the impingement of their right to commons. Darder (2002: 11) echoes the sentiment, 'the forces of the marketplace and the interests of the corporations also drive educational rhetoric and classroom curricula'. Walton (2011: 20) maps this trend from thirty years of neoliberal history,

> the dominant ideology under Blair as under Thatcher (and Major), was an almost religious faith in markets and competition which paid no heed to the existing wealth of understanding and experience in academe ... and took as its sole aim the materialist goals of preparing students for the corporate labour market.

This is good for neither students nor academics as Crowther *et al.* (2005: 4) testify:

> the contemporary academy – certainly in the rich world – is a hotbed of market ideology orchestrated by the dictates of the new managerialism. In the era of academic capitalism university knowledge has become a commodity, and the successful academic is now a trader in the educational market place.

Freedman (2011: 10) agrees with Neary and SaP when he says, 'we ... have [a] responsibility, to defend the idea of university education as a public good that is reducible neither to market values nor to instrumental reasoning'. Cavanagh (in Borg & Mayo, 2007: 46) insists that

> the mainstreaming of popular education could ... be a part of creating a more just society. But we cannot be naïve about this. We must be vigilant to ensure that the ethics of justice and compassion and love remain vital within popular education.

It should be remembered however, that SaP was implemented within the confines of a modern university, students were still paying high fees to attend and it could not escape the enclosure of some of the language of the market being adopted in their own literature:

> Student as Producer supports the career preparation and aspirations of students, in the form of a traditional route into the professions, working within an SME, creating a new start business, employment within the growing third sector or going on to further study. Student as Producer maintains that research-engaged teaching and learning is more likely to result in graduates who are better prepared to cope with a globalised labour market which is characterised by ever-changing technology and working practices.
>
> (Student as Producer, 2010)

This language is a warning that we must 'avoid romanticising situations that capture our imagination and offer much hope' (Borg & Mayo, 2007: xi). However, this should not denigrate the initiative, as mentioned earlier, SaP was meant not only as a reorganisation of the university, but also as a starting point for a conversation about how we teach and learn. SaP had to be subversive and adopt the language of market driven policy in order to survive the gaze of the boundary policing authorities mentioned earlier. However, its literature betrayed its apparent commitment to dominant ideology with extracts such as 'the emphasis on the Student Voice ... *allowing for the space of dissensus and disagreement, driven by engaged and participatory pedagogies*' (Student as Producer, 2010, my italics). Student Voice in dominant ideology is about the voice of the consumer, as Williams (2013: 8) explains:

> it is argued that the operation of consumer choice within a marketised HE sector will drive up standards, and therefore the student as consumer is a positive force: the 'good' student will exercise consumer choice and 'drive up the quality' of HE for others. Such assumptions may suggest that HE is a commodity designed to be packaged and consumed, and that it has an inherent financial value which can, once purchased, be traded in in the post-graduate labour market.

However, Williams (2013: 10) also argues, 'in treating students as consumers needing to be satisfied, universities can play a role in infantilising students through reducing intellectual challenge to the completion of modules and replacing academic relationships with customer care contracts'. SaP managed, in principle, to avoid this infantilising – despite students being in the same financial position and therefore positioned as 'customers' there as anywhere else – by assuring that 'Student as Producer promotes the involvement and engagement of students in the design and delivery of modules and programmes' (University of Lincoln, 2012: 5). Again, we see this aspect of choice and agency, so when, as Giroux (2001: xxii) says, 'the only form of citizenship increasingly being offered to young people is consumerism', the SaP initiative claimed to be offering agency, choice and control to students over their own learning. It can therefore be seen as potential for a strong defence of the notion of the university as a public good, ready and primed to be radicalised into a political project par excellence. Crowther *et al.* (2005: 1) insist that 'the radicalisation of intellectual work ... is an important, necessary and urgent task ... at a time when universities are being drawn inexorably away from social and political engagement'. This was well supported by Neary and Amsler's (2012: 122) insistence that SaP gives students 'the sense that they are part of creating the future – as subjects/makers rather than objects/victims of history'; this effect, they claim, occurs during their time at university and when students leave. Although without engaging the student politically as Neary insisted they did not, it is unclear how, exactly, students come to see themselves this way. These points give a clear understanding that SaP is, as

Neary and Amsler (2012: 124) insist, 'set firmly 'within and against' the idea of the university as a neoliberal institution'. These points also clearly support Freedman's (2011: 10) notion that the university should be 'a public service, a social entitlement, a space for critical thinking and a place of discovery', which are reminiscent of what TCU was for Occupy, and indeed the SSC is and therefore links can be built between the different sites.

If indeed, Neary's (2012: 234) suggestion that 'at the very most, teaching politically can be used to reinvent higher education as a revolutionary political project' is to be used as a linkage point, assertions can begin to be made about the potential that SaP had to use the learning from Occupy and the SSC to build on the initiative and create a popular-based education within, against and beyond academe. For example, as suggested earlier and supported here by Crowther *et al.* (2005: 1),

> university based teachers and researchers …. use their work to support popular struggles for greater democracy, equality and social justice – and to do so at a time when all the demands being made upon them are, seemingly, towards institutional disengagement from social and political action.

SaP seemed to begin to do this at a time when, as Bahruth and Steiner (2000: 119) suggest, 'students have learned to respond to the expectations of the teacher: parroting, memorising, and regurgitating from a series of facts and official bodies of knowledge promoted by the mainstream canon'. SaP attempted to circumvent 'the resulting "stupidification" (Macedo 1993)' and 'demands a counter-hegemonic pedagogy' (ibid). SaP had the potential not only to create academics who may as Crowther *et al.* suggested 'use their work to support popular movements', but who may also see their work as part of an emergent popular movement to re-engage students in HE. This potential arises because of tenets such as these:

> Research-based learning …. includes: Design of learning activities based on authentic research problems in the public domain that involve engagement with the wider community.
>
> (Student as Producer, 2010)

The understanding of, or making intellectual and practical connections between, such issues as frontiers of disciplines, research methodologies, authentic research problems and engagement with the wider community, suggest that SaP had indeed the potential to create a popular education within the university, but not only that. SaP had the potential to support social movements and grass roots popular education, such as Occupy by researching them throughout the curriculum. Newman (2005: 28) says, 'critical learning is a political act. It helps us see through ourselves and so become better at seeing through others. It makes us much less susceptible to hegemonic control', thus enabling learners to research movements beyond hegemonic conceptions of activism and without the elitist attitude that some HE institutions pass on to their graduates. This is substantiated by Couldry (2011: 44) who insists that, in the face of the neoliberalisation of the university,

> the best response (perhaps obvious, but the obvious needs saying in the face of a neoliberal culture that grows by not allowing certain types of 'obvious' to be said) is to build a counter-culture within the English university, a culture and a life which embeds a counter-rationality into neoliberalism.

This counter-rationality is evident in the work being done by some who were involved with designing SaP around militant co-research; 'from the position of militant/co-research and self-education the political subjectivity of the author is not regarded as detrimental to the research process, but is the essential objective reality out of which the research is derived' (Neary, 2012: 234). This position in militant/co-research (see Shukaitis & Graeber, 2007) was built into the SaP initiative as a central point, it was however, understandably not mentioned as militant/co-research on University literature, but is there

> [a] definition of research-engaged teaching and learning might be: 'a fundamental principle of curriculum design, where students learn primarily by engagement in real research projects, or projects which replicate the process of research in their discipline. Engagement is created through active collaboration amongst and between students and academics, underpinned by the effective use of information resources.
> (University of Lincoln, 2011–2012: 6)

And

> Student as Producer ... strongly promotes the use of Creative Commons licenses, as well as other ways of making publicly and openly accessible the intellectual products that are developed at UL.
> (University of Lincoln, 2011–2012: 15)

These extracts can be argued as having traits of what Neary and Amsler (2012: 107) call 'occupying the curriculum': 'we consider here how attempts to occupy the university curriculum, not as a programme of education but as the production of critical knowledge, may also constitute "a new pedagogy of space and time"'. This new pedagogy of space and time is an interesting concept and connects with Crowther et al.'s (2005: 6) insistence that within popular education 'pedagogy is a matter of principle and purpose rather than mere technique. Methods of teaching and learning must therefore be developed and deployed in ways which enable the teacher to learn and the learner to teach'. Research-engaged teaching and learning does this, as Faulkner

(2011: 28) argues, 'it unites practice and theory, skills and critique, the knowledge to do things with an understanding of purpose and consequence'. In addition, Neary and Amsler (2012: 122) insist that we wonder 'what are the spatial learning landscapes within which teaching is set: at the geographical level of the classroom, the campus and beyond: but also as a horizontal space within which collaborations can multiply'. Collini (2012: 91) maintains, 'the governing purpose [of the university] involves extending human understanding through open-ended enquiry'. Neary and Amsler (2012: 109) extend this purpose by explaining that

> in practical terms, this means that 'education' cannot be separated from 'life' in institutions, and that thinking about education cannot be separated from the spaces and times in which we produce knowledge – which in this formulation, are potentially everywhere and always.

This idea of the spaces we produce knowledge – or learn – being 'potentially everywhere and always', ties SaP, the SSC and Occupy together in a continuum of knowledge production sites, thus presenting the opportunity for imagining that they could be connected in a plethora of other ways. This, coupled with the notion of co-production of knowledge, creates the condition wherein, as Neary & Winn (2012: 12) state,

> students and academics [are] working together as a form of political praxis, so that the production of knowledge becomes a key principle of self-organisation and radical subjectivity (Roggero, 2011). And in the middle of all this the concept of the 'common' is re-established.

Therefore, if SaP could have re-established a form of academic commons, there seems to be little reason why that commons could not have extended outwards from the confines of the university to encompass social movements, alternative education provision (such as the SSC) and community groups, all involved in a form of political praxis, creating new, extended radical subjectivities. This reiterates Neary's notion above that the SSC and SaP were two ends of the same project to dissolve the neoliberal university (Neary & Amsler, 2012: 124) and reconstitute education as another form of 'social knowing' (Neary & Hagyard, 2011). Neary and Amsler (2012: 121) take the connections between all the sites further and insist that 'like Occupy, Student as Producer is an anti-curriculum, whose substance is not simply teaching and learning but the production of knowledge as a revolutionary political project'. Williams (2013: 5) agrees and argues for a form of radical dissolution of the university structure: 'I argue for students to be considered as active participants in their education, who have the potential to become the intellectual equals of their lecturers and make a contribution to society's knowledge and understanding of the world'.

To connect SaP to the pedagogical verities in our grounded theory exploration, SaP connects very much with the democratic power sharing pedagogy espoused by Shor (1996). So much so that this extract from Shor (1996: 56) could almost have been included verbatim in one of their reports:

> in the critical pedagogy I have been defining here and elsewhere, teachers don't stop being authorities or academic experts, but they deploy their power and knowledge as democratic authorities who question the status quo and negotiate the curriculum rather than as authoritarian educators who unilaterally make the rules and lecture on pre-set subject matters.

It is at this point, then, that I will turn to the lines of continuity (Holloway, 2010) between the three sites. In the face of it, the connections between the sites in this work may seem spurious, particularly between Occupy and SaP, but as already discussed, albeit tentatively, there are connections. It is time now to make those lines explicit, and create a solidarisitic movement between them – to join the cracks.

# 6 In the beginning Occupy created camps
## Thinking through the implications

Holloway insists that 'what is important is not to draw dividing lines, but see the lines of continuity' (2010); it is therefore necessary, whilst accepting the narrative of failure and despair, to bring out the hopeful narrative that runs through the sites thus explored. Consequently, this chapter will argue that there is at least the potential to build strong connections for promoting voice, equality and democracy in the current socio-political juncture and will ask questions about possible ways forward. Once more, thinking through Bricolage is activated to allow the imagination of what might be, and how it might be constituted. This chapter will attempt to further uncover and identify what Cho (2013: 78) calls a 'world of alternative values and practices' in the sites. Connections between the sites that indicate attempts at providing this world of alternatives are explored through the themes of 'story and experience'; 'occupation and reclamation'; and 'conscientization'. I argue that, at the current moment, there may well be a need for forms of organisation that have clear pedagogical direction accompanied by strong and collective procedures and mechanisms that are able, and encouraged, to subvert and constrain any emergent vanguards in order to eventually dispense with current forms and create more organic, non-hierarchical and fluid forms of education. Here, I will also discuss whether the connections that are uncovered between the sites could constitute a learning loop which can cycle as a form of praxis, creating the proposed 'grand action research cycle'.

Cowden and Singh (2013: 3) describe the current political and educational problems, including the commodification of the university and the further standardisation of schooling, as 'a crisis of thinking, feeling and doing' and insist, 'it is crucial to understand the wider linkages'. Therefore, linking these attempts at restructuring, through a solidarisitic cycle of praxis becomes paramount so that educators might be ready to ensure the 'crisis of thinking, feeling and doing' does not become pervasive throughout education and indeed society.

As mentioned above, running throughout this chapter and the sites explored are the somewhat contentious themes of story and experience (the telling, feeling and doing in the world of the human subject), occupation and reclamation (of space, of cities, of the intellectual subject, of the heart and the mind), and conscientization (of the individual, the collective, and the human as political animal). I argue that it is through this bricolage, or juxtaposition of themes, that the strongest lines of continuity of practice and solidarity for a potentially revolutionary pedagogy of escape can be seen. This is because, as Kincheloe et al. (2011: 164) state, critical theory should not be treated as a universal grammar of revolutionary thought objectified and reduced to discrete formulaic pronouncements, therefore a juxtaposition of potential viewing points seems appropriate. It is here, then, that those imaginative elements of the bricolage, of thinking beyond what exists and seeing the world that exists not yet, are employed to see the negatives from the sites, but also to tease out what is hopeful and could carry us forward.

Here the three sites explored throughout the book are tied together in order, not to assimilate or indoctrinate each other, but to create a dialogue through their juxtaposition; to disquiet tensions, to assist each other to grow, to become more, and to uncover the possible imaginative resolutions to the crisis of thinking and feeling described above by Cowden and Singh.

## Story and experience

Cho (2013: 78) states that 'the voices of those who are marginalised can/do provide 'evidence for a world of alternative values and practices whose experience gives the lie to hegemonic constructions of social worlds' (Scott, 1992: 24)', this makes these stories from the margins important for escaping the enclosure of the TINA (there is no alternative) syndrome. Ollis (2012: 213) adds to this notion by insisting that 'adult learners are rich sites of knowledge ... their capacity to take on new knowledge is dynamic because they are agentic', especially, it is argued here, when educational activity takes place in conducive and insurgent settings. The use of bricolage here has allowed 'education' to be uncovered beyond its usual confinements in formal institutions and community halls, through the leaving behind of the traditional discourses on education that reside mainly in the revision of schooling. Seeing through the bricolage lens has allowed a view of the pedagogical Other and an understanding of experience as pedagogy and social action as an educational institution. Perhaps the stories from the fieldwork sites assert that the notion of activist needs redefining to encompass all learners who are beginning to 'occupy' their minds? It is this, and the public performance in the sites of other social relations, that makes the pedagogy activism in and of itself.

The role of experience and storytelling is of particular significance in both bricolage and higher education (HE). Story telling can be thought of as a bricolage form in itself; the telling of experience provides a feedback loop between speaker and listener, in this case researcher and researched. As Kincheloe and Berry (2004: 130) insist, 'feedback looping purposely works to evoke imaginary, virtual spaces; that is spaces that are packed with infinite possibilities to create new realities that are inclusive, diverse, socially just, equitable and respectful of agency and democratic, equal participation', the purpose of the mutually useful conversations discussed earlier. In HE, through this notion of the feedback loop, seen as a bricolage essential for creating these new realities, connections with activist groups and ordinary people can ground what happens in the academy. For example, in research carried out by Johnston (2005: 71) one academic

> specifically stressed her involvement with a young anarchist group as a 'wake-up call', a challenge to our assumptions as educators, demonstrating a 'need to reinvigorate ourselves from time to time staying in touch with new ideas'

The specific stress on this involvement suggests that the power of this interaction created this lens to see this feedback loop spoken of by Kincheloe and Berry. Therefore, I would argue there is evidence that the university can benefit from involving itself with activists who engage in the sharing of experience. This involvement is an opening up of new spaces, new feedback loops, new bricolages. These can lead to the mutually useful conversations that are a practice of the bricolage, allowing both the researcher and the researched to de-construct common sense notions, the taken for granted. Kincheloe *et al.* (2011: 171) say that in bricolage 'we are looking at the degree to which research moves those it studies to understand the world and the way it is shaped in order for them to transform it', but perhaps more is happening? Perhaps this involvement helps in the researcher's own conscientization, an opening up, through the practice of bricolage, which affects both researcher and researched, creating new places to be re-occupied by our conscientized selves. These are bricolaged connections, where the collective action of expelling the elites from our world views enable a new form of occupation; that of ourselves.

## Occupation

Brown (2012: 56) argues that 'the target of occupation is no longer just physical spaces or objects, but everything, everywhere – including ourselves to begin with'. Of particular interest here is the burgeoning movement to 'occupy the curriculum' in higher education and learning, and as Bigelow (2011) reiterates, 'we don't need to take tents and sleeping bags to our town squares to participate ... we can also "occupy" our classrooms, "occupy" the curriculum, and then collect the stories about what we have done'. Neary and Amsler (2012: 114) agree: 'we are particularly interested in the possibility ... of appropriating the social space and time of education in ways to enable us to articulate what, how and why people learn'. This is the basis of occupation in this work: that people occupy the *space and time of the event*. Otherwise, as Shantz (2013: 14) says, 'the thrill of immediacy of the street eruptions quickly subsides, leaving little of real gain in its wake'. The Occupy movement may feel like this to many, but from a popular, critical pedagogical point of view, the energy that was spent there could be recouped and learnt from. Holloway (2010: 30–1) explains the notion of capturing these 'happenings', these street explosions like this:

> Often such explosions are seen as failures because they do not lead to permanent change, but this is wrong: they have a validity of their own, independent of the long-term consequences. Like a flash of lightening, they illuminate a different world ... the impression that remains on our brain and in our senses is that of an image of the world we can (and did) create. The world that does not yet exist displays itself as a world that exists not-yet.

This world that exists not-yet in the case of Occupy is one of relations attended to otherwise, experimental democracy and, of particular interest here, politically charged education in a place where the agora is reclaimed; reclaimed through filling the empty place of power with discussion, creativity and liberated desires to commune. These practices, thus far limited, need to be extended if the social world is to escape from enclosure.

This world that exists not-yet could possibly become the new space of occupation. If this is so then, as stated earlier, Merrifield (2011a: 133) has a point when he asserts that

> we need another zone of indistinguishability, another space of slippage, a space in which there's a lot of spontaneous energy as well as a few signs indicating where to go and what time the action begins. We need a new space of slippage in which we can organise and strategize, act without self-consciously performing, encounter others without walls, and hatch en masse a daring Great Escape from capitalism.

Therefore, it is argued that occupation can be viewed as a less public or explicit transgressive act, as well as an overt, physical act. The sites explored here and the future imagined sites, transgress to varying degrees, the normative rules in education and instead attempt to occupy the creative imaginations of those who wander/wonder in. However, as Foust (2010: 3) states,

> transgressive actions incite reactions due to their relationship to norms: Transgressions violate unspoken or explicit rules that maintain a particular social order. Yet, as scholars and practitioners have figured it, transgression's threat to social order runs deeper than violating the rules and expectations that govern what is normal.

The occupation of our newly emancipated selves through a practice of bricolage also transgress those unspoken and explicit rules and indeed, bricolage's threat to the normative order of social research runs deeper than violating the rules and expectations that govern what is normal. Bricolage has deep potential power, the power to critically awaken those who practice it and those they practice with. The transgression of the elitism of positivistic research paradigms, and even some more liberal ways of thinking about social research, mean that individuals can reclaim their occupied selves because bricolage can have a 'catalytic validity' which can have a 'reality-altering impact of the inquiry process and directs this impact so that those under study will gain self-understanding and self-direction' (Kincheloe, et al., 2011: 171).

## Reclamation

When individuals occupy, their task is then to reclaim. Bricolage can help with this reclamation, as suggested above; as 'in this complex ontological view, bricoleurs understand that social structures do not *determine* individual subjectivity but *constrain* it in remarkably intricate ways' (Kincheloe, et al., 2011: 171). Therefore, reclaiming the determination of subjectivity from those constraints takes an alternative way of thinking about social structures.

Peters and Freeman-Moir (2006: 2) insist that the individual 'political will to imagine much beyond the present seems hardly to exist. And the idea of utopia or the value of utopian thinking is easily dismissed as idle and silly. ...Nothing like an alternative to global capitalism seems remotely possible'. However, in Occupy, individuals attempted to begin the collective task of finding the solidarity required to create the will to escape from their ordinary lives and to find others to work with; in the SSC the pedagogical project had the *potential* to create a greater awareness of how to dream, how to use utopian thought, to find an alternative; and in the SaP project, the *potential* was there to create an organisational structure that can support the theorising and the building of such alternatives: As Kincheloe et al. (2011: 169) insist 'a basic dimension of an evolving criticality involves a comfort with the existence of alternative ways of analysing and producing knowledge'. Therefore, it could be argued that these three sites were practicing elements of bricolage in their day-to-day business This can be argued as, when seeing through the lens of bricolage, Kincheloe and Berry (2004: 15) tell us that the bricoleur is 'not aware of where the empirical ends and the philosophical begins, because such epistemological features are always embedded in one another'; in the context here, it is argued that the as yet unseen potential is no less important than the empirical evidence.

If the mass schooling, and therefore enclosure and dulling of our creative imaginations, is to be challenged, then the assertion of the right to freely associate, to assemble, to imagine and to produce our own knowledge, here seen as education, should be reclaimed. As we heard earlier from Foust (2010: 3) 'transgressions that are permitted or escape the notice and discipline of boundary-policing authorities, push the boundaries further', therefore, what is acceptable tomorrow will be *different* to what is acceptable today. In the case of SaP and the SSC, I would argue that if they had been able to escape the 'notice of the boundary policing authorities' they could have become accepted and normative practices, but only if they were celebrated for their reclamation of thought, imagination and a popular curriculum.

However, due to the full enclosure of all spheres of social life (Shantz, 2012) and the notion that 'the political will to imagine much beyond the present seems hardly to exist', the first urgent reclamation can be argued to be that of *ourselves*. I argue that it is true, as von Kotze (2012: 109) says, that 'creative collective experiences can help break through from seeing others as barriers rather than essential allies and make conscious the potential of solidarity in action'. This entails reclaiming sociality: reclaiming what is common to us all, creating, in other words, commons. According to Dyer-Witheford (2010: 106), 'the notion of the commons presupposes collectivities – associations and assemblies – within which sharing is organised'. Shantz (2013: 19) adds to this 'in commonism we re-appropriate our own productive power, taking it back as our own'. Therefore, an educational philosophy that enhances the reclamation of sociality seems essential for initiating the process.

## Conscientization

Neary and Amsler (2012: 132) say that

> the essential aspect of critical practical reflexivity is that it questions the validity of its own concepts, which it does by recognising itself as inhering in the practical social world emerging out of, and inseparable from, the society it is attempting to understand.

This type of reflexivity is a practice of bricolage and should be emergent from authenticity of the human experience, Freire (1998: 31–2) understood that 'when we live our lives with the authenticity demanded by the practice of teaching that is also learning, we are participating in a total experience that is simultaneously directive, political, ideological, gnostic, pedagogical, aesthetic and ethical'. In this work, it is this collective experience, through both communing and the practice of bricolage, of questioning the validity of our own concepts, which brings us into a state of conscientization. The prefigurative, and therefore intensely pedagogical, nature of Occupy makes this questioning inevitable. This prefigurative nature is echoed in the practice and lenses of bricolage as the laying out of a set of fixed characteristics is contrary to the desire of the bricoleur (Kincheloe, *et al.*, 2011), bricolage prefigures not only a new social vision through its practices, but also a new research paradigm through its use of eclectic methods and discourses. 'Popular educators/activists in social movements would say radical interventions happen through the concerted, purposive building of critical consciousness, through analysing power relations, through fashioning a constantly vigilant attitude' (von Kotze, 2012: 104), this is reminiscent of the rhetoric from both the SSC and SaP and the aims of bricolage. Neary and Amsler (2012: 113) report that Occupy 'asserted that because it was primarily an idea or collectivised sense of agency, it could never be "evicted" from social relations', and so once the idea of conscientization is planted and exercised, it becomes part of the emergent and flourishing social relations and part of a potential new era of research.

## Creating a dialogue between the pedagogies: finding the trajectory

Ollis (2012: 8) argues that 'all activism, in fact all politicisation, is an invitation to learning. To be politicised is to learn'. Here I would turn that argument on its head and assert that all learning is (should be) politicisation, in fact, all learning (including research) is (should be) activism. It is from this premise that I will attempt to construct an interruptive cycle from the sites.

Newman (2005: 22) insists 'to practice popular education ... we need to form an understanding of action, identify the kinds of action open to us, and consider the implications of engaging in each kind'. However, not every kind of action is open to everyone and, I assert, it need not be.

Each of the sites was considered a form of activism, a form of reflection, a form of prefiguration and a form of knowledge (co)production. The potential cycle between them can be constructed from this view, through a lens of bricolage that sees process rather than fixity, which sees the political alongside the pedagogical, can see a bricolaging of a form of pedagogical activism that extends to the trajectory I now wish to explore. As Kincheloe *et al.* (2011: 169) state, 'the bricolage hopes to contribute to an evolving criticity'.

However, the first task is to answer some questions as follows: who has the time, space and inclination to apply the learning from the knowledge generated? Who is in a position to take up any new theory that has been produced from these activities and turn it into a sustainable project of experimentation and implementation? In addition, who can set up new ways of doing interruptional activism based on the activities of the rest? The answers to these questions are for each individual to decide and reflect upon at different times in their own lives and a bricolage of experience may be built up as each individual travels through these roles for 'the bricolage is dedicated to a form of rigour that is conversant with numerous modes of meaning making and knowledge production – modes that originate in diverse social locations' (Kincheloe, *et al.*, 2011: 169).

However, there are some constants: academic researchers are in a position to record, reflect upon, and theorise what is happening; organisations such as the SSC could be positioned to take the learning and implement it in ever increasingly sustainable ways; those we currently identify as social movements are in a position to take the theories and apply them as new forms of interruptional activism.

The argument follows that we must find each other, dialogue and create, thus forging networks of solidarity, feedback loops of the learning that is needed to enclose the enclosers, to escape from the fatalism of the neoliberal agenda.

Ollis (2012: 9) says of theory that it can 'help you find your voice; it can help you to understand inequality and hegemony. Theory can also provide insight into what needs to be challenged and changed'. Kincheloe *et al.* (2011: 169) add to this that 'a basic dimension of an evolving criticality involves a comfort with the existence of alternative ways of analysing and producing knowledge', therefore, bricolage also helps you to 'find your voice', as Ollis puts it, by not only examining theory, but also producing it through a comfort with alternative ways of coming to know. Therefore, if the attention of an initiative like SaP, wherever possible, were to be directed at scenarios where there was a goal of social change – for example, Occupy – then new knowledges, theories and even epistemologies could be (co)produced; studying differences, begins an understanding of how 'dominant power operates to exclude and certify particular forms of knowledge production and why ... we gain new appreciations of how power tacitly shapes what we know and how we came to know it' (Kincheloe, *et al.*, 2011: 170). This production could become fully co-production, without the need for bracketing any contribution. The co-production would include not only the students and academics in the university, but also the activists carrying out the projects. This is not a new idea, I know, however, these new theories, these tales, ideas and philosophies could then be fed through an organisation such as the SSC: open, democratic and inclusive, where anyone could openly study them in order to exploit their explanations of the world to the ends of improving actions for transformation. This can be argued to be employing bricolage because it recognises that process sensitive scholars recognise

> all observers view an object of inquiry from their own vantage points ... no portrait of social phenomenon is ever exactly the same as another. Because all physical, social, cultural, psychological and educational dynamics are connected in a larger fabric, researchers will produce different descriptions of an object of inquiry depending on what part of the fabric they have focussed on.
>
> (Kincheloe, *et al.*, 2011: 170)

If the SSC model were to be improved and spread to more sites: who carefully challenged ideologies not compatible with equality and social justice; used as teaching points culturally hegemonic behaviours; discussed as a central tenet the dynamics of its members in a non-threatening way, then activists and academics alike may find these spaces places to reflect upon the theories about the actions of the activists. This enables, as Kincheloe *et al* (2011: 170) suggest, that

> everyone leaves the table informed by the dialogue in a way that idiosyncratically influences the research methods they subsequently employ. The point of the interaction is not standardised agreement as to some reductionist notion of the 'proper interdisciplinary method' but awareness of the diverse tools in the researcher's toolbox.

Through this lens, they come to understand that

> in social research, the relationship between individuals and their contexts is a central dynamic to be investigated. This relationship is a key ontological and epistemological concern of the bricolage; it is a connection that shapes the identities of human beings and the nature of the complex social fabric.... Recognising the complex ontological importance of relationships alters the basic foundations of the research act and knowledge production process. Thin reductionist descriptions of things-in-themselves are no longer sufficient in critical research
> 
> (Kincheloe, *et al.*, 2011: 170)

This is how the 'grand' cycle of action research could conceivably come about, producing in its wake a wave of countervailing discourses about the transformation of social life where a multitude of democratic voices could be heard.

If indeed the relations between activists and academics were to change to become equals in the same struggle, understanding what the limitations are for each other, the insider/outsider dichotomy presented in the Occupy Research Collective would become redundant. This is where the need to reassess the nature and practice of research plays a role, seeing research through the lens of the bricolage methodology assists in this reassessment as 'bricoleurs act on the concept that theory is not an explanation of nature – it is more an explanation to our relationship to nature' (Kincheloe, *et al.*, 2011: 168). Roggero (2011: 5) says that 'co-research questions the borders between research and politics, knowledge and conflicts, university and social context, work and militancy' and it is these borders that, I would argue, not only need to be questioned, but to be redefined if learning loops and feedback systems are to be produced. These are, indeed, it is argued, a bricolage of learning spaces and their borders can be seen as shifting, fluid or even disintegrating when viewed through a bricolage lens, their individual, discipline-bound epistemologies informing each other and building a cohesive and complex view of the social world. Shantz (2013: 1) insists,

> in the period of crisis and opportunity, movements of the global North have been largely perplexed by questions of how to advance, to build strength on a sustainable basis in a way that might pose real challenges to states and capital.

Shantz also hints here at the idea of the inclusion of other epistemologies, other modes of struggle, other imaginaries of change being brought into the consciousness of the movements of the global North, building a 'new language of an emerging constellation of struggle' (Holloway, 2010: 12). As Kincheloe and Berry (2004: 15) insist, 'in its critical concern for just social change the bricolage seeks insight from the margins of Western societies and the knowledge and ways of knowing of non-Western peoples. Such insight helps bricoleurs reshape and sophisticate social theory, research methods, and interpretive strategies', 'bricolage is dedicated to a form of rigour that is conversant with numerous modes of meaning making and knowledge production – modes that originate in diverse social locations' (Kincheloe, et al., 2011: 169). This is also where universities have something distinctive to offer; not only the co-production of knowledge, but the exchange of global knowledges and ways of thinking, acting and being.

## Thinking through education.

If there were strong 'learning loops' – feedback systems that cycle learning from one group to the next, such as those implied in the practice of bricolage: 'feedback looping purposely works to evoke imaginary, virtual spaces; that is spaces that are packed with infinite possibilities to create new realities that are inclusive, diverse, socially just, equitable and respectful of agency and democratic, equal participation' (Kincheloe & Berry, 2004: 130) – the impossibility of large scale social change starts to crack. The more learning is shared, the stronger solidarity becomes; 'we gain new appreciations of how power tacitly shapes what we know and how we came to know it' (Kincheloe, et al., 2011: 170). As a result, the less 'impossible' the task of changing the world becomes, because all turning back seems even more impossible than to stay where we were.

It seems that one of the lessons from all the sites, Occupy in particular, is that skilled pedagogues and bricoleurs are needed to initiate the required change, well versed in popular education and research and who understand the nuances of oppressive behaviour, although the SSC provides us with a warning that this does not always work. However, with careful and skilful monitoring, these behaviours; the classroom banter containing sexism, racism, homophobia, ableism and other forms of oppressive and colonial attitudes, could be picked up immediately and be treated as teaching points. As mentioned earlier, this must not be a pedagogical vanguard, but a democratic and challengeable direction that starts the process of change through power sharing pedagogies. Any pedagogical leadership must be willing, able, and encouraged, to relinquish its leadership through mechanisms that 'wither away the teacher', as Shor (1992) insists should happen, and allow an intellectual public to emerge and continuously educate each other and future generations, without the need for leadership. This is initially in contrast to Rancière's notions, but in keeping with the ideas of critical pedagogy; that conscientization is needed in order that the oppressed may begin the project of self-liberation. As Bahruth and Steiner (2000: 129) say of their experience:

> if we do not postpone the syllabus and utilize the organic teachable moments …we merely 'cover' the curriculum. The curriculum becomes the antagonist of non-engagement while contributing to the development

of false concepts about teaching and learning ... critical pedagogues are aware of the 'hidden' curriculum and are politically motivated to be counter-hegemonic.

This awareness of the hidden curriculum comes with experience and the practice of a critical gaze. This is because the bricoleur understands that

> the relationship between individuals and their contexts is a central dynamic to be investigated. This relationship is a key ontological and epistemological concern of the bricolage; it is a connection that shapes the identities of human beings and the nature of the complex social fabric.
> (Kincheloe, *et al.*, 2011: 170)

The study undertaken for this book suggests that revolutionary education cannot do without a skilled pedagogue, at least initially. Whilst it is acknowledged that vanguards tend to take this line – that they will be a temporary leadership – it is not vanguardism that is expressed here, as any vanguardism is countered by the power sharing pedagogy, which constantly monitors the elitism of the teacher and uncovers the attempts at manipulation and suppression. Does it however, suggest that the pedagogue must be an expert in what is being taught? As heard, Rancière insists not. Nonetheless, Bahruth and Steiner (2000: 122–3) insist that 'teachers must recognise both conscious and unconscious attempts to derail the discourse'; can these attempts be recognised if the teacher does not have a good understanding of the subject the learners are grappling with?

Freire (1998: 74) says,

> One of the basic questions that we need to look at is how to convert merely rebellious attitudes into revolutionary ones in the process of the radical transformation of society.... It is necessary to go beyond rebellious attitudes to a more critical and revolutionary position, which is in fact a position not simply of denouncing injustice but announcing a new utopia. Transformation of the world implies a dialectic between two actions: denouncing the process of de-humanization and announcing the dream of a new society

I would argue that to ensure that knowledges are not lost, subjugated or simply missed, an expert is needed to ensure that any dialogue encompasses 'Other' views and epistemologies. Freire also adds this: 'It is precisely because ingenuous curiosity does not automatically become critical that one of the tasks of progressive educational praxis is the promotion of a curiosity that is critical, bold and adventurous' (1998). Without understanding the material that the students or learners are grappling with, the pedagogue may not be able to effectively assist in the development of a critical understanding. The non-expertise of the pedagogue in this view, may also allow despots and vanguards to emerge as the materials, and therefore the learners, are manipulated by persons that do understand the topics and are able therefore to steer the discussions to a certain conclusion without the pedagogue realising what is happening. Occupy illustrated the desire for experts by inviting in 'experts' to assist with their ongoing inquiry into the state of things and what to do about it, but not being entirely led by them. In addition, Brookfield (2001) argues that people do not spontaneously become critical thinkers, and that even when they do, it is a painful process that needs to be nurtured by skilled helpers. This process maybe made easier by a skilled pedagogue asking the questions alongside the learner of a corpus of information that the pedagogue knows well and can therefore anticipate the pitfalls, the cul-de-sacs and the potential triumphs.

However, what is indicated here is that this process of developing critical thinking has to start with a belief in the equality of intelligence in order to ensure that the learner is able to become agentic in the process. I have argued that 'critical pedagogy changes the relationship between teachers and students. It changes teachers from givers/authority figures to "co-learners" with students' (Cho, 2013: 88); the SaP project, along with the SSC were examples of this, but this seems, from the studied sites to be especially true when a power sharing within the classroom is enacted with an emphasis on research engaged teaching and learning. The ignorant schoolmaster, however, cannot share power, but must hand it over to his/her students. This handing over of power could lead to despots emerging in the learning process, manipulating the learners as we saw in some cases in Occupy. An expert pedagogue might have picked this up and challenged it. For example, the Occupy GAs were intensely educative and concretised the norms and hegemonies of the movement. However, the deconstruction of the GAs may have been thought necessary by an attending pedagogue whose expertise lies in gender theory, or democratic participation, who would have noticed this behaviour had they been mandated to carry out this task.

On analysis of the data, the ignorant schoolmaster thesis is flawed on several levels, first there has to be someone in the learning process to guide the newer learners to credible sources in their field, to suggest paths of learning often happens in the SSC. Therefore, at least initially, Rancière's thesis cannot be supported as a way immediately forward, except in terms of recognising that essential equality of intelligence mentioned earlier and central in Rancière's work. It is accepted in *The Ignorant School Master* as it is in critical pedagogy texts and in bricolage that each and every person brings valuable experience to the learning space, and that pedagogues must recognise both their ignorance and their unique contribution alongside that of the learners, thus rendering a hierarchy of intelligence between teacher and student defunct. This important recognition is essential in the struggle against manipulation and enclosure of the learning materials as well as the vigilance against the formation of vanguards as the experienced person, the pedagogue, adopts the stance of equal among a community of learners who come together to dialogue, debate and commune: the pedagogue is there to provide guidance when necessary and pick up those damaging oppressive behaviours. Therefore, as Kincheloe *et al.* (2011: 165) state,

> the authority of the critical teacher is dialectical; as teachers relinquish the authority as truth providers, they assume the mature authority of facilitators of student inquiry and problem posing. In relation to such teacher authority, students gain their freedom – they gain the ability to become self-directed human beings capable of producing their own knowledge.

The SaP initiative did for a while allow for cross fertilisation and an opening up of disciplinary fields through interdisciplinary working in a research engaged atmosphere therefore could have been capable of evoking bricolage. This could well have led to a post-disciplinary epoch for many subjects and therefore a whole systems view of the world and its relations, connection and of course, lines of continuity. The same applies to social movements: 'a task for critical education is to provide the space to bring those informal learning processes [in social movements] to consciousness, to reflect on them and to develop further strategies for action in exchange with others' (Steinklammer, 2012: 33). This is particularly applicable when utilising bricolage to connect the levels through research as 'the bricolage enables researchers to produce new forms of knowledge that inform ... political action in general' (Kincheloe, *et al.*, 2011: 169).

Bringing out informal learning processes to consciousness, reflecting upon them and developing further strategies for action in exchange with others is something that can be done jointly by researchers and pedagogues (who, of course, can be one and the same). This is also why, I argue, it is important to have some researchers/pedagogues who are relatively external to the political process going on in the social movement; because they need a critical distance to ensure that they can observe the crucial moments when these informal learning processes take place. Seeing these processes through the bricolage paradigm can assist in this by understanding the learning process as a whole process rather than a separate activity to those undertaken in the everyday activities of social movements by distorting the pedagogical lens. This is because 'bricolage hopes to contribute to an evolving criticity ... a basic dimension of an evolving criticality involves a comfort with the existence of alternative ways of analysing and producing knowledge' (Kincheloe, *et al.*, 2011: 169).

Newman (2005: 29–30) insists,

> we can teach about different forms of social action. We can provide an analysis of the different social sites where popular education might be located. We can teach the different domains of learning. We can teach different kinds of social control.

Resulting in politically literate, critically engaged independent learners for whom education has a different meaning than the schooled consuming of official knowledge.

To these ends, the democratic power-sharing that is attempted in the SSC, and to some extent in Occupy, seems the most productive organisation of learning for popular education, both outside and within the academy.

von Kotze (2012: 108) explains that the participants in their study of a social movement,

> having internalized how conditions of competition for scarce resources translate into competitive behaviour rather than sharing it took a while to recognise just how deep the 'cut-throat' mentality had permeated all aspects of their lives to the degree that it had become naturalised as normal. Reimagining relations as cooperative and reciprocal was a major step – and one that had to be made over and over in different sessions.

This experience illustrates the necessity for gently handing over to the students if the goal is mass conscientization and not marginalisation of efforts toward change: sharing power, nurturing resistance, taking up incongruent and solipsistic behaviours as teaching points. For some students, even those with much schooling, 'education' is quite a new experience and to think of education as a political act, even more so. Bricolage assists with this notion of the midwifing, as Freire (1993a) might call it, of individuals into this new criticality as bricolage 'displays the reality-altering impact of the inquiry process and directs this impact so that those under study will gain self-understanding and self-direction' (Kincheloe, et al., 2011: 171), therefore assisting individuals to come to a conscientization. These ideas start to look like a sharp contrast to some of the ideas expressed so far in this work; however, this is a misconception. Holloway (2010) talks about every small act of rebellion – such as reading a book in the park on a sick day from work – being an act of resistance that cracks capitalism; there is consensus in the literature that old revolutionary theory is no longer useful: there is no aim here to overthrow the governments and enter a violent and bloody revolution. The argument in the literature, and here, is summed up by the Zapatistas notion that we walk, because we are going very far. The ideas contained here are not a coming insurrection, as The Invisible Committee put it, but a quiet and sustained rebellion, a revolt, a mutiny. Education is not an uprising on its own, it may be preparation for one, but that is for the people to decide, and for educational researchers to follow, witness, and attempt to assist.

## Thinking through research

We cannot decouple education or activism from research; as bricolage suggests, they are, or perhaps should be, one and the same. However, tensions arise, as a critique of activities can seem like misunderstanding or misrepresentation if the relationship is not handled sensitively. Bricoleurs understand that 'social structures do not determine individual subjectivity but constrain it in remarkably intricate ways' (Kincheloe, *et al.*, 2011: 171) and therefore it is often individually problematic to espouse solidarity whilst *appearing* to make judgements through research activities. Perhaps, then, if we organise education systems to allow people to relish tensions in their social relations, recognise the informal education in everyday life and begin to see, as explored earlier, the political as pedagogical and the pedagogical as political, research interventions will become a recognised and valued part of our growth and evolution as a human species, especially if, as in bricolage, they are not compartmentalised and seen as an elite overview of the social worlds of others because the job of the bricoleur is to 'commit their knowledge work to helping address the ideological and informational needs of marginalized groups and individuals' (Kincheloe, *et al.*, 2011: 169). This achieved, people will then be able to build in the cycles of action research in all parts of the social world as the tensions, the critiques, and the research interventions, will be just another element of the positive social relations being built. This is particularly possible, I would argue, with the use of bricolage and its embrace of complexity, its acceptance of tensions and its relationship with creating new (research) relationships. The use of bricolage allows for the gathering of people in solidarity because it subverts and transgresses the boundaries of traditional research and embraces epistemologies not necessarily familiar to its practitioners. Therefore, it is particularly useful as a research paradigm that encourages an active role for research, researchers and most importantly, research participants: those in conversation with the world around them.

The sites in this study have given us what Burdick and Sandlin (2010: 3) call

> glimpses of the pedagogical Other – forms and practices of pedagogy that exist independently of, even in opposition to, the knowledge within the common sense 'research imagination' (Kenway & Fahey, 2009) found in the general body of scholarly discourse on education.

Burdick and Sandlin argue that without a careful and imaginative approach to researching these sites of learning outside formal institutions, 'researchers risk taking on an institutionalised form of the colonial gaze, applying reductive logics to or even completely failing to witness phenomena that are not easily resolved in dominant cultural meanings and images of teaching and learning' (Burdick & Sandlin, 2010: 3); again, bricolage can avoid this through its insistence that researchers should construct 'a far more active role for humans in shaping both reality and in creating the research process and narratives that represent it' (Kincheloe, *et al.*, 2011: 168). Researchers need, therefore, to understand that, as stated earlier, 'these moments embody not just practices to adapt and creatively redeploy, but are in themselves ways of understanding the world and forms of research in action' (Shukaitis & Graeber, 2007: 37). I would argue that researchers of these types of public and popular pedagogy are there to help make this 'understanding the world' and forms of research explicit and effective, of which bricolage is capable. Nonetheless, 'defining and capturing critical public pedagogies through the lens of traditional educational research has the potential to arrest the potency of such activism' (Burdick & Sandlin, 2010: 8) and therefore using bricolage to 'expand research methods and construct a more rigorous mode of knowledge about education' (Kincheloe & Berry, 2004: 1) does seem appropriate.

## The future of the academy, the community and change agents

> What intellectual and political tactics might be appropriate for conceptualising an occupation of curriculum? What are the spaces and times of curriculum that we might inhabit otherwise? And what external macro- and micro-politics must this project be connected to in order for it to have any transformative potential beyond individual perception?
> 
> (Neary & Amsler, 2012: 116)

The above questions posed by Neary and Amsler are central to the ideas in this section, and indeed this book. Kane (2005: 40) has this to say:

> In my experience, the rhetoric of 'academic freedom' still allows us, mostly, to be honest about what we think.... Our role is to use our relative autonomy to develop critical consciousness amongst our students, both through posing questions – and making explicit their ideological underpinnings – and, more generally, by exposing students to a range of ideas and literature which is often ignored or not seen as relevant to the dominant instrumentalism.

It could be argued that there was the potential for this in the SaP initiative, through the model of research-engaged teaching and learning. Could this model still spread?

Crowther and Villegas (2012: 58) insist that 'the [current political] trend all looks very favourable for the educator committed to a democratic project for social justice and equality'. Steinklammer (2012: 30) concurs and adds, 'it is necessary to connect the claims that education should have an empowering effect with the perspective of resistance'.

It is worth noting here, as Peters and Freeman-Moir (2006: 3) do, 'that every great educational theory is imbued with elements of what might be called the utopian disposition' and this work is no different. It is worth using Peters and Freeman-Moir's description of utopia to illustrate the interpretation of utopian thinking subscribed to here, as this notion of utopian thinking, engages once more, with the attempt here of thinking through bricolage:

> Utopianism is not about specific solutions but rather the opening of the imagination to speculation and open exploration.... In this education of

desire the status quo is opened up to question but the challenge is not restricted to the short comings of the present. The utopian thinker is also free to think of ways of living that lie completely beyond what is currently envisaged.

(Peters & Freeman-Moir, 2006: 4)

As society moves to a more popular ethos for its education, pedagogues must 'ensure that critique and the creative imagination fertilize one another' (von Kotze, 2012: 111). The potential for this to have happened in the researched sites and elsewhere, including in the explored research paradigm of bricolage, is already there. It is worth mentioning here the recent rise in the number of 'free universities' (for examples see http://sustainingalternatives.wordpress.com/), where volunteer academics teach courses for which there is no fee. Also, public pedagogy initiatives such as The University for Strategic Optimism' (http://universityforstrategicoptimism.wordpress.com/) a group of mainly postgraduate students who do teach-outs in banks, on the streets, and in other sites of political dissatisfaction.

However, there is no need to give up free time, or teach-out in banks to be part of the struggle (although efforts are redoubled if people do); scholars can contribute both within, against and beyond the university, eventually realising the ambition of dissolving the walls of the university and turning whole cities into explicitly pedagogical sites and generating 'questions previously unimagined' (Kincheloe, *et al.*, 2011: 170) through their research activities. However, until this is a reality, Shantz (2013: 72) thinks 'there is a pressing need ... for institutions, organisations, and relations that can sustain people as well as building capacities for self-defence and struggle'. He calls these 'infrastructures of resistance'.

Denzin (2010: 20), building on the work of others, says, 'we need to become more accomplished in linking these interventions to those institutional sites where troubles are turned into public issues, and public issues transformed into social policy (Nespor, 2006: 124; Mills 1959; Charmaz, 2005)'. Real opposition to what is happening requires more than momentary joy (Holloway, 2010; Shantz, 2013), 'it requires foundations and infrastructures that contribute to significant advances while maintaining a basis for ongoing struggles' (Shantz, 2013: 15). The SSC and SaP, extended and reproduced could constitute those foundations and infrastructures, making both models productive sites of struggle.

This, then, is the utopian future for educational institutions, one where alliances can be made in order to dissolve the essentialised dichotomies of teacher and learner, researcher and researched, through a bricolage of knowledges and ways of knowing. Of course, there are plenty of people who have said this before, however as Kincheloe and Tobin (2006: 4) say, 'while we deeply respect those who have come before us and have helped us to get where we are, we are ambitious – we want to go farther into the epistemological and ontological fog'. The time seems to be right, society seems to be in a socio-political juncture that lends itself to the possibility of radical change, capitalisms crises have reached the point of destabilisation, there are uprisings all over the world and people are edgy. As the neoliberal agenda of policy makers tightens its grip on institutions, they must transgress that grip and intervene as teachers and researchers in any/every way they can.

The move to a more popular based pedagogy in these institutions appears as an effective way to transgress. I have discussed that individual's thoughts, minds and hearts are places that are essential to occupy as they are enclosed in a way that is easily transgressed and escaped if people join their efforts. 'Popular education is concerned with learning to identify, use and resist various kinds of social control' (Newman, 2005: 28); this justifies it becoming the transgressive norm in university institutions. Popular education, coupled with bricolage research is also concerned with pedagogy that comes from the interests and needs of the 'people', the students, the community members, the populace, the Multitude. They are, therefore, very effective at raising the volume of the silenced and subjugated voices. This challenge to the hegemonic regime of truth constitutes in those members of the group who have not been subjugated a form of awareness raising:

> Education is not a habitus, but a force that objects to every kind of habitualisation of habits that chain the human being to what already exists.... On the other hand, this cannot be done in isolation from practice, since the practical sense is structured by practice and at the same time has a structuring effect. Therefore, practical experiences and action learning are necessary for a new practice to be developed and for the practical sense to be worked in interaction with the social world.
>
> (Steinklammer, 2012: 31)

This is where a grand action research cycle comes into its own, with the notion that the resistance that education provides to habitualisation cannot be fully achieved in isolation from practice. Peters and Freeman-Moir (2006: 3) say of utopian pedagogy that 'utopia links the special dimension of living with the temporal dimension of learning and in that sense any utopian methodology can be said to ground education in the everyday fabric of the imagined society'. However, if that society is merely imagined then where is the practical experience insisted upon by Steinklammer? The practical experience that students of higher education can have is creating alliances with groups prefiguring these utopian futures – starting dialogues in order that they may create mutual benefit by setting up action research projects with stable groups, or as witness to protests, street demonstrations and occupations, practicing the larger, slower action research cycle there. As these groups of activists and people living otherwise in our society currently have limited access to institutions of HE, groups such as the SSC are ideal grounds for the presentation of findings and discussion of results. Groups such as the SSC could therefore, not only be autonomous education providers, but could also provide an essential link between the universities and activist groups. That is, until the divisions are dissolved. This bricolage process gives everyone, academics, community members, activists and any other interested parties equal (subversive) access to theory and interruptional thought. This should result in the academic voice being heard in the protest and the community action and the subjugated voices of activist communities being heard in the academy: a bricolaging of the Multitude. This potentially results in a praxis where theory informs the practice of those outside the academy and practice informs the theory of those inside. The future of this process contains several possibilities: the dissolution of the barriers of HE in terms of the dissemination of knowledge and access to academic thinkers; the inclusion of more voices and experiences in academic work; and the disappearing necessity for public intellectuals in favour of an intellectual public; and the rise and continuation of a radical democracy that encounters and celebrates countervailing discourses as a matter of necessity.

Ollis (2012: 8) says of her own research, and I would like to think of mine in the same way, that 'this research, in itself, is a process of activism'. Nevertheless, I want to suggest that more is done than merely 'give voice' to the pedagogical Other. I want to assert that HE institutions and researchers *become*, wherever possible and to whatever extent, the pedagogical Other and make that Other the norm, a wonderful destabilised, unbalanced, temporal and utopian norm.

It has been said by feminist activists for a long time that the personal must become the political, but the personal should now perhaps become more, it should become *pedagogical*: '"society is not composed of individuals", says Marx.... What constitutes society is the system of its social relations, in which individuals live, work and struggle' (Leonardo, 2006: 82).

Education, like insurrection, requires building from the ground up, enclosed as it often is in the mechanisms of schooling, testing and surveillance. Therefore, the future of education, like the future of all social relations, should hold the promise of 'comradeship, dignity, amorosity, love, solidarity, fraternity, friendship, ethics' (Holloway, 2010: 43). Each person's struggles within education, to occupy the curriculum that emerges in the academy, in the community and on the streets, have, then, to be connected to the wider struggles, if they are not connected by those in the struggle, they will be connected by those they stand in opposition to. Indeed, they already are. Therefore, choosing and taking sides becomes a necessity; 'it is only by taking sides that it becomes possible to understand the whole, and to transform it' (Roggero, 2011: 6).

## The escape from enclosure

Illich (2011: 2) once famously said that 'not only education but social reality itself has become schooled'. Shor recognises this and adds that

Even if critical pedagogy in particular and education in general cannot by themselves reverse these conditions, they can break the silence moving us into the worst world possible. Interfere by teaching your heart out. Interfere with where we are headed by making classrooms public spaces whose discussions grapple with what is happening to us. Shine bright lights on the mechanisms of power.... Critical classrooms are opportunities to circulate unauthorised democratic discourse against the status quo.

(Shor in Macrine, 2009: 128–9)

Milojevic (2006: 24) asserts that 'the main problem with the prevalence of the dystopian genre is its capacity to legitimise fears while delegitimising hope'. This makes escape from enclosure difficult, if not impossible. This, then, is the reality with which we are faced, a reality that Giroux (2001: xxiii), building on Adorno, accuses of being a 'prohibition on thinking itself'. Therein, I would argue, lays the solution: *thinking itself*. And, as Esteva (2010: 29) insists, a necessity to begin 'enclosing the enclosers', making Shor's plea to 'interfere by teaching your heart out' a painfully hopeful space for educators to inhabit.

I argue then that what has come to light in this investigation is that what is needed now is a social connection based on trust, solidarity, generosity and gift, but as Holloway (2010) warns, for the moment this can only exist as an oppositional form. The imperative for escape, then, needs to be hopeful, utopian, but also in opposition to, against, united by a common enemy; this is a battle ground in a class war. In the sites in this work, it was acknowledged that Occupy was *against* the banking system, austerity and the corruption in our political system; SaP was *against* the student as consumer model of the neoliberal university; the SSC is *against* the commodification of knowledge and the elitism of the university institution. But all are, or were, hopeful – hopeful of the actuality of new social relations. All believed in the positive possibilities and I argue that there is something very instructive to be learnt from that hope.

Their hope has been, and continues to be, realistic and grounded. Hope is the will to accept and overcome difficulties, as autonomous projects in a collective struggle. The evidence of these sites suggests, therefore, that individuals need to organise and strategize for hope, for institutions of the commons, for the future of free thought itself. These struggles have to take place within, against and beyond our current enclosure because 'there is no longer an outside within contemporary capitalism' (Roggero, 2011: 9).

## Final words of radical hope

This book has suggested that what will create the change needed for the escape from enclosure are the individual and collective thoughts and actions of people in their newly occupied selves. Social movements here are seen as essential sites of slippage, of experimentation, of the collective occupation of space and time.

They practice essential forms of public pedagogy and are furtive sites for bricolage research to bring out the subjugated voices of the oppressed.

However, as we have seen, social movements can also become sites of reproduction, activism is fast paced and deeply embedded cultural hegemonies are missed in the confusion and urgency of the action, especially when it is focused on external tensions. Therefore, it is my view that when the action, the volcano of anger and emotion is spent – watched, witnessed and recorded as the *pedagogical moment* – activists should have the opportunity to regroup into their, now more pedagogical, institutions of the commons. Reflecting and learning, extending the knowledge and the scope ready for the next action alongside academics who through a bricolage of research have reached that catalytic validity that allows a strengthening in the efficacy of the movement, embedding new learning at a personal and collective level in order to live otherwise now.

In this scenario, the researcher is not distant or detached; they are inside the pedagogical moment. They do not then 'teach' the activists where they went wrong, or how to be 'better' at activism, but start a dialogue, accepting the equality of intelligence but mindful of the essential roles each group plays in the activities of the other, sharing the power. They dialogue about their findings; what was missed, what should be celebrated and how change was elicited, both inside and outside the movement. The critical distance of the bricolage researcher becomes an ally for the group; not the ritualised objectivity of a detached observer but the friend who picks you up when your energy is depleted. It is this space where more organisations such as the SSC are required, these places where activist and community members can insert their own biographies into the action, where camaraderie, solidarity and equality can be discovered between individuals who have previously seen each other from a cultural distance; research performed through the bricolage lens has the viable potential to bridge this gap. Now the various groups occupy space and time in creative and intellectual ways. Moving collectively toward a fulfilling and vital intellectual public. Then perhaps one day, this organisational ideology could become what we now think of as academe.

Merrifield (2011a) asserts that the time for critique is over. I would disagree, the time for critique is rife, but that critique must escape the enclosure of the divided spectrum: the walls of academe and the activist circles and become a people's critique: a popular critique. Bricoleurs are what Kincheloe et al. (2011: 170) call 'process sensitive scholars'. They are able to follow this popular critique as they 'watch the world flow by like a river in which the exact contents of the water are never the same'. They understand that

> no portrait of social phenomenon is ever exactly the same as another. Because all physical, social, cultural, psychological and educational dynamics are connected in a larger fabric, researchers will produce different descriptions of an object of inquiry depending on what part of the fabric they have focussed on – what part of the river they have seen.

Therefore the knowledge they produce about it will not be reductionist but celebratory and imaginative, producing hope. However, to echo Holloway (2010) once more, we need to do more, we need to go further, we need now not only a collective critique, but also collective and individual action, infused with collective theorising – making socially good use of the emergent intellectual public.

Williams' (1989) sentiment that to be truly radical is to make hope possible rather than despair convincing, has been echoed by the sites under examination here, and although it is acknowledged that this is a sentiment out of context, it has been useful to the thinking about what is needed to be done. What is required when Marx and Engels (1846/ 2007: 123) insist that philosophers only interpreted the world: 'the point, however, is to change it'. The answer from the sites also seems to be to make hope possible, rather than despair convincing.

# 7 Capturing future resistance in education

So, what has this snapshot of these three actions told us? I want to return here to the overall argument that this book has presented and make some concluding remarks about how this all hangs together. I also want to indicate here what new questions the research has produced and how we might proceed.

The first question asked in the beginning of this work regarded what pedagogical experiments occurred in Occupy and what models of practice were identifiable? Judged by the theoretical explorations used here, the individuals in Occupy attempted to democratically share power in a critically orientated pedagogical structure that fell short of being sustainable for many reasons. It is argued here that one of those reasons may have been that actually the term 'Occupy' turned out to be an empty signifier; it became, and somewhat continues to be, a 'bucket' into which the engaged multitude could pour its discontents sometimes in a focussed way, sometimes not. The viewpoints that are brought together in this empty signifier do not necessarily have a homogenous message or vision to move toward, they do not necessarily want precisely the same thing. However, they are all *against* the same thing, united by the perceived common enemy of corruption and greed at the top. However, the ambiguity of that emptiness could also be seen to be its greatest strength, allowing the notion of occupation to contain many thoughts, ideas and countervailing discourses, allowing new pedagogical experiments, and new models of practice, therefore, Occupy may not ever be able to be spoken about in a past tense, the political/pedagogical experiment could have continued for as long as the empty signifier seems a useful way to link the struggles in diverse ways. This form of fluidic, spatially and temporally contextualised voice of Occupy had the possible potential of creating and organising spaces that could be both creative and politically progressive. This should be because they do not silence dissent, but relish its ability to add to the constitution of new identities and new forms of relations and organisations that may eventually replace the corrupt and greed ridden institutions that the multitude of heterogeneous voices argue against.

The book has therefore argued that there are lines of continuity between the three sites explored, which may have been enough to begin the constitution of new organisational principles that have the potential to lead to a revolutionary pedagogy of solidarity if thought about differently and organised in more sustainable ways.

A second question was that of the relevance of the pedagogical experiment within Occupy to other radical experiments, specifically, the SSC and SaP projects. The answer, viewed through the pedagogical and political lenses discussed here, seems to be that the pedagogical project initiated by members of the Occupy London encampment had a great deal to teach other projects about the nature of organic pedagogy. Specifically, the work done here and elsewhere uncovered situations of oppression, such as the subjugated voices of women and the silencing of internal dissent, that can arise in these fast flowing and organic pedagogical situations, situations that other, more stable projects would need to be aware of and address if they are to support radical and revolutionary change. The SSC seem to have attempted to address this by their internal monitoring – discussing relations of gender and other aspects of social life and relating them to their experience in the group – but elsewhere they seemed absent in my research. It is therefore argued here that the notion of a pedagogue being needed to ensure that the pedagogical project does not fall foul of co-option and despotism is borne out in the explorations of Occupy London and it is further argued that although Rancière's notions in *The Ignorant Schoolmaster* have proved useful for discussion, they do not stand up to scrutiny in this context and that some kind of organised pedagogical direction, albeit constituted through an organic curriculum, is essential in order for hegemonic and dominant conditioned behaviours to be challenged when they arise.

The third question that was initially asked was could a form of 'learning loop' or broad action research type cycle be established between the three different pedagogical actions as a way to connect different forms of learning within in social movements, community groups, and higher education establishments, so that they might support each other and find ways to share and contribute to each other's knowledge and tactics for creating transformative change?

The main obstacle to this, which considering the ethos of Occupy London came as a surprise, was that of the insider/outsider division between academics and activists, although this may eventually be challenged through the rise of autonomous higher learning initiatives that are being set up around the world. However, this work has argued that, particularly through a bricolage research paradigm, there is no reason for this dichotomy to be present. Research can be thought of as activism, but only under the proviso that an activist pedagogy is enacted to engender a reciprocal relationship between activism and academe. Thinking about the two current ends of a strata becomes thinking about a cycle of solidarity, knowledge share and activism; the SSC seemed to represent an embryonic form of organisation that had the potential to make this relationship possible. However, this is a temporally situated notion, as the rise of autonomous higher learning initiatives suggests that the university may possibly become irrelevant to the struggle. Nonetheless, it has been argued here that this potential trajectory of popular, critical pedagogies that cycle from the streets to the academy has been explored and is worthy of further exploration to concretise the ideas explored here.

There is a notion of unfinishedness in this research which contributes to the thinking about the power of the bricolage to expand research methods. This is because the research was thought about through the post-disciplinary lens of bricolage, which enabled the imagining of how possibilities and potentialities might be extended into research projects to allow full explorations of their enactments. In this work, bricolage has been utilised to understand the phenomena under study in creative and imaginative ways; talking not only about what was there and what could be seen, but extending those theories and practices into the realms of imaginative possibility. One of the weaknesses with bricolage is that, as Kincheloe and Berry warned, it is a lifelong pursuit, and therefore making claims about reaching the status of fully fledged bricoleur are absent here. Bricolage is a wide lens, which whilst allowing for a great deal of freedom for the researcher, can become overwhelming in any research project. The strength of bricolage, I would argue, is that it allows the researcher to think freely about their research without the constraints of the 'recipe book' methods of some research paradigms. It is very difficult within the constraints of one piece of research, especially at the beginning of a research career, to carry out a genuine piece of bricolage research and therefore from my point of view the *ethos* of bricolage has been useful and the strengths of a lens that this provides: the acceptance of complexity and the notion of carrying out the research in a post-disciplinary way, allowing the researcher to dispense with the preconceived notions about their area of study. I would argue for the further use of bricolage, because I understand it as being a robust and liberating paradigm for research; I would argue it does have the potential power, once practiced to fully competent level, to extend the thoughts of researchers in many directions; I would argue it has assisted me to think in ways that I may not have thought had I not adopted this position. Bricolage does not claim to be a method; indeed, I would argue that it is the antithesis to 'method', singular. It is a *methodology*, a way of thinking about research, which is why it leaves the individual researcher, in their individual context, to decide on their own methods, to become contextualised methodological negotiator, whilst allowing the ability to think across boundaries, through complexity and understand the power of their research.

The underlying arguments in this book are that for Occupy to have become a global force for social change, it needed to concentrate on resolving its own, internal tensions. This would mean creating the conditions for internal monitoring of conditioned behaviours through their pedagogical experiments, whilst continuing to offer up, and to take relish in, counter-vailing discourses. This could be helped, it is argued, by the introduction of feedback loops and 'grand' action research type cycles from other levels of education provision and research.

The argument that arose from these broad aims was that the various sites under exploration here are offering, to various degrees, a vision of alternative ways of doing, relating and living. These visions include socially just and democratic ways of learning together, communing and cooperating beyond the social relations imposed by global capitalism – all offered through pedagogical paradigms. It was because each site was not only claiming to offer, but also making attempts at offering, alternative methods – such as mutual aid, in the case of Occupy, cooperation in the case of the SSC and agentic knowledge production in the SaP program, and generally of education that was political and aimed at social change – that it was argued that a potential 'loop of learning' or 'grand action research cycle' was a possibility between them. The work was therefore able to argue that the various experiments – the Occupy London movement, the Social Science Centre in Lincoln, and The University of Lincoln – could have had the potential for a solidarisitic interrelationship that would bring the 'levels' of learning into dialogue with each other and improve their efficacy to affect social change for a more just world.

It is therefore argued that firstly, pedagogical practices that were contextualised in that particular socio-political climate of 2011/2012 in the UK were emerging and they did have the possible potential to represent revolutionary practices. The *Crack Capitalism* thesis presented by Holloway (2010) and the critical, power sharing pedagogy of Shor (1996) supported these notions. The practices included sharing power amongst all learners and 'teachers', inserting biographies into the wider socio-political contexts and creating research led teaching and learning to give agency to the undergraduate learner in higher education. This revolutionary potential was indicated and supported by the evidence of the sites as a new form of revolutionary theory that consists of the activism of political pedagogy enabling and encouraging just social changes, such as the production of democratic citizens who relish tension and the democratisation of public life through a raising of social consciousness. This had the potential to be achieved through the interaction of various levels of learning through from social movements to academe, thus eventually rupturing the social fabric of capitalism, through the cracks created by these new pedagogical and prefigurative relations. It seemed that there was no desire in the sites to overthrow a government, but to form a new thesis of revolution that involves the interplay between theory and action; a job, I have argued, that popular, critical education has the potential to be instrumental in.

In relation to the first question asked in this research – that of what pedagogical experiments occurred in Occupy and what models of practice were identifiable – it seemed, as the ongoing project of occupation moved around the globe in the years following Occupy, a question remained for other initiatives and I hope the conversation will continue; the significantly 'empty bucket' of Occupy moving across continents and peoples, linking them together in a plethora of struggles, and more initiatives such as the SSC will be needed to link the learning from one to the other to keep cycles going. Therefore, from a pedagogical point of view, it is felt that we need to understand how to maintain the explicitly pedagogical aspects of any future vessel for discontent in order to understand how people learn to act otherwise in these situations.

It was the *pedagogical* and prefigurative nature of the Occupy London movement and encampment that was so interesting and potentially important; if this nature is lost, how will we practice to 'crack capitalism'?

It also is felt that these explorations and examinations of the possibilities of the sites under exploration have allowed new questions, about how to proceed in the quest for a revolutionary education to come to the fore and to emerge, as was hoped, from the specific context under study, thus creating further hope that change could be elicited from a pedagogic structure.

However, in order for the nature of any changes or new initiatives to begin to be understood, those questions need to be formed explicitly and further research is deemed necessary to answer them:

One of the significant questions still begging an answer, I would argue, is that of if Occupy's hope of seeing the end of capitalism did not bear fruit, what is it that would actually make change happen and how can education play a part? The argument made here was that capitalism has to be 'cracked' as understood in the writings of Holloway (2010). The rise of Occupy as an empty signifier has the possibility to be significant in this context. It is felt now that it is important to 'watch this space', the space of future events, happenings, interruptions in the hegemonic political flow and to witness, record and analyse what potential forms of relations and organisations arise there. As stated earlier, Occupy seemed unfinished and will potentially continue to inspire if the 'Occupation' in Hong Kong, Occupy Central and other places is anything to go by.

A second significant question relating to this understanding that arose was that of if the enclosure of higher education as a radical space of free and utopian thought continues, what are the possibilities for the future of pedagogical experimentation? This is a question that particularly interests me in my position in the academy, as teacher and as researcher. It looks, in the sites explored, as if the fight must take place within, against and beyond the academy, as seemed to be happening in Lincoln with the SSC and the SaP project as two ends of the same initiative, as Neary insisted they were – using the university classroom to take the first step and encouraging radical spaces beyond for those ready to join the struggle to become involved in. There are many experiments in higher learning as discussed, and it is argued that some of these may have the potential, such as the SSC, to become sustainable organisations, but some may not. So as Shantz (quoted earlier) says, it may be time to build 'infrastructures of resistance' in our existing institutions as sustainable alternatives are explored and hopefully found, but these need to recorded, witnessed and further researched to ensure their sustainability and their real commitment to radical social change.

As was determined by the third question here, concerning the possible trajectory from one project to another, this work attempted to understand, as its contribution to on-going debates, whether there were enough lines of continuity, enough connections and understandings, to enable the creation of such a trajectory from one pedagogical project to another and this main question is answered as a tentative possibility. The problems with this possibility are many, as discussed throughout, and each would need to be addressed in turn through a combination of research and pedagogical practices. This begins to look more like traditional action research at some of its points, as where possible action research projects should be set up with the more stable linking initiatives to assure their efficacy. Where this is not possible, because of the fluidity of a situation or the temporality, then the 'grand' action research type cycle could come into play as a way to see whether changes in the solidarity between the pedagogical levels has taken place, or where it could with some extra 'tinkering'.

The notion has also been explored here that perhaps, the traditional university can never be this space of activism. And despite the watering down and deconstruction that has since happened to the SaP initiative, I would still argue that it is worth continuing research in this vein to see what happens as the Student as Producer ethos seemed to create the possibilities for the trajectory. Therefore, had it continued to succeed and grow, then the university might become a useful site of struggle, however, if we keep trying and others like it are also subsumed by the neoliberal agenda in HE, then I would suggest that the university is no longer a useful institution for this type of struggle and the struggle will need to be taken elsewhere.

Even with the loss of the SaP initiative in its original political form, the potential trajectory of popular, critical pedagogies that cycle from the streets to the academy that has been explored here is worthy of further exploration to concretise the ideas and to find other potentials, other possibilities. This exploration may take the form of many different research projects at every stage of the overall trajectory and cycle, with many different actors taking part. This research would need to seek to understand the attitudes at each level about the others and what barriers need to be overcome to begin to implement such a cycle.

The next step in this form of action is to connect the politics of the university to the classroom, to discuss our collective situation with our students in higher education, to collectively plan and strategize. There is a disjoint between student politics and university politics in the UK currently, which mirrors the dysfunctional relationship between teacher and student. This chasm needs to be filled with debate concerning where we are and how we got here, with creating connections outside the walls of the academy, with making hope possible.

As discussed earlier on in this conclusion, the notion of Occupy as a continuing empty signifier makes the answering of the initial research question problematic as instead of being an answer, it is more a contribution to ongoing debates that perhaps attempt to understand whether there are enough lines of continuity to create trajectories, not just from one form of pedagogical intervention to another, but also from one struggle to another. The case study of Occupy presents as an attempt to do just this, to create these 'empty' spaces to be filled with, at times, antagonistic dissenting voices in the potential hope of forming a new democratic public. However, on closer examination, Occupy failed to do this, with internal voices of dissent silenced when criticising the central experiment of Occupy London, that of consensus decision making, as was discussed in Chapter 6. In addition to the failing to give equal status and voice to socially subjugated groups, such as women, within the movement meant that Occupy failed to use fully the potential power of what they had created. This thesis has been a snapshot of a stage in the development of Occupy as a movement of ideas, people and issues, and explores the strengths and weaknesses of a certain aspect of the pedagogical practices of that snapshot and cannot therefore claim to be a definitive assessment of what Occupy could, or may, become but a contribution to ongoing debates. As for the other sites explored in this thesis, I would argue here that they have the potential to assist future Occupy actions along these lines, but only if the insider/outsider dichotomy can be resolved, otherwise the voices of those that wish to see just social change – the subjugated, the timid, the voices of those unable to join such street eruptions for a myriad of reasons (ill health, vulnerability, pressures of family and caring responsibilities, etc.) – will be missed in the voices of the multitude.

As has been discussed in relation to the second research question, situations of oppression have been uncovered by the research, such as the subjugated voices of women and the silencing of internal dissent, and as discussed, these often do arise in fast flowing and organic pedagogical situations. Nonetheless, I would argue that the contribution to knowledge about the nature of these emergent social movements and their prefigurative constitution is that they still have a long way to go in terms of real conscientization, in terms of actually ridding themselves of oppressive internal behaviour. I am not the only person to argue this as has been seen; however, it is important that this knowledge is not glossed over in the name of hope and expectation.

This understanding also led to the argument that Occupy's Tent City University's attempt at organic organisation and horizontalism within the realm of teaching and learning gave rise to the notion that perhaps the cultural and pedagogical imperatives needed to dispense with the teacher in the learning space are not yet in place, this speaks to other initiatives that might wish to try this form of pedagogical horizontalism.

Therefore, the conclusion here is that the notion, defined in this work through Shor (1996) – of the critical democratic power sharing pedagogy – is most conducive for producing change agents and conscientised individuals who are able to challenge the status quo of dominant relations. It has been argued here that this power sharing pedagogy would enable countervailing discourses to emerge in the classrooms creating a familiarity with tensions, counter-hegemonic desires and the disquieting effects of a radically democratic social life of the Multitude. Therefore, an intellectual public that understands the necessity of the constant and revolutionary democratisation of public life could emerge from institutions of learning in order to reconstitute social relations to promote justice for all. It was only by exploring the organic horizontalism of the pedagogic aspects of Occupy London that this knowledge became unveiled in this thesis and has the possible potential to allow those in initiatives such as the SSC and SaP to understand better the role of the pedagogues in creating these conditions for revolutionary change.

This work has attempted to understand, as its contribution to on-going debates, whether there are enough lines of continuity, enough connections and understandings, to enable the creation of a trajectory from one pedagogical project to another and this main question has been answered as a tentative possibility. It is seen this way because, as discussed in the last section, there needs to be more work, more research before this can become more than a tentative possibility. But this work has attempted to contribute to the thinking about the possibilities of this kind of solidarisitic way of working toward a goal of using pedagogical techniques in a specific way to bring about change by improving the 'sharpness' of the educative tool at several levels.

I would also argue that the thesis contributes to the thinking about research methods and the use of bricolage. The thesis has found that one of the weaknesses with bricolage is that, as Kincheloe and Berry warned, it is a lifelong pursuit, as discussed above and in Chapter 4. This thesis has been experimental in several ways and one of those ways was to begin the bricolage and see where it took me. It has many strengths, as discussed above and in Chapter 6, but perhaps it is not wise to begin the journey to bricoleur in doctoral study. Nonetheless, bricolage has allowed me to explore my own position in the research and in the world and it is my hope that it will contribute to the thinking of others about this kind of radical methodology.

The thesis argued overall, then, that a solidarisitic grand action research type cycle may be both possible and desirable to enable pedagogical and research practices to add to the efficacy of the struggle for social justice, both within the university and outside, accepting of course, that the university may not be able to re-constitute itself as an effective site of struggle. The cornerstone of this cycle was, in the case of this work, the Social Science Centre – or at least organisations like it – so the question that arises on this issue, then, is that of whether the SSC can indeed become the linking form of organisation to bring together academics and activists (who, of course, can always be one and the same); is it 'portable' enough to respond to these 'Occupy' situations and create this cornerstone of ideas shares and knowledge production? It is argued here that if the aims of the Centre were adjusted slightly, it could have the potential to be the essential 'step' that enables the grand action research type cycle to be possible. However, the main issue – that it is claimed the members of the centre are working on, but would have to be fully resolved – is the tension between teacher and student. This leads me to the overall conclusion of this work: until the tension between those seen as *learned* and those seen as *learners* is resolved and it is a generally accepted principle that although some may be 'experts' in certain areas of knowledge, each and every person is both learned and learner – or has as Rancière would put it, an equality of intelligence – the cycle of solidarisitic struggle that is argued for here may never be possible.

This is a first step to enable the potential enactment of a revolutionary pedagogy. This is because, as was seen in all the sites, there remains this tension, which has been problematic for many years of progressive and revolutionary education; the argument here is not that this is the only tension that needs to be resolved, far from it, because as discussed in the book and above in this conclusion, there are many potential points at which the education being experienced becomes just another form of repressive cultural invasion, but I would argue that this tension resolution between teacher and student, learner and learned, is an important first step as it has been brought up across all three sites, it has been a generative theme, a line of continuity between them, which has been posed as a main issue that prevents the pedagogy moving from progressive toward revolutionary – and it presents as a sticking point, a tension that is enduring attempts at resolution. Therefore, it may be one of the issues, if a revolutionary pedagogy is to be enacted, that requires immediate attention, before other tensions are addressed.

# References

Adelman, C., Kemmis, S. and Jenkins, D. (1980) 'Rethinking Case Study: Notes from the Second Cambridge Conference'. In Simon, H. (Ed.) *Towards a Science of the Singular*. Norwich: Centre for Applied Research in Education, University of East Anglia, pp. 45–61.
Agamben, G. (1998) *Homo Sacer: Sovereign Power and Bare Life*. Stanford: Stanford University Press.
Allen, M. and Ainley, P. (2007) *Education Make You Fick, Innit?: What's Gone Wrong in England's Schools, Colleges and Universities and How to Start Putting it Right*. London: The Tufnell Press.
Allman, P. (1987) 'Paulo Freire's Education Approach: A Struggle For Meaning'. In Allen, G. (Ed.) *Community Education: An Agenda for Educational Reform*. Open University Press.
Allman, P. (2010) *Critical Education Against Global Capitalism: Karl Marx and Revolutionary Critical Education*. Rotterdam, Boston, Taipei: Sense Publishers.
Amsler, S. (2011a) 'From "Therapeutic" to Political Education: The Centrality of Affective Sensibility in Critical Pedagogy'. *Critical Studies in Education*, 52(1), pp. 47–64.
Amsler, S. (2011b) 'Beyond All Reason: Spaces of Hope and Struggle for England's Universities'. *Representations*, 116, pp. 90–114.
Amsler, S., Canaan, J., Cowden, S., Motta, S. and Singh, G. (Eds) (2010) *Why Critical Pedagogy and Popular Education Matter Today*. Birmingham: Centre for Sociology, Anthropology and Politics.
Anonymous (2012) 'Occupy – The End of the Affair'. *Social Movement Studies: Journal of Social, Cultural and Political Protest*, 11(3–4), pp. 441–445.
Apple, M. W., Au, W. and Gandin, L. A. (2009) 'Mapping Critical Education'. In Apple, M. W., Au, W. and Gandin, L. A. (Eds) *The Routledge International Handbook of Critical Education*. London, New York: Routledge, pp. 3–20.
Apps, J. W. (1985) *Improving Practice in Continuing Education: Modern Approaches for Understanding the Field Determining Priorities*. San Francisco: Jossey-Bass.
Arber, S. (2001) 'Designing Samples'. In Gilbert, N. (Ed.) *Researching Social Life*, 2nd ed., London, Thousand Oaks, New Delhi: Sage Publications, pp. 58–84.
Arditi, B. (2008) *Politics on the Edges of Liberalism: Difference, Populism, Revolution, Agitation*. Edinburgh: Edinburgh University Press.
Arditi, B. (2012) 'Insurgencies Don't have a Plan – They are the Plan: Political Performativities and Vanishing Mediators 2011'. *JOMEC, Journalism, Media and*

*Cultural Studies*. [Online] [Accessed August 2014] http://1arditi.files.wordpress.com/2012/2010/arditi_insurgencies_jomec_2012.pdf

Aronowitz, S. (1993) 'Freire's Radical Democratic Humanism'. In McLaren, P. and Leonard, P. (Eds) *Paulo Freire: A Critical Encounter*. Oxon, New York: Routledge, pp. 8–24.

Ashman, D. (2012) Dan Ashman Litigant-In-Person. Sent through personal communication: www.channel4news.com

Au, W. and Apple, M. W. (2009) 'Rethinking Reproduction: Neo-Marxism in Critical Education Theory'. In Apple, M. W., Au, W. and Gandin, L. A. (Eds) *The Routledge International Handbook of Critical Education*. London, New York: Routledge, pp. 83–95.

Avritzer, L. (2002) *Democracy and the Public Space in Latin America*. Princeton, Oxford: Princeton University Press.

Backhaus, H.-G. (1992) 'Between Philosophy and Science: Marxian Social Economy as Critical Theory'. In Bonefeld, W., Gunn, R. and Psychopedis, K. (Eds) *Open Marxism: Dialectics and History*. Vol. 1. London: Pluto Press, pp. 54–92.

Badiou, A. and Žižek, S. (2009) *Philosophy in the Present*. Cambridge, Malden: Polity Press.

Bahati Kuumba, M. (2001) *Gender and Social Movements*. Oxford, Walnut Creek: Altamira Press.

Bahl, V. and Callahan, M. (1998) 'Minorities and Mentoring in the Postcolonial Borderlands'. *Radical History Review*, 72 (Fall), pp. 21–31.

Bahruth, R. E. and Steiner, S. F. (2000) 'Upstream in the Mainstream: A Pedagogy Against the Current'. In Steiner, S. F., Krank, H. M., McLaren, P. and Bahruth, R. E. (Eds) *Freirean Pedagogy, Praxis, and Possibilities: Projects for the New Millennium*. New York, London: Falmer Press, pp. 119–146.

Bailey, M. (2011) 'The Academic as Truth Teller'. In Bailey, M. and Freedman, D. (Eds) *The Assault on Universities: A Manifesto for Resistance*. London: Pluto Press, pp. 91–102.

Bailey, M. and Freedman, D. (Eds) (2011) *The Assault on Public Universities: A Manifesto for Resistance*. London, New York: Pluto Press.

Balibar, E. (2012) *Politics and the Other Scene*. London, New York: Verso.

Balibar, E. (2014) *Equaliberty*. Duke University Press.

Barber, P. (2006) *Becoming a Practitioner Researcher: A Gestalt Approach to Holistic Inquiry*. Hendon: Middlesex University Press.

Bassey, M. (1999) *Case Study Research in Educational Settings*. Buckingham, Philadelphia: Open University Press.

Bella, K. (2011) *Bodies in Alliance: Gender Theorist Judith Butler on the Occupy and Slut Walks Movement*. Truthout.

Berman, M. (1982) *All That is Solid Melts into Air: The Experience of Modernity*. London, New York: Verso Books.

Bernays, E. L. (1928) *Propaganda*. New York: Horace Liveright.

Bernays, E. L. (1947) 'The Engineering of Consent'. *The Annals of the American Academy of Political and Social Science*, 250.

Berrett, D. (2011) 'Intellectual Roots of Wall Street Protest lie in Academe', *The Chronicle of Higher Education*, 16.

Bey, H. (1985) *The Temporary Autonomous Zone, Ontological Anarchy, Poetic Terrorism*. New York: Autonomedia.

Biesta, G. (1998) 'Say You Want a Revolution… Suggestions for the Impossible Future of Critical Pedagogy'. *Educational Theory*, 48(4) pp. 499–510.

Biesta, G. and Bingham, C. (2010) *Jacques Rancière: Education, Truth, Emancipation*. London, New York: Continuum.
Bigelow, B. (2011) Occupy the Curriculum, *Blog: Rethinking Schools*.
Blass, T. (Ed.) (2000) *Obedience to Authority: Current Perspectives on the Milgram Paradigm*. Mahwah, New Jersey, London: Lawrence Erlbaum Associates, Publishers.
Bloch, E. (1964) *Tübinger Einleitung in die Philosophie* (2 vols). Frankfurt: Suhrkamp.
Bloch, E. (1986) *The Principle of Hope*, Vol. 1. Cambridge, MA: The MIT Press.
Bloom, C. (2012) *Riot City: Protest and Rebellion in the Capital*. Basingstoke, New York: Palgrave Macmillan.
Blumer, H. (1992) *Symbolic Interactionism: Perspective and Method*. University of California Press.
Bonefeld, W. (1992) 'Social Construction and the Form of the Capitalist State'. In Bonefeld, W., Gunn, R. and Psychopedis, K. (Eds) *Open Marxism: Dialectics and History*, Vol. 1. London: Pluto Press, pp. 93–132.
Bonefeld, W. (1995) 'Capital as Subject and the Existance of Labour'. In Bonefeld, W., Gunn, R., Holloway, J. and Psychopedis, K. (Eds) *Emancipating Marx: Open Marxism*, Vol. 3. London: Pluto Press, pp. 182–212.
Bonefeld, W., Gunn, R. and Psychopedis, K. (1992) 'Introduction'. In Bonefeld, W., Gunn, R. and Psychopedis, K. (Eds) *Open Marxism: Dialectics and History*, Vol. 1. London: Pluto Press, pp. ix–xx.
Bonefeld, W., Gunn, R., Holloway, J. and Psychopedis, K. (1995) 'Introduction: Emancipating Marx'. In Bonefeld, W., Gunn, R., Holloway, J. and Psychopedis, K. (Eds) *Emancipating Marx: Open Marxism*, Vol. 3. London: Pluto Press, pp. 1–6.
Bonnett, A. (2013) 'Something New in Freedom'. *Times Higher Education online*.
Borg, C. and Mayo, P. (Eds) (2007) *Public Intellectuals, Radical Democracy and Social Movements: A Book of Interviews*. New York, Washington D.C., Baltimore, Bern, Frankfurt am Main, Berlin, Brussels, Vienna, Oxford: Peter Lang.
Boser, S. (2006) 'Ethics and Power in Community-Campus Partnerships for Research'. *Action Research*, 4(1), pp. 9–21.
Bourdieu, P. (1977) *Outline of a Theory of Practice*, Vol. 16. Cambridge, New York: Cambridge University Press.
Bovens, L. (1999) 'The Value of Hope'. *Philosophy and Phenomenological Research*, 59(3), pp. 667–681.
Brkich, A. and Barko, T. (2012) '"Our Most Lethal Enemy?": Star Trek, the Borg and Methodological Simplicity'. *Qualitative Inquiry*, 18(9), pp. 787–797.
Brookfield, S. (2001) *Developing Critical Thinkers: Challenging Adults to Explore Alternative Ways of Thinking and Acting*. Milton Keynes: Open University Press.
Brookfield, S. (2005) *The Power of Critical Theory for Adult Learning and Teaching*. Maidenhead: Open University Press.
Brookfield, S. and Holst, J. D. (2011) *Radicalizing Learning: Adult Education for a Just World*. San Francisco: Jossey-Bass.
Brown, N. (2012) 'Occupations: Oakland'. *Radical Philosophy*, January-February, pp. 53–54.
Brown, G. and Pickerill, J. (2009) 'Space for Emotions in the Spaces of Activism'. *Emotion, Space and Society*, 2(1), pp. 24–35.
Bryant, A. and Charmaz, K. (2007) 'Introduction: Grounded Theory Research: Methods and Practices'. In Bryant, A. and Charmaz, K. (Eds) *The Sage Handbook of Grounded Theory*. Los Angeles, London, New Delhi, Singapore, Washington DC: Sage, pp. 1–27.

Brydon-Miller, M. (2009) 'Covenantal Ethics and Action Research: Exploring a common Foundation for Social Research'. In Mertens, D. M. and Ginsburg, P. E. (Eds) *The Handbook of Social Research Ethics*. Los Angeles, London, New Delhi, Singapore, Washington DC: Sage.

Brydon-Miller, M., Greenwood, D. and Maguire, P. (2003) 'Why Action Research?' *Action Research*, 1(1), pp. 9–28.

Burbules, N. C. (2000) 'The Limits of Dialogue as a Critical Pedagogy'. In Trifonas, P. P. (Ed.) *Revolutionary Pedagogies: Cultural Politics, Instituting Education, and the Discourse of Theory*. New York, London: Routledge Falmer, pp. 251–273.

Burdick, J. and Sandlin, J. (2010) 'Inquiry as Answerability: Toward a Methodology of Discomfort in Researching Critical Public Pedagogies'. *Qualitative Inquiry Online First*, pp. 1–12.

Byrne, J. (Ed.) (2012) *The Occupy Handbook*. New York, Boston, London: Back Bay Books.

Campbell, E. R. A. (2011) 'A Critique of the Occupy Movement from a Black Occupier'. *The Black Scholar*, 41(4) pp. 42–51.

Carrigan, M. (2011) *The Social Science Centre. Campaign for the Public University*. [Online] [Accessed 03. 11. 2012] http://publicuniversity.org.uk/2011/04/19/the-social-science-centre

Casas-Cortes, M. and Cobarrubias, S. (2007) 'Drifting Through the Knowledge Machine'. In Shukaitis, S., Graeber, D. and Biddle, E. (Eds) *Constituent Imagination: Militant Investigations, Collective Theorization*. Edinburgh, Oakland: AK Press, pp. 112–126.

Castells, M. (2012) *Networks of Outrage and Hope: Social Movements in the Internet Age*. Cambridge, Malden: Polity Press.

Cavanagh (2007) 'Popular Education, Social Movements and Story Telling: Interview with Chris Cavanagh'. In Borg, C. and Mayo, P. (Eds) *Public Intellectuals, Radical Democracy and Social Movements: A Book of Interviews*. New York, Washington DC, Baltimore, Bern, Frankfurt am Main, Berlin, Brussels, Vienna, Oxford: Peter Lang, pp. 41–48.

Charmaz, K. (2003) 'Grounded Theory: Objectivist and Constructivist Methods'. In Denzin, N. K. and Lincoln, Y. S. (Eds) *Strategies of Qualitative Inquiry*, 2nd ed. Thousand Oaks, London New Delhi: Sage Publications, pp. 249–291.

Charmaz, K. (2005) 'Grounded Theory in the 21st Century: A Qualitative Method for Advancing Social Justice Research'. In Denzin, N. K. and Lincoln, Y. (Eds) *Handbook of Qualitative Research*, 3rd ed. Thousand Oaks: Sage, pp. 507–535

Chetkovich, C. and Kunreuther, F. (2006) *From the Ground Up: Grassroots Organisations Making Social Change*. Ithaca, London: Cornell University Press.

Cho, S. (2013) *Critical Pedagogy and Social Change: Critical Analysis on the Language of Possibility*. New York, London: Routledge.

Chomsky, N. (2012) *Occupy*. London, New York and Worldwide: Penguin Books.

Christians, C. (2000) 'Ethics and Politics in Qualitative Research'. In Denzin, N. K. and Lincoln, Y. (Eds) *Handbook of Qualitative Research*, 2nd ed. Thousand Oaks: Sage.

Clarke, A. E. and Friese, C. (2007) 'Grounded Theorizing Using Situational Analysis'. In Bryant, A. and Charmaz, K. (Eds) *The Sage Handbook of Grounded Theory*. Los Angeles, London, New Delhi, Singapore, Washington DC: Sage, pp. 363–397.

Clarke, H. (Ed.) (2009) *People Power: Unarmed Resistance and Global Solidarity*. New York: Pluto Press.

Clarke, S. (1992) 'The Global Accumulation of Capital and the Periodisation of the Capitalist State Form'. In Bonefeld, W., Gunn, R. and Psychopedis, K. (Eds) *Open Marxism: Dialectics and History*, Vol. 1. London: Pluto Press, pp. 133–150.

Class War University (2013) *Occupying the City with the Social Science Centre – an Interview with Mike Neary*. Class War University. [Online] [Accessed 09. 10. 2013] http://www.classwaru.org/2013/09/02

Cleaver, H. (1992) 'The Inversion of Class Perspective in Marxian Theory: From Valorisation to Self-Valorisation'. In Bonefeld, W. (Ed.) *Open Marxism*, Vol. 2. London: Pluto Press, pp. 106–144.

Cleaver, H. (2000) *Reading Capital Politically*. Leeds, Edinburgh, San Francisco: AK Press, Anti Theses.

Clennon, O. D. (2014) *Alternative Education and Community Engagement: Making Education a Priority*. Basingstoke, New York: Palgrave Macmillan.

Coffey, A. (1999) *The Ethnographic Self: Fieldwork and the Representation of Identity*. London, Thousand Oaks, New Delhi: Sage Publications.

Collini, S. (2012) *What Are Universities For?* London, New York and Worldwide: Penguin Books.

Conant, J. (2010) *A Poetics of Resistance: The Revolutionary Public Relations of the Zapatista Insurgency*. Edinburgh, Oakland, Baltimore: AK Press.

Costanza-Chock, S. (2012) 'Mic Check! Media Cultures and the Occupy Movement'. *Social Movement Studies: Journal of Social, Cultural and Political Protest*, 11(3–4), pp. 375–385.

Coté, M., Day, R. and de Peuter, G. (Eds) (2007) *Utopian Pedagogy: Radical Experiments Against Neoliberal Globalisation*. Toronto: University of Toronto Press.

Couldry, N. (2011) 'Fighting for the University's Life'. In Bailey, M. and Freedman, D. (Eds) *The Assault on Universities: A Manifesto for Resistance*. London: Pluto Press, pp. 37–46.

Cowden, S. and Singh, G. (2013) 'Introduction: Critical Pedagogy and the Crisis in the Contemporary University'. In Cowden, S., Singh, G., with Amsler, S., Canaan, J. and Motta, S. (Eds) *Acts of Knowing: Critical Pedagogy In, Against and Beyond the University*. New York, London, New Delhi, Sydney: Bloomsbury, pp. 1–12.

Crouch, C. (2011) *The Strange Non-Death of Neo-liberalism*. Cambridge, Maldon: Polity Press.

Crowther, J. and Villegas, E. L. (2012) 'Reconnecting the Intellect and Feeling: Marx, Gramsci, Williams and the Educator's Role'. In Hall, B. L., Clover, D. E., Crowther, J., and Scandrett, E. (Eds) *Learning and Education for a Better World: The Role of Social Movements*. Rotterdam: Sense Publishers, pp. 57–68.

Crowther, J., Galloway, V. and Martin, I. (2005) 'Introduction: Radicalising Intellectual Work'. In Crowther, J., Galloway, V. and Martin, I. (Eds) *Popular Education: Engaging the Academy, International Perspectives*. Leicester: National Institute for Adult Continuing Education, pp. 1–10.

Dalla Costa, M. (1995) 'Capitalism and Reproduction'. In Bonefeld, W., Gunn, R., Holloway, J. and Psychopedis, K. (Eds) *Emancipating Marx: Open Marxism*. Vol. 3. London: Pluto Press, pp. 17–39.

Darder, A. (2002) *Reinventing Paulo Freire: A Pedagogy of Love*. Cambridge MA, Oxford: Westview Press.

Davis, A. (2011) 'Economic Alternatives in the Current Crisis: ConDem and Financier Economic Narrative … And Other Fairy Tales'. In Bailey, M. and Freedman, D.

(Eds) *The Assault on Universities: A Manifesto for Resistance*. London, New York: Pluto Press, pp. 49–58.
Debord, G. (1977) *Society of the Spectacle*. Detroit: Black & Red.
Denzin, N. K. (2009) *Qualitative inquiry Under Fire: Toward a New Paradigm dialogue*. Walnut Creek: Left Coast Press Inc.
Denzin, N. K. (2010) *The Qualitative Manifesto: A Call to Arms*. Walnut Creek: Left Coast Press Inc.
Denzin, N. K. and Lincoln, Y. (Eds) (2000) *Handbook of Qualitative Research*, 2nd ed. Thousand Oaks: Sage.
Dewey, J. (1927/1954) *The Public and its Problems*. Chicago: Swallow Press.
Dewey, J. (1937) *How We Think*. Boston: Heath.
Dewey, J. (1965) *Dewey on Education: Selections*. New York: Teachers College Press.
Dewey, J. (1997) *Experience and Education*, reprint ed. New York: Touchstone.
Drahos, P. (2004) 'Trading in Public Hope'. *The Annals of the American Academy of Political and Social Science*, 592, pp. 18–38.
Duncan-Andrade, J. (2009) 'Note to Educators: Hope Required When Growing Roses in Concrete'. *Harvard Educational Review*, 19(2), pp. 181–194.
Dyer-Witheford, N. (2007) 'Commonism'. *Turbulence*1, pp. 28–29.
Dyer-Witheford, N. (2010) 'Commonism'. In Turbulence Collective (Eds) *What Would it Mean to Win?* Oakland: PM Press, pp. 105–112.
Eagleton, T. (1991) *Ideology: An Introduction*. London: Verso.
Earl, C. (2013) 'Being Realistic by Demanding the Impossible: Beginning the Bricolage'. *Enquire*, 8 Special Edition (1), pp. 14–36.
Earl, C. (2014) 'Education and Social Change: A Theoretical Approach'. In Clennon, O. D. (Ed.) *Alternative Education and Community Engagement: Making Education a Priority*. Basingstoke: Palgrave Macmillan, pp. 37–52.
Eckstein, H. (2000) 'Case Study and Theory in Political Science'. In Gomm, R., Hammersley, M. and Foster, P. (Eds) *Case Study Method*. London, Thousand Oaks, New Delhi: Sage Publications Ltd, pp. 119–164.
Ellsworth, E. (1992) 'Why Doesn't this Feel Empowering? Working Through the Repressive Myths of Critical Pedagogy'. In Luke, C. and Gore, J. (Eds) *Feminisms and Critical Pedagogy*. New York: Routledge, pp. 90–119.
Esteva, G. (2010) 'Enclosing the Enclosers'. In Turbulence Collective (Ed.) *What Would it Mean to Win?* Oakland: PM Press, pp. 23–29.
Faulkner, N. (2011) 'What is a University Education For?' In Bailey, M. and Freedman, D. (Eds) *The Assault on Universities: A Manifesto for Resistance*. London: Pluto Press, pp. 27–36.
Fendler, L. (1999) 'Making Trouble: Prediction, Agency and Critical Intellectuals'. In Pokewitz, T. S. and Fendler, L. (Eds) *Critical Theories in Education: Changing Terrains of Knowledge and Politics*. New York: Routledge, pp. 169–189.
Fenton, N. (2011) 'Impoverished Pedagogy, Privatised Practice'. In Bailey, M. and Freedman, D. (Eds) *The Assault on Universities: A Manifesto for Resistance*. London: Pluto Press, pp. 103–110.
Fielding, M. and Moss, P. (2011) *Radical Education and the Common School: A Democratic Alternative*. Oxon, New York: Routledge.
Fielding, N. and Thomas, H. (2001) 'Qualitative Interviewing'. In Gilbert, N. (Ed.) *Researching Social Life*. London, Thousand Oaks, New Delhi: Sage Publications, pp. 123–144.

Fine, R. (1995) 'Hegel's Philosophy of Right and Marx's Critique: A Reassessment'. In Bonefeld, W., Gunn, R., Holloway, J. and Psychopedis, K. (Eds) *Emancipating Marx: Open Marxism*. Vol. 3. London: Pluto Press, pp. 84–109.

Fisher, M. (2009) *Capitalist Realism: Is There no Alternative?*, Ropley: Zero Books.

Flyvbjerg, B. (2011) 'Case Study'. In Denzin, N. K.. and Lincoln, Y. (Eds) *The Sage Handbook of Qualitative Research*, 4th ed. Los Angeles, London, New Delhi, Singapore, Washington DC: Sage, pp. 301–316.

Foley, G. (2004) *Learning in Social Action: A Contribution to Understanding Informal Education*. London: Zed Books.

Fordham, E. (2012) 'The School of Ideas'. *Occupied Times*.

Foster, R. (1997) 'Addressing Epistemologic and Practical Issues in Multimethod Research: A Procedure for Conceptual Triangulation'. *Advances in Nursing Education*, 202(2).

Foucault, M. (1997) 'The Masked Philosopher'. In Rabinow, P. (Ed.) *Michel Foucault: Ethics, Subjectivity and Truth – The Essential Works of Michel Foucault*. New York: The Free Press, pp. 321–328.

Foust, C. (2010) *Transgression as a Mode of Resistance: Rethinking Social Movements in an Era of Corporate Globalisation*. Lanham, Boulder, New York, Toronto, Plymouth UK: Lexington Books.

Freedman, D. (2011) 'An Introduction to Education Reform and Resistance'. In Bailey, M. and Freedman, D. (Eds) *The Assault on Universities: A Manifesto for Resistance*. London: Pluto Press, pp. 1–10.

Freire, P. (1974) *Cultural Action for Freedom*. Middlesex, Baltimore, Ringwood, Au: Penguin Books.

Freire, P. (1976) 'A Few Notes about the Word "Conscientisation"'. In Dale, R., Esland, G. and MacDonald, M. (Eds) *Schooling and Capitalism*. London: Routledge, pp. 224–227.

Freire, P. (1978) *Pedagogy in Process: The Letters to Guinea-Bissau*. New York: Writers and Readers Publishing Cooperative.

Freire, P. (1985) *The Politics of Education: Culture, Power and Liberation*. Westport: Greenwood Publishing Group, Inc.

Freire, P. (1986) 'Keynote Address'. *In The Workshop on Worker Education*. New York:City College of New York Centre for Worker Education.

Freire, P. (1993a) *Pedagogy of the Oppressed*. London, New York, Worldwide: Penguin Books.

Freire, P. (1993b) *Pedagogy of the City*. New York: Continuum.

Freire, P. (1996) *Letters to Christina: Reflections on My Life and Work*. New York: Routledge.

Freire, P. (1997) *Pedagogy of the Heart*. New York: Continuum.

Freire, P. (1998) *Pedagogy of Freedom: Ethics, Democracy, and Civic Courage*. Lanham, Boulder, New York, Oxford: Rowman & Littlefield Publishers, Inc.

Freire, P. (2004) *Pedagogy of Hope: Reliving Pedagogy of the Oppressed*. London, New York: Continuum.

Freire, P. (2005) *Teachers as Cultural Workers: Letters to Those Who Dare to Teach*, expanded ed. Boulder: Westview Press.

Freire, P. (2007) *Daring to Dream: Toward a Pedagogy of the Unfinished*. Boulder: Paradigm Publishers.

Freire, P. (2008) *Education for a Critical Consciousness*. London, New York: Continuum.

Freire, P. and Faundez, A. (1989) *Learning to Question: A Pedagogy of Liberation*. Geneva: WCC Publications.

Freire, P., Escobar, M., Fernandez, A. and Guevara-Niebla, G. (1994) *Paulo Freire on Higher Education*. Albany: SUNY Press.

Gadamer, H. G. (1989) *Truth and Method*. New York: Continuum Press.

Gamson, W. A. and Sifry, M. L. (2013) 'The #Occupy Movement: An Introduction'. *The Sociological Quarterly*, 54, pp. 159–228.

Gatto, J. T. (2009) *Weapons of Mass Instruction: A School Teacher's Journey Through the Dark World of Compulsory Schooling*. Gabriola Island: New Society Publishers.

Gerstenberger, H. (1992) 'The Bourgeois State Form Revisited'. In Bonefeld, W., Gunn, R. and Psychopedis, K. *Open Marxism: Dialectics and History*. Vol. 1. London: Pluto Press, pp. 151–176.

Giroux, H. (1988) *Teachers as Intellectuals: Toward a Critical Pedagogy of Learning*. South Hadley MA: Bergin & Garvey.

Giroux, H. (1992) *Border Crossings*. New York: Routledge.

Giroux, H. (2001) *Theory and Resistance in Education: Towards a Pedagogy of the Opposition*. Westport, CT: London: Bergin and Garvey.

Giroux, H. (2011) *On Critical Pedagogy*. New York, London: Continuum.

Giroux, H. (2012) 'The Occupy Movement and the Politics of Educated Hope'. *Truthout*.

Giroux, H. and McLaren, P. (1989) *Critical Pedagogy, the State and Cultural Struggle*. Albany NY: State University of New York Press.

Gitlin, T. (2013) 'Occupy's Predicament: The Moment and Prospects for the Movement'. *The British Journal of Sociology*, 64(1), pp. 3–25

Glaser, B. G. and Strauss, A. L. (2009) *The Discovery of Grounded Theory: Strategies for Qualitative Research*. New Brunswick, London: Aldine Transaction.

Glasius, M. and Pleyers, G. (2013) 'The Global Movement of 2011: Democracy, Social Justice and Dignity'. *Development and Change*, 44(3), pp. 547–567.

Gledhill, J. (2012) 'Collecting Occupy London: Public Collecting Institutions and Social Protest Movements in the 21st Century'. *Social Movement Studies: Journal of Social, Cultural and Political Protest*, 11(3–4) pp. 342–348.

Goffman, I. (1959) *The Presentation of Self in Everyday Life*. London, New York and Worldwide: Penguin Books.

Goodlad, J. I. (1984) *A Place Called School: Prospects for the Future*. New York: McGraw Hill Book Company.

Gorz, A. (1997) *Farewell to the Working Class*. Chadlington: Pluto Press.

Graeber, D. (2004) *Fragments of an Anarchist Anthropology*. Chicago: Prickly Paradigm Press.

Graeber, D. (2011) 'Occupy Wall Street's Anarchist Roots'. *Aljazeera*, (30 November 2011).

Graeber, D. (2013) *The Democracy Project: A History. A Crisis. A Movement*. London, New York and Worldwide: Allen Lane.

Gramsci, A. (1971) *Selections from the Prison Notebooks*. London: Lawrence & Wishart.

Grandin, G. (2005) 'The Instruction of Great Catastrophe: Truth Commissions, National History and State Formations in Argentina, Chile and Guatemala'. *American Historical Review*, pp. 46–67.

Greenwood, D. and Levin, M. (2003) 'Reconstructing the Relationship Between Universities and Society Through Action Research'. In Denzin, N. K. and Lincoln, Y.

(Eds) *The Landscape of Qualitative Research: Theories and Issues*, 2nd ed. Thousand Oaks, New Delhi, London: Sage Publications, pp. 131–166.

Griffiths, M. (2003) *Action for Social Justice: Fairly Different*. Maidenhead: Open University Press.

Guba, E. (1981) 'Criteria for Assessing the Trustworthiness of Naturalistic Inquiries'. *Educational Communications and Technology*, 29, pp. 75–81.

Gunn, R. (1989) 'Marxism and Philosophy: A Critique of Realism'. *Capital and Class*, 13(1) pp. 87–116.

Gunn, R. (1992) 'Against Historical Materialism: Marxism as First-Order Discourse'. In Bonefeld, W., Gunn, R. and Psychopedis, K. (Eds) *Theory and Practice: Open Marxism*, Vol. 2. London: Pluto Press, pp. 1–45.

Habermas, J. (1979) *Communication and the Evolution of Society*. Boston: Beacon Press. cited in Brookfield, S. (1987) *Developing Critical Thinkers: Challenging Adults to Explore Alternative Ways of Thinking and Acting*. Milton Keynes: Open University Press.

Hage, G. (2002) 'On the Side of Life – Joy and the Capacity of Being: A Conversation with Ghassan Hage'. In Zournazi, M. (Ed.) *Hope: New Philosophies for Change*. London: Lawrence Wishart.

Hall, B. (2003) 'Introduction'. In Minker, M. and Wallerstein, N. (Eds) *Community-Based Participatory Research for Health*. San Francisco: Jossey-Bass, pp. xiii–xiv.

Hall, B. (2012) '"A Giant Human Hashtag": Learning and the #Occupy Movement'. In Hall, B. L.. Clover, D. E.., Crowther, J., and Scandrett, E. (Eds) *Learning and Education for a Better World: The Role of Social Movements*. Rotterdam: Sense, pp. 127–140.

Halvorsen, S. (2012) 'Beyond the Network? Occupy London and the Global Movement'. *Social Movement Studies: Journal of Social, Cultural and Political Protest*, 11(3–4), pp. 427–433.

Hammersley, M. and Gomm, R. (2000) 'Introduction'. In Gomm, R., Hammersley, M. and Foster, P. (Eds) *Case Study Method: Key Issues, Key Texts*. London, Thousand Oaks, New Delhi: Sage Publications.

Haplin, D. (2003) *Hope and Education: The Role of the Utopian Imagination*. London, New York: Routledge.

Harber, C. (2004) *Schooling as Violence: How Schools Harm Pupils and Societies*. New York: Routledge.

Hardt, M. and Negri, A. (2000) *Empire*. Cambridge, MA, London: Harvard University Press.

Hardt, M. and Negri, A. (2004) *Multitude: War and Democracy in the Age of Empire*. New York and Worldwide: Penguin Books.

Hardt, M. and Negri, A. (2009) *Commonwealth*. Cambridge MA, London: The Belknap Press of Harvard University Press.

Hardt, M. and Negri, A. (2012) *Declaration*. New York: Argo Navis Author Services.

Harvey, D. (2000) *Spaces of Hope*. Edinburgh: Edinburgh University Press.

Harvey, D. (2003) *The New Imperialism*. Oxford: Oxford University Press.

Harvey, D. (2011) *The Enigma of Capital and the Crisis of Capitalism*. London: Profile Books.

Harvey, D. (2012) *Rebel Cities: From the Right to the City to the Urban Revolution*. London, New York: Verso.

Heaney, T. (1993) 'Identifying and Dealing with Vocational, Social, and Political Issues'. *New Directions for Adult and Continuing Education*, 60, pp. 13–20.

## References

Hensby, A. (2014) 'Networks, Counter-Networks and Political Socialisation – Paths and Barriers to High-Cost/Risk Activism in the 2010/11 Student Protests Against Fees and Cuts'. *Contemporary Social Science: Journal of the Academy of Social Science*, 9(1), pp. 92–105.

Herman, E. S. and Chomsky, N. (1994) *Manufacturing Consent: The Political Economy of the Mass Media*. New York, Toronto, London: Vintage Books.

Hessel, S. (2011) *Time for Outrage! (Indignez-vous!)*. London: Charles Glass Books.

Hilsen, A. I. (2006) 'And They Shall be Known by Their Deeds: Ethics and Politics in Action Research'. *Action Research*, 4(1), pp. 23–36.

Holloway, J. (1995) 'From Scream of Refusal to Scream of Power: The Centrality of Work'. In Bonefeld, W., Gunn, R., Holloway, J. and Psychopedis, K. (Eds) *Emancipating Marx: Open Marxism*. Vol. 3. London: Pluto Press, pp. 155–181.

Holloway, J. (2003) 'In the Beginning was the Scream'. In Bonefeld, W. (Ed.) *Revolutionary Writings: Common Sense Essays in Post-Political Politics*. New York: Autonomedia, pp. 15–24.

Holloway, J. (2005) *Change the World Without Taking Power: The Meaning of Revolution Today*, new ed. London, Ann Arbor, MI: Pluto Press.

Holloway, J. (2010) *Crack Capitalism*. London, New York: Pluto Press.

Holloway, J., Matamoros, F. and Tischler, S. (2009) *Negativity and Revolution: Adorno and Political Activism*. London: Pluto.

Holmes, B. (2007) 'Continental Drift: Activist Research, From Geopolitics to Geopoetics'. In Shukaitis, S., Graeber, D. and Biddle, E. (Eds) *Constituent Imagination: Militant Investigations Collective Theorization*. Oakland, Edinburgh, West Virginia: AK Press, pp. 39–43.

Holst, J. D. (2002) *Social Movements, Civil Society, and Radical Adult Education*. Westport, London: Bergin & Garvey.

Holt, D. (1989) 'Complex Ontology and Our Stake in the Theatre'. In Shotter, J. and Gergen, K. (Eds) *Texts of Identity*. London: Sage.

hooks, b. (1994) *Teaching to Transgress: Education as the Practice of Freedom*. New York, London: Routledge.

Horton, M. and Freire, P. (1990) *We Make the Road by Walking: Conversations on Education and Social Change*. Philadelphia: Temple University Press.

Hou, J. (Ed.) (2010) *Insurgent Public Space: Guerrilla Urbanism and the Remaking of Contemporary Cities*. London, New York: Routledge.

Howe, K. R. and MacGillivary, H. (2009) 'Social Research Attuned to Deliberative Democracy'. In Mertens, D. M.. and Ginsburg, P. E. (Eds) *The Handbook of Social Research Ethics*. Los Angeles, London, New Delhi, Singapore, Washington DC: Sage.

Hughes, R. (2000, November 20) 'The Phantom of Utopia'. *Time*, pp. 84–85.

Hydra, S. (2012) 'Notes on a Radical Pedagogy'. *Occupied Times*.

Ife, J. and Tesoriero, F. (2006) *Community Development: Community-Based Alternatives in an Age of Globalisation*, 3rd ed. Crows Nest, NSW: Pearson Education.

Illich, I. (2011) *Deschooling Society*. London, New York: Marion Boyard Publishers Limited.

Jaramillo, N. (2012) 'Occupy, Recuperate and Decolonise'. *Journal for Critical Education Policy Studies*, 10(1) pp. 67–75.

Jardine, D. W. (2006) 'On Hermeneutics: "Over and Above our Wanting and Doing"'. In Kincheloe, J. L. and Tobin, K. (Eds) *Doing Educational Research: A Handbook*. Rotterdam, Taipei: Sense Publishers, pp. 269–288.

Jasper, J. (2009) 'The Emotions of Protest'. In Jasper, J. and Goodwin, J. (Eds) *The Social Movements Reader: Cases and Concepts*, 2nd ed. Chichester: Wiley Blackwell, pp. 175–184.
Jesson, J. and Newman, M. (2004) 'Radical Adult Education and Learning'. In Foley, G. (Ed.) *Dimensions of Adult Learning: Adult Education and Training in a Global Era*. Crows Nest NSW: Allen & Unwin.
Johnson, R. (1988) 'Really Useful Knowledge, 1790–1850: Memories for Education in the 1980's'. In Lovett, T. (Ed.) *Radical Approaches to Adult Education*. London: Routledge.
Johnston, R. (2005) 'Popular Education and the Academy: The Problem of *Praxis*'. In Crowther, J., Galloway, V. and Martin, I. (Eds) *Popular Education: Engaging the Academy, International Perspectives*. Leicester: National Institute of Adult Continuing Education, pp. 63–76.
Kane, L. (2005) 'Ideology Matters'. In Crowther, J., Galloway, V. and Martin, I. (Eds) *Popular Education: Engaging the Academy, International Perspectives*. Leicester: National Institute of Adult Continuing Education, pp. 32–42.
Kant, I. (1982) 'Über Pädagogik [On Education]'. In Kant, I. (Ed.) *Schriften zur Anthropologie, Geschichtsphilosophie, Politik und Pädagogik*. Frankfurt am Main: Insel Verlag, pp. 695–761.
Katsiaficas, G. (2006) *The Subversion of Politics: European Autonomous Movements and the Decolonization of Everyday Life*. Oakland, Edinburgh: AK Press.
Kemmis, S. (1980) 'The Imagination of the Case and the Invention of the Study'. In Simon, H. (Ed.) *Towards a Science of the Singular*. Norwich: Centre for Applied Research in Education, University of East Anglia, pp. 96–142.
Kenny, S. (2006) *Developing Communities for the Future*, 3rd ed. Melbourne: Nelson Thompson.
Kerton, S. (2012) 'Tahrir, Here? The Influence of the Arab Uprisings on the Emergence of Occupy'. *Social Movement Studies: Journal of Social, Cultural and Political Protest*, 11(3–4) pp. 302–308.
Khatib, K., Killjoy, M. and McGuire, M. (Eds) (2012) *We Are Many: Reflections on Movement Strategy from Occupation to Liberation*. Oakland, Edinburgh, Baltimore: AK Press.
Kincheloe, J. L. and Berry, K. S. (2004) *Rigour and Complexity in Educational Research: Conceptualizing the Bricolage*. Maidenhead, New York: Open University Press.
Kincheloe, J. L. and Steinberg, S. R. (Eds) (1998) *Unauthorized Methods: Strategies for Critical Teaching*. London, New York: Routledge.
Kincheloe, J. L. and Tobin, K. (2006) 'Doing Educational Research in a Complex World'. In Kincheloe, J. L. and Tobin, K. (Eds) *Doing Educational Research: A Handbook*. Rotterdam, Taipei: Sense Publishers, pp. 1–14.
Kincheloe, J. L., McLaren, P. and Steinberg, S. R. (2011) 'Critical Pedagogy, and Qualitative Research: Moving to the Bricolage'. In Denzin, N. K. and Lincoln, Y. S. (Eds) *The Sage Handbook of Qualitative Research*, Vol. 4. Los Angeles, London, New Delhi, Singapore, Washington DC: Sage, pp. 163–178.
Kindon, S., Pain, R. and Kesby, M. (2010) 'Participatory Action Research: Origins, Approaches and Methods'. In Kindon, S., Pain, R. and Kesby, M. (Eds) *Participatory Action Research Approaches and Methods: Connecting People, Participation and Place*. London, New York: Routledge, pp. 9–19.
Kohl, H. (1983) 'Examining Closely What We Do'. *Learning*, 12(1). pp. 28–30.
Köksal, I. (2012) 'Walking in the City of London'. *Social Movement Studies: Journal of Social, Cultural and Political Protest*, 11(3–4), pp. 446–453.

Kroll, A. (2011) 'How Occupy Wall Street Really Got Started'. In van Gelder, S. and the Staff of YES! Magazine (Eds) *This Changes Everything: Occupy Wall Street and the 99% Movement*. San Francisco: Berrett-Koehler Publishers, Inc.

Kvale, S. and Brinkman, S. (2009) *Interviews: Learning the Craft of Qualitative Research Interviewing*, 2nd ed. Los Angeles, London, New Delhi, Singapore: Sage.

La Boétie, E. (1548/2002) *Le Discours de la Servitude volontair/ Anti-Dictator*. New York: Columbia Press.

Laclau, E. and Mouffe, C. (1985) *Hegemony and Socialist Strategy: Towards a Radical Democratic Politics*. London: Verso.

Lather, P. (1986) 'Issues of Validity in Openly Ideological Research: Between a Rock and a Soft Place'. *Interchange*, 17(4), pp. 63–84.

Lather, P. (1992) 'Post-critical Pedagogies: A Feminist Reading'. In Luke, C. and Gore, J. (Eds) *Feminisms and Critical Pedagogy*. New York: Routledge, pp. 120–137.

Lather, P. (1998) 'Critical Pedagogy and its Complicities: A Praxis of Stuck Places'. *Educational Theory*, 48(4), pp. 487–498.

Lave, J. and Wenger, E. (1991) *Situated Learning: Legitimate Peripheral Participation*. New York: Cambridge University Press.

Lefebvre, H. (1991) *The Production of Space*. Malden, Oxford, Carlton: Blackwell Publishing.

Lefort, C. (1988) *Democracy and Political Theory*. Cambridge: Polity Press.

Leonardo, Z. (2002) 'The Souls of White Folk: Critical Pedagogy, Whiteness Studies and Globalisation Discourse'. *Race, Ethnicity and Education*, 5(1), pp. 29–50.

Leonardo, Z. (2006) 'Reality on Trial: Notes on Ideology, Education and Utopia'. In Peters, M. and Freeman-Moir, J. (Eds) *Edutopias: New Utopian Thinking in Education*. Rotterdam, Taipei: Sense Publishers, pp. 79–98.

Leonardo, Z. (Ed.) (2005) *Critical Pedagogy and Race*. Malden: Blackwell. cited in Cho, S. (2013) *Critical Pedagogy and Social Change: Critical Analysis on the Language of Possibility*. New York, London: Routledge.

Levitas, R. (2007) 'The Imaginary Reconstitution of Society: Utopia as Method'. In Moylan, T. and Baccolini, R. (Eds) *Utopia Method Vision*. Oxford: Peter Lang, pp. 47–68.

Lincoln, Y. (2001) 'An Emerging New Bricoleur: Promises and Possibilities'. *Qualitative Inquiry*, 7, pp. 639–649.

Lippmann, W. (1922) *Public Opinion*. New York: Harcourt Brace and Company.

Lippman, W. (1927) *The Phantom Public*. New York: Macmillan.

Lockhart, J. (1997) '*After Freire: A Continuing Pedagogy*'. [Online] [Accessed 21. 06. 2013] www.williamtemplefoundation.org.uk/publications/

Lotringer, S. and Marazzi, C. (2007) 'Introduction'. In Lotringer, S. and Marazzi, C. (Eds) *Autonomia: Post-Political Politics*. Los Angeles: Semiotext(e).

Lukacs, G. (1971) *History and Class Consciousness*. Cambridge: The MIT Press.

Luke, C. and Gore, J. (Eds) (1992) *Feminisms and Critical Pedagogy*. New York: Routledge.

Lunghi, A. and Wheeler, S. (Eds) (2013) *Occupy Everything: Reflections on Why it's Kicking Off Everywhere*. Wivenhoe, New York, Port Watson: Minor Compositions.

Macedo, D. (1993) 'A Dialogue with Paulo Freire'. In McLaren, P. and Leonard, P. (Eds) *Paulo Freire: A Critical Encounter*. Oxon, New York: Routledge,

MacKenzie, I. (2011) *How the Occupy Movement is Hacking Your Consciousness*. Matador Network. [Online] [Accessed February 2012] http://matadornetwork.com/bnt/occupy-movement-hacking-consciousness

Macrine, S. L. (2009) 'What is Critical Pedagogy Good For? An Interview with Ira Shor'. In Macrine, S. L. (Ed.) *Critical Pedagogy in Uncertain Times: Hopes and Possibilities*. New York: Palgrave Macmillan, pp. 119–136.

Madison, D. S. (1998) 'Performances, Personal Narratives and the Politics of Possibility'. In Dailey, S. J. (Ed.) *In the Future of Performance Studies: Visions and Revisions*. Annandale: National Communication Association.

Mair, P. (2013) *Ruling the Void: The Hollowing Out of Western Democracy*. London, New York: Verso.

Marx, K. (1844/1975) 'Introduction to the contribution to the critique of Hegel's philosophy of law'. In Marx, K. and Engels, F. (Eds) *Collected Works: Vol. 3*. London: Lawrence and Wishart.

Marx, K. (1858) *Grundrisse: Foundations of the Critique of Political Economy (Rough Draft)*. London, New York: Penguin Books in Association with New Left Review, 1993.

Marx, K. (1867/1990) *Capital: Vol. 1*. Harmondsworth, UK: Penguin, 1976.

Marx, K. (1869/2013) *The 18th Brumaire of Louis Bonaparte: 2nd Edition*. Hamburg / New York: International Publishers/Wildside Press.

Marx, K. and Engels, F. (1846/ 2007) *The German Ideology*. Moscow: Progress.

Marx, K. and Engels, F. (1848/2003) *The Communist Manifesto*. London: The Merlin Press.

Mason, J. (2009) *Qualitative Researching*, 2nd ed. London, Thousand Oaks, New Delhi: Sage.

Mason, P. (2012) *Why It's Kicking Off Everywhere: The New Global Revolutions*. Brooklyn: Verso.

Mason, P. (2013) *Why It's Still Kicking Off Everywhere: The New Global Revolutions*. Brooklyn: Verso.

May, T. (2001) *Social Research: Issues, Methods and Process*, 3rd ed. Maidenhead, New York: Open University Press.

Mayo, P. (2004) *Liberating Praxis: Paulo Freire's Legacy for Radical Education and Politics*. Westport, CT: London: Praeger.

McGettigan, A. (2013) *The Great University Gamble: Money, Markets and the Future of Higher Education*. London, New York: Pluto Press.

McIntosh, P. (2010) *Action Research and Reflective Practice: Creative and Visual Methods to Facilitate reflection and Learning*. London, New York: Routledge.

McLaren, P. (1995) *Critical Pedagogy and Predatory Culture: Oppositional Politics in a Postmodern Era*. London, New York: Routledge.

McLaren, P. (1997) *Revolutionary Multiculturalism: Pedagogies of Dissent for the New Millennium*. Boulder CO: Westview Press.

McLaren, P. (1998a) 'Revolutionary Pedagogy in Post-Revolutionary Times: Rethinking the Political Economy of Critical Education'. *Education Theory*, 48(4), pp. 431–462.

McLaren, P. (1998b) *Life in Schools: An Introduction to Critical Pedagogy in the Foundations of Education*, 3rd ed. New York, Mexico City, Madrid, Amsterdam: Longman.

McLaren, P. (2000a) 'Paulo Freire's Pedagogy of Possibility'. In Steiner, S. F., Krank, H. M., McLaren, P. and Bahruth, R. E. (Eds) *Freirean Pedagogy, Praxis, and Possibilities: Projects for the New Millennium*. New York, London: Falmer Press, pp. 1–22.

McLaren, P. (2000b) *Che Guevara, Paulo Freire and the Pedagogy of Revolution*. Lanham MD: Rowman & Littlefield.

McLaren, P. and Jaramillo, N. (2007) *Pedagogy and Praxis in the Age of Empire: Towards a New Humanism.* Rotterdam: Sense Publisher.
McLaren, P. and Leonard, P. (Eds) (1993) *Paulo Freire: A Critical Encounter.* Oxon, New York: Routledge.
McNair, B. (2011) *An Introduction to Political Communication.* Oxon, New York: Routledge.
McNiff, J. (2002) *Action Research: Principles and Practice*, 2nd ed. London, New York: Routledge Falmer.
Meighan, R. (2002) *John Holt: Personalised Learning Instead of Uninvited Teaching.* Nottingham: Educational Heretics Press.
Meighan, R. and Harber, C. (2007) *A Sociology of Educating*, 5th ed. London, New York: Continuum.
Melucci, A. (1989) *Nomads of the Present: Social Movements and Individual Needs in Contemporary Society.* Philadelphia: Temple University Press.
Members of the Social Science Centre (2013) 'An Experiment in Free, Co-operative Higher Education'. *Radical Philosophy*, 182, pp. 66–67.
Merleau-Ponty, M. (1962) *Phenomenology of Perception.* London: Routledge.
Merrifield, A. (2011a) *Magical Marxism: Subversive Politics and the Imagination.* London, New York: Pluto Press.
Merrifield, A. (2011b) *Lefebvre: A Critical Introduction.* New York, London: Routledge.
Mezirow, J. (1995) 'Kriittinen reflektio uudistavan oppimisen käynnistäjänä'. In Mezirow, J. (Ed.) *Uudistava oppiminen. Kriittinen reflektio aikuiskoulutuksessa.* Helsinki: Helsingin yliopiston Lahden tutkimus- ja koulutuskeskus, pp. 17–37. Cited in Suoranta, J. (2010) *Jacques Rancière on Radical Equality and Adult Education.* In Peters, M. and Ghiraldelli, B. (Eds), *Encyclopedia of Educational Philosophy and Theory.* [Online] [Accessed 15. 01. 2014] https://link.springer.com/referencework/10.1007/978-981-287-532-7/page/all/1
Milgram, S. (1974) *Obedience to Authority: An Experimental View.* New York:Pinter & Martin Ltd.
Mills, C. W. (1957/2000) *The Sociological Imagination*, 40th anniversary ed. Oxford, New York and Worldwide: Oxford University Press.
Milojevic, I. (2006) 'Hegemonic and Marginalised Educational Utopias in the Contemporary Western World'. In Peters, M. and Freeman-Moir, J. (Eds) *Edutopias: New Utopian Thinking in Education.* Rotterdam, Taipei: Sense Publishers, pp. 21–44.
Mitchell, W., Harcourt, B. and Taussig, M. (2013) *Occupy: Three Inquiries in Disobedience.* Chicago, London: The University of Chicago Press.
Moltmann, J. (1967) *Theology of Hope.* London: SCM Press.
Montuori, A. (2008) 'Forward: Transdisciplinarity'. In Nicolescu, B. (Ed.) *Transdisciplinarity: Theory and Practice.* Cresskill, NJ: Hampton Press, Inc.
Mouffe, C. (1999) 'Deliberative Democracy or Agonistic Pluralism?' *Social Research*, 66(3), pp. 745–758.
Mouffe, C. (2005) *The Return of the Political.* London, Brooklyn: Verso.
Mouffe, C. (2013) *Agonistics: Thinking the World Politically.* London, New York: Verso.
Mowbray, M. (2010) 'Blogging the Greek Riots: Between Aftermath and Ongoing Engagement'. *Resistance Studies Magazine*, (1), pp. 4–15.
National Communication Association, cited in Denzin, N. K. (2010) *The Qualitative Manifesto: A Call to Arms.* Walnut Creek: Left Coast Press Inc., pp. 276–286.
Neary, M. (2004) 'Travels in Moishe Postone's Social University: A Contribution to a Critique of Political Cosmology'. *Historical Materialism*, 12(3), pp. 239–269.

Neary, M. (2012) 'Teaching Politically: Policy, Pedagogy and the New European University'. *Critical Journal for Education Policy Studies*, 10(2), pp. 232–257.
Neary, M. and Amsler, S. (2012) 'Occupy: A New Pedagogy of Space and Time'. *Critical Journal of Education Studies*, 10(2), pp. 106–138.
Neary, M. and Hagyard, A. (2011) 'Pedagogy of Excess: An Alternative Political Economy of Student Life'. In Molesworth, M., Scullion, R. and Nixon, E. (Eds) *The Marketisation of Higher Education and Student as Consumer*. London, New York: Routledge.
Neary, M. and Winn, J. (2012) 'Open Education: Commons, Commonism and the New Commonwealth'. *Ephemera: Theory & Politics in Organization*, 12(4).
Neary, M., Stevenson, H. and Bell, L. (Eds) (2013) *Towards Teaching in Public: Reshaping the Modern University*. London, New York: Bloomsbury.
Negri, A. (1992) 'Interpretation of the Class System Today: Methodological Aspects'. In Bonefeld, W., Gunn, R. and Psychopedis, K. (Eds) *Theory and Practice: Open Marxism*, Vol. 2. London: Pluto Press, pp. 69–105.
Nespor, J. (2006) 'Methodological Inquiry: The Uses and Spaces of Paradigm Proliferation', *International Journal of Qualitative Studies in Education*, 19(6), pp. 115–128.
Newman, M. (2005) 'Popular Teaching, Popular Learning and Popular Action'. In Crowther, J., Galloway, V. and Martin, I. (Eds) *Popular Education: Engaging the Academy, International Perspectives*. Leicester: National Institute of Adult Continuing Education, pp. 22–31.
Newman, S. (2011) *The Politics of Postanarchism*. Edinburgh: Edinburgh University Press.
Ng, E. and Toupin, S. (2013) 'Feminist and Queer Practices in the Online and Offline Activism of Occupy Wall Street'. *Networking Knowledge: Media, Communication and Cultural Studies Association*, 6(3), pp. 90–114.
Nixon, J. (2011) 'Re-Imagining the Public Good'. In Bailey, M. and Freedman, D. (Eds) *The Assault on Universities: A Manifesto for Resistance*. London: Pluto Press, pp. 59–70.
Nocella, A. J., Best, S. and McLaren, P. (Eds) (2010) *Academic Repression: Reflections from the Academic-Industrial Complex*. Edinburgh, Oakland, Baltimore: AK Press.
Occupy London LSX (2011) *About*. [Online] [Accessed 26. 07. 2013] http://occupylondon.org.uk/about-2
Occupy Research Collective (2012) *Ethical Guidelines for Activist Research*. [Online] [Accessed 23. 12. 2013] http://piratepad.net/XqLMuhCau8
Ollis, T. (2012) *A Critical Pedagogy of Embodied Education: Learning to Become an Activist*. New York: Palgrave MacMillan.
Orum, A. M., Feagin, J. R. and Sjoberg, G. (1991) 'The Nature of Case Study'. In Orum, A. M., Feagin, J. R. and Sjoberg, G. (Eds) *A Case for the Case Study*. Chapel Hill, London: The University of North Carolina Press, pp. 1–26.
Otto, W. and Stallard, C. (1976) 'One Hundred Essential Site Words'. *Visible Language*, 10(3), pp. 247–252.
Oxford English Dictionary (2007) *Shorter Oxford English Dictionary: On Historical Principles*, 6th ed., Vol. 2. Oxford and Worldwide: Oxford University Press.
Panayotakis, C. (2009) 'Reflections on the Greek Uprising'. *Capitalism Nature Socialism*, 20(2), pp. 97–101.
Parker, I. (2007) *Revolution in Psychology: Alienation to Emancipation*. London: Pluto Press.

## 184  References

Patrick, J. (1973) *A Glasgow Gang Observed*. London: Methuen.
Peters, M. and Freeman-Moir, J. (2006) 'Introducing Edutopias: Concept, Genealogy, Futures'. In Peters, M. and Freeman-Moir, J. (Eds) *Edutopias: New Utopian Thinking in Education*. Rotterdam, Taipei: Sense Publishers, pp. 1–20.
Pickerill, J. and Krinsky, J. (2012) 'Why Does Occupy Matter?' *Social Movement Studies: Journal of Social, Cultural and Political Protest*, 11(3–4), pp. 279–287.
Pinar, W. F. (2001) 'The Researcher as Bricoleur: The Teacher as Public Intellectual'. *Qualitative Inquiry*, 7, pp. 696–700.
Polletta, F. (2006) *It Was Like a Fever: Story Telling in Protest and Politics*. Chicago, London: The University of Chicago Press.
Postman, N. (1993) *Technopoly: The Surrender of Culture to Technology*. New York: Vintage Books. Cited in Milojevic, I. (2006) 'Hegemonic and Marginalised Educational Utopias in the Contemporary Western World'. In Peters, M. and Freeman-Moir, J. (Eds) *Edutopias: New Utopian Thinking in Education*. Rotterdam, Taipei: Sense Publishers, pp. 21–44.
Pratt, M. L. (1991) 'Arts of the Contact Zone'. In *Profession '91*. New York: Modern Language Association, pp. 33–40.
Psychopedis, K. (1992) 'Dialectical Theory: Problems of Reconstruction'. In Bonefeld, W., Gunn, R. and Psychopedis, K. (Eds) *Open Marxism: Dialectics and History*, Vol. 1. London: Pluto Press, pp. 1–53.
Pusey, A. (2010) 'Social Centres and the New Cooperativism of the Common'. *Affinities: A Journal of Radical Theory, Culture and Action*, 4(1), pp. 176–198.
Rancière, J. (1991) *The Ignorant Schoolmaster: Five Lessons in Intellectual Emancipation*. Stanford CA: Stanford University Press.
Rancière, J. (1995) *On the Shores of Politics*. London, New York: Verso.
Rancière, J. (1998) *Disagreement: Politics and Philosophy*. Minneapolis MN: University of Minnesota Press.
Rancière, J. (2001) 'Ten Theses on Politics'. *Theory & Event*, 5(3).
Rancière, J. (2003) *The Philosopher and his Poor*. Durham, London: Duke University Press.
Rancière, J. (2004) *The Politics of Aesthetics*. London: Continuum.
Rancière, J. (2011) *Dissensus: On Politics and Aesthetics*. London, New York: Continuum.
Razsa, M. and Kurnik, A. (2012) 'The Occupy Movement in Žižek's Hometown: Direct Democracy and a Politics of Becoming'. *American Ethnologist*, 39(2), pp. 238–258.
Really Open University. (2010) What do We Mean by 'Strike, Occupy, Transform'?, *Blog: Really Open University*.
Reason, P. and Rowan, J. (1981) 'Issues of Validity in New Paradigm Research'. In Reason, P. and Rowan, J. (Eds) *Human Inquiry: A Sourcebook for New Paradigm Research*. New York: John Wiley.
Reason, P. and Bradbury, H. (Eds) (2006) *Handbook of Action Research*. London: Sage.
Reitz, C. (2000) 'Liberating the Critical in Critical Theory: Marcuse, Marx and a Pedagogy of the Oppressed: Alienation, Art and the Humanities'. In Steiner, S. F., Krank, H. M., McLaren, P. and Bahruth, R. E. (Eds) *Freirean Pedagogy, Praxis, and Possibilities: Projects for the New Millennium*. New York, London: Falmer Press, pp. 41–66.
Riesman, D. (1969) *The Lonely Crowd: A Study of the Changing American Character*. New Haven, London: Yale University Press.

Robson, C. (2002) *Real World Research: A Resource for Social Scientists and Practitioner Researchers*. Malden, Oxford, Carlton: Blackwell Publishing.
Roggero, G. (2011) *The Production of Living Knowledge: The Crisis of the University and the Transformation of Labour in Europe and North America*. Philadelphia: Temple University Press.
Rorty, R. (1999) *Philosophy and Social Hope*. London:Penguin.
Rose, M. (1990) *Lives on the Boundary*. New York: Penguin Books.
Ross, J. (2006) *¡Zapatistas!: Making Another World Possible, Chronicles of Resistance 2000–2006*. New York: Nation Books.
Rycroft, C. (1979) 'Steps to an Ecology of Hope'. In Fitzgerald, R. (Ed.) *The Sources of Hope*. Rushcutters Bay: Pergamon Press, pp. 3–23.
Sahasrabudhey, S. (2009) 'Management of Knowledge vs. Production of Knowledge'. In The Edu-Factory Collective (Eds) *Toward a Global Autonomous University*. Brooklyn: Autonomedia, pp. 42–44.
Sandlin, J., O'Malley, M. and Burdick, J. (2011) 'Mapping the Complexity of Public Pedagogy Scholarship: 1894–2010'. *Review of Educational Research*, 81(3), pp. 338–375.
Sartre, J.-P. (1943) *L'être et le néant*. Paris: Gallimard. Cited in Merrifield, A. (2011) *Magical Marxism: Subversive Politics and the Imagination*. London, New York: Pluto Press.
Schmitt, C. (1996) *The Concept of the Political*. Chicago: University of Chicago Press.
Schön, E. (1983) *The Reflective Practitioner: How Professionals Think in Action*. New York: Basic Books
Schostak, J. (1983) *Maladjusted Schooling: Deviance Social Control and Individuality in Secondary Schooling*. Oxon, New York: Routledge.
Schostak, J. (2014) Personal communication. Manchester Metropolitan University.
Schostak, J. and Schostak, J. (2008) *Radical Research: Designing, Developing and Writing Research to Make a Difference*. Oxon, New York: Routledge.
Schostak, J. and Schostak, J. (2013) *Writing Research Critically: Developing the Power to Make a Difference*. London, New York: Routledge.
Schratz, M. and Walker, R. (1995) *Research as Social Change: New Opportunities for Qualitative Research*. London, New York: Routledge.
Schutz, A. (1944) 'The Stranger: An Essay in Social Psychology'. *American Journal of Sociology*, 49(6), pp. 499–507.
Scott, J. (1992) 'Experience'. In Butler, J. and Scott, J. (Eds) *Feminists Theorize the Political*. New York: Routledge, pp. 22–40.
Shantz, J. (2013) *Commonist Tendencies: Mutual Aid Beyond Communism*. Brooklyn: Punctum Books.
Sharp, G. (2012) *From Dictatorship to Democracy: A Conceptual Framework for Liberation*. London: Serpent's Tail.
Shor, I. (1992) *Empowering Education: Critical Teaching for Social Change*. Chicago, London: The University of Chicago Press.
Shor, I. (1996) *When Students Have Power: Negotiating Authority in a Critical Pedagogy*. Chicago, London: The University of Chicago Press.
Shor, I. and Freire, P. (1987) *A Pedagogy for Liberation: Dialogues on Transforming Education*. Westport, Connecticut, London: Bergin & Garvey.
Shukaitis, S. and Graeber, D. (2007b) 'Moments of Possibility/Genealogies of Resistance: Introduction'. In Shukaitis, S., Graeber, D. and Biddle, E. (Eds) *Constituent*

*Imagination: Militant Investigations Collective Theorization*. Oakland, Edinburgh, West Virginia: AK Press, pp. 36–38.
Sitrin, M. (2012) 'Horizontalism and the Occupy Movements'. *Dissent*, 59(2), pp. 74–75.
Skinner, J. (2011) 'Social Media and Revolution: The Arab Spring and the Occupy Movement as Seen through Three Information Studies Paradigms'. *Sprouts: Working Papers on Information Systems*, 11(169).
Smith, J. and Glidden, B. (2012) 'Occupy Pittsburgh and the Challenges of Participatory Democracy'. *Social Movement Studies: Journal of Social, Cultural and Political Protest*, 11(3–4), pp. 288–294.
Smith, N. (1984) *Uneven Development: Nature, Capital and the Production of Space*. London, New York: Verso.
Smith, W. A. (1976) *The Meaning of Conscientização: The Goal of Paulo Freire's Pedagogy*. Centre for International Education.
Smyth, J. (2011) *Critical Pedagogy for Social Justice*. New York, London: Continuum.
Smyth, J., Down, B. and McInerney (2014) *Socially Just Schooling: Making Space for Youth to Speak Back*. London: Springer.
Snow, D. A. and Anderson, L. (1991) 'Researching the Homeless: The Characteristic Features and Virtues of Case Study'. In Orum, A. M., Feagin, J. R. and Sjoberg, G. (Eds) *A Case for the Case Study*. Chapel Hill, London: The University of North Carolina Press, pp. 148–173.
Social Science Centre. (2012) [Online] [Accessed 05. 03. 2012] socialsciencecentre.org.uk
Solnit, D. and Solnit, R. (Eds) (2010) *The Battle of the Story of the Battle of Seattle*. Oakland, Edinburgh: AK Press.
Spinoza, B. (2006) *The Essential Spinoza: Ethics and Related Writings*. Indianapolis, Cambridge: Hackett Publishing Company Inc.
Stake, R. E. (1978) 'The Case Study Method in Social Inquiry'. *Educational Researcher*, 7(5), pp. 5–8.
Stake, R. E. (1995) *The Art of Case Study Research*. Thousand Oaks, London, New Delhi: Sage Publications.
Stake, R. E. (2000) 'The Case Study Method in Social Inquiry'. In Gomm, R., Hammersley, M. and Foster, P. (Eds) *Case Study Method: Key Issues, Key Texts*. London, Thousand Oaks, New Delhi: Sage Publications, pp. 19–26.
Stake, R. E. (2010) *Qualitative Research: Studying How Things Work*. New York, London: The Guilford Press.
Stanley, L. and Wise, S. (1990) 'Method, Methodology and Epistemology in Feminist Research Processes'. In Stanley, L. (Ed.) *Feminist Praxis: Research, Theory and Epistemology in Feminist Sociology*. London: Routledge, pp. 3–19.
Star, S. L. (2007) 'Living Grounded Theory: Cognitive and Emotional Forms of Pragmatism'. In Bryant, A. and Charmaz, K. (Eds) *The Sage Handbook of Grounded Theory*. Los Angeles, London, New Delhi, Singapore, Washington DC: Sage, pp. 75–93.
Steinberg, S. R. (2007) 'Preface'. In Borg, C. and Mayo, P. (Eds) *Public Intellectuals, Radical Democracy and Social Movements: A Book of Interviews*. New York, Washington DC, Baltimore, Bern, Frankfurt am Main, Berlin, Brussels, Vienna, Oxford: Peter Lang, pp. vii–viii.
Steinklammer, E. (2012) 'Learning to Resist: Hegemonic Practice, Informal Learning and Social Movements'. In Hall, B. L., Clover, D. E., Crowther, J. and Scandrett, E. (Eds) *Learning and Education for a Better World: The Role of Social Movements*. Rotterdam: Sense Publishers, pp. 23–40.

Stenhouse, L. (1985) 'A Note on Case Study and Educational Practice'. *Field Methods in the Study of Education*, pp. 263–271.
Stenhouse, L. (1988) 'Case Study Methods'. In Keeves, J. P. (Ed.) *Educational Research, Methodology, and Measurement: An International Handbook*, 1st ed. Oxford: Pergamon, pp. 49–53.
Stryker, S. (1980) *Symbolic Interactionism*. New Jersey: The Blackburn Press.
Stryker, S. (2000) 'Identity Competition: Key to Differential Social Movement Participation'. In Stryker, S., Owens, T. J. and White, R. W. (Eds) *Self, Identity and Social Movements*. Minneapolis, London: University of Minnesota Press, pp. 21–41.
Student as Producer. (2010) *Key Features*. University of Lincoln. [Online] [Accessed 07. 10. 2012] http://studentasproducer.lincoln.ac.uk
Sturman, A. (1994) 'Case Study Methods'. In Keeves, J. P. (Ed.) *Educational Research, Methodology, and Measurement: An International Handbook*, 2nd ed. Oxford: Pergamon, pp. 61–66.
Suoranta, J. (2010) 'Jacques Rancière on Radical Equality and Adult Education'. In Peters, M. and Ghiraldelli, B. (Eds), *Encyclopaedia of Educational Philosophy and Theory*. [Online]
Suoranta, J. (2011) 'Learners and Oppressed Peoples of the World, Wikify! Wikiversity as a Global Critical Pedagogy'. In Stephenson Malott, C. and Porfilio, B. (Eds) *Critical Pedagogy in the Twenty-First Century: A New Generation of Scholars*. Charlotte, NC: Information Age Publishing, pp. 497–520.
Tandon, R. (2005) 'Social Transformation and Participatory Research'. In Tandon, R. (Ed.) *Participatory Research: Revisiting the Roots*. New Delhi: Mosaic Books, pp. 203–215.
Taylor, P. (1993) *The Texts of Paulo Freire*. Open University Press. Cited in Lockhart, J. (1997) 'After Freire: A Continuing Pedagogy'. [Online] [Accessed 21. 06. 2013] www.williamtemplefoundation.org.uk/publications/
Temple-Raston, D. (2005) *Justice on the Grass: Three Rwandan Journalists, Their Trial for War Crimes, and a Nation's Quest for Redemption*. New York, London, Toronto, Sydney: Free Press.
Tent City University (2012) *Welcome to Tent City University*. [Online] [Accessed 07. 01. 2012] http://tentcityuniversity.org/
The Contributors (Eds) (2011) *Occupy! Scenes from Occupied America*. London, Brooklyn: Verso.
The Edu-Factory Collective (2009) *Towards a Global Autonomous University: Cognitive Labour, The Production of Knowledge, and Exodus from the Education Factory*. Brooklyn: Autonomedia.
The Free Association (2007) 'Worlds in Motion'. *Turbulance*1, pp. 26–27.
The Invisible Committee (2009) *The Coming Insurrection*. Paris, Los Angeles: Semiotext(e).
The School of Barbiana (1969) *Letter to a Teacher*. Aylesbury: Penguin Books Ltd.
Thomas, J. (2000) *The Battle in Seattle: The Story Behind the WTO Demonstrations*. London, Minneapolis: Fulcrum Group.
Thompson, N. (2007) *Power and Empowerment*. Lyme Regis: Russell House Publishing.
Thorpe, S. (2013) 'Rights, Constitution and Radical Democracy in Occupy Wall Street and Occupy London'. *Birkbeck Law Review*, 1(2), pp. 225–280.
Thrasher, F. M. (1927) *The Gang: A Study of 1,313 Gangs in Chicago*. Chicago: The University of Chicago Press.

Tiger, L. (1999) 'Hope Springs Eternal'. *Social Research*, 66(2), pp. 611–623.
*Time Magazine* (2011) *What is Occupy? Inside the Global Movement*. New York: Time Books.
Toscano, A. (2011) 'The University as a Political Space'. In Bailey, M. and Freedman, D. (Eds) *The Assault on Universities: A Manifesto for Resistance*. London: Pluto Press, pp. 81–90.
Trifonas, P. P. (Ed.) (2000) *Revolutionary Pedagogies: Cultural Politics, Instituting Education and the Discourse of Theory*. New York, London: Routledge Falmer.
Turbulence (2008) 'Introduction: Present Tense, Future Conditional'. *Turbulence* (Leeds), 4(3).
Tyler, I. (2013) *Revolting Subjects: Social Abjection and Resistance in Neoliberal Britain*. London, New York: Zed Books.
Uitermark, J. and Nichols, W. (2012) 'How Local Networks Shape a Global Movement: Comparing Occupy in Amsterdam and Los Angeles'. *Social Movement Studies: Journal of Social, Cultural and Political Protest*, 11(3–4), pp. 295–301.
University and College Union. (2013) *Over Half of Universities and Colleges use Lecturers on Zero-Hour Contracts*. Online: UCU. [Online] [Accessed 07. 03. 2014] http://www.ucu.org.uk/6749
University of Lincoln. (2011–2012) *Student as Producer: Research Engaged Teaching and Learning at the University of Lincoln*. University of Lincoln.
van Gelder, S. and the Staff of YES! Magazine (Eds) (2011) *This Changes Everything: The Occupy Wall Street Movement and the 99%*. San Francisco: Berrett-Koehler Publishers, Inc.
Van Stekelenburg, J. (2012) 'The Occupy Movement: Product of This Time'. *Development* 55(2), pp. 224–231.
Vodovnik, Ž. (Ed.) (2004) *¡Ya Basta! Ten Years of the Zapatista Uprising: Writings of the Subcomandante Insurgente Marcos*. Oakland, Edinburgh: AK Press.
von Kotze, A. (2012) 'Composting the Imagination in Popular Education'. In Hall, B. L., Clover, D. E., Crowther, J. and Scandrett, E. (Eds) *Learning and Education for a Better World: The Role of Social Movements*. Rotterdam: Sense Publishers, pp. 101–112.
Vygotsky, L. S. (1962) *Thought and Language*. Cambridge: Harvard University Press.
Waller, W. (1932) *The Sociology of Schooling*. New York, London: John Wiley/Chapman and Hall.
Walton, J. K. (2011) 'The Idea of the University'. In Bailey, M. and Freedman, D. (Eds) *The Assault on Universities: A Manifesto for Resistance*. London: Pluto Press, pp. 15–26.
Wassall, T. (2011) 'John Holloway's "Crack Capitalism"'. *Blog: Capitalism – Crisis and Critique*.
Waterworth, J. (2004) *A Philosophical Analysis of Hope*. Basingstoke: Palgrave.
Webb, D. (2010) 'Paulo Freire and "the need for a kind of education in hope"'. *Cambridge Journal of Education*, 40(4), pp. 327–339.
Weems, M. (2002) *I Speak from the Wound in my Mouth*. New York: Peter Lang. Cited in Denzin, N. K. (2010) *The Qualitative Manifesto: A Call to Arms*. Walnut Creek: Left Coast Press Inc.
Weldon, S. L. (2012) *When Protest Makes Policy: How Social Movements Represent Disadvantaged Groups*. Ann Arbor: University of Michigan Press.
West, G. and Blumberg, R. L. (Eds) (1990) *Women and Social Protest*. Oxford, New York: Oxford University Press.
Whitehead, J. and McNiff, J. (2006) *Action Research Living Theory*. London, Thousand Oaks, New Delhi: Sage Publications.

Whyte, W. F. (1943) *Street Corner Society: The Social Structure of an Italian Slum*. Chicago: The University of Chicago Press.
Williams, J. (2013) *Consuming Higher Education: Why Learning Can't Be Bought*. London, New Delhi, New York, Sydney: Bloomsbury.
Williams, R. (1989) *Resources of Hope: Culture, Democracy, Socialism*. London, New York: Verso.
Williams, R. (2011) *The Long Revolution*. Cardigan: Parthian.
Willis, P. (1977) *Learning to Labour: How Working Class Kids Get Working Class Jobs*. Farnborough: Saxon House.
Winn, J. (2010) 'A Co-operatively Run "Social Science Centre"', *Blogs at Lincoln* (Vol. 2012): The University of Lincoln.
Wolcott, H. F. (2008) *Ethnography: A Way of Seeing*, 2nd ed. Lanham, New York, Toronto, Plymouth, UK: AltaMira Press.
Yin, R. K. (2009) *Case Study Research: Design and Methods*, 4th ed. Thousand Oaks, New Delhi, London, Singapore: Sage.
Zacharakis-Jutz, J. (1991) *Highlander Folkschool and the Labour Movement, 1932–1953*. Chicago, IL: ERIC Document Reproduction Service No. ED 331 940.
Žižek, S. (2008) *The Sublime Object of Ideology*. London, New York: Verso.
Žižek, S. (2009) *First as Tragedy, Then as Farce*. New York, London: Verso.
Žižek, S. (2012) *The Year of Dreaming Dangerously*. London, New York: Verso.
Žižek, S. (2013) 'The Simple Courage of Decision: A Leftist Tribute to Thatcher'. *New Statesman*. [Online] [Accessed 25. 08. 2014] www.newstatesman.com/politics/politics/2013/04/simple-courage-decision-leftist-tribute-thatcher
Žižek, S. (2014) 'The Impasses of Today's Radical'. *Crisis and Critique*, 1(1). [Online] [Accessed 20. 08. 2014] http://materializmidialektik.org/wp-content/uploads/2014/2001/Zizek_Politics.pdf

# Index

academia, market values in 132
action: and anger 67–8; and bricolage 39; and case study approach 29; collective 86; and popular education 144
action research 3, 39–40, 131, 146, 165
activism: and learning 144; research as 156, 161
activists, professional 103
alienation 57, 64, 65, 111; *see also* cultural invasion
anger: and action 67–8; Freire on 64
Arab Spring 8, 13, 84
Arditi, B. 19, 45, 46

Bahruth, R.E., and Steiner, S.F. 128, 134, 147–8
Bonnett, A. 120
Borg, C., and Mayo, P. 131
bricolage 3, 5, 6, 26–7, 31; and action 39; and change 31; complexity 49, 152; connections 140, 150, 156; and conscientization 151; and criticity 150; and data 36; eclecticism 33–4; essence of 10, 31; ethical issues 42; etymology 33; intertextuality 46–7; and knowledge in process 90; and knowledge production 9, 32, 41, 147; as methodology 162; as multidisciplinary approach 32, 33; of the multitude 156; in Occupy movement 142; and possibility 138, 139, 147; post-disciplinary 32, 33, 34, 35, 40–1; and reclamation 142; research paradigm 146, 153, 161, 162, 167; serendipity element 36–7; storytelling as 139; strengths and weaknesses 162; subversiveness of 39, 40, 142; and transgression 141–2

bricoleur 32, 40, 142; becoming 33; and critique 158–9; role 152
Brookfield, S. 67, 68, 81, 99
Brydon-Miller, M. 39, 42, 45, 46
Burdick, J., and Sandlin, J. 152

capitalism: cracks in 55, 60, 61, 63, 67, 72, 95, 151, 164; as enclosure 2, 5, 53, 63, 64; manipulation of society 53
case studies approach 28–9; and action 29; alternative interpretations 30
Castells, M. 67–8, 90, 123; on construction of meaning 97; on social movements 117
Cavanagh, Chris 4, 132
change: and bricolage methodology 31; and critical mass 90; resistance to 99–100; and social structure 128
character masks, Holloway on 73, 92
Cho, S. 128, 129, 138
choice, and SaP initiative 130, 133
Chomsky, Noam 13, 14, 19; on cooperative communities 17
Christians, C. 52
Clarke, A.E., and Friese, C. 30
Coffey, A. 45–6, 47
commonism 143; creation of 76, 136; theories 38
communication, and proximity 20
communities: cooperative, Chomsky on 17; imagined 19
conscientization 52, 72, 90, 99, 143–4; and bricolage 151
consciousness, critical: Freire on 58, 68, 72, 89; *see also* self-awareness
consensus model, disillusionment with 110–11
context, knowledge production in 109

# Index 191

conviviality, and learning 108
Couldry, N. 128, 135
critical mass: and change 90; and multitude notion 90
critical pedagogy *see* popular education
critical thinkers 67–8; engagement with life 130
critical thinking 90; and popular education 58
criticity, and bricolage 150
critique: and the bricoleur 158–9; and hope, contrast 9–10; politics of 94
Crowther, J., and Villegas, E.L. 153
cultural invasion 64–5; Freire on 65–6; *see also* alienation
culture: collective 81; critical 75
curiosity: epistemological 89, 90; need to promote 148
curriculum, hidden 147–8

Darder, A. 132; on democracy 5, 7
data 52n1; and bricolage 36; interpretations 51–2; and intertextuality 50; and theory 37–8
Davis, A. 90
Debord, G., *Society of the Spectacle* 102
democracy: Darder on 5; deliberative 76; and education 5; and hope 7, 117
Denzin, N.K. 35, 154
despair, and hope 107
differences, articulation of 106
discovery, by doing 63
disobedience 64
doing: discovery by 63; revolt of 65
Dyer-Witheford, N. 143

education: autonomous 124; balanced approach 130; and democracy 5; divergent attitudes to 100; and equality of intelligence 74; and life 136; schooling, distinction 4; Shor on 108, 157; and social action 4; as social movement 116–17; Steinklammer on 58, 110, 153, 155; taking of 76; and values 82; *see also* higher education; learning; popular education; university education
educators, as political actors 59
enclosure: battle against 9; capitalism as 2, 5, 53, 63, 64; escape from 156–7; of higher education 164; neoliberalism as 53–4; of social life 143; of social relations 8
escapism, Occupy LSX camp 21

ethics 45–6; bricolage 42; covenantal 42, 46
experts: need for 149; in SSC 121; in TCU 90–1, 113, 114

Faulkner, N. 135–6
Foust, C., on transgression 34, 35, 141, 142
free universities 154
Freedman, D. 132
Freire, Paulo 1, 5, 50–1, 54; on anger 64; on critical consciousness 58, 68, 72, 89; on cultural invasion 65–6; hard and soft readings of 56; on knowledge 89; on oppressors and the oppressed 82; *Pedagogy of the Oppressed* 56, 66; and pedagogy of the oppressed 70; philosophy, and Occupy movement 56; on rebellion and revolution 148; reinvention of 66–7; on schooling 57; on the self and the social 59; on teaching and learning 143

gender issues, Occupy LSX 92–3
General Assemblies: Occupy LSX 16–17, 81–2, 82–3, 84, 149; tensions in 106
Giroux, H. 106
Gitlin, T. 18
Glaser, B.G., and Strauss, A. 37
Gorz, A. 54, 63
Greenpeace 103
grounded theory 30, 36, 38, 49–50; and SaP 136–7

Halvorsen, S. 13, 16, 17
Hardt, M., and Negri, A. 20, 100, 124; *Declaration* 14; *Multitude* 14
Heaney, T. 58
hegemony: exploration of contexts 128; logic of 119; of marketplace 132
higher education: breakdown of barriers 156; enclosure of 164; feedback loop 140; storytelling in 139; *see also* university education
Holloway, John 2, 5, 7, 53, 58, 61–2, 63, 65, 91–2, 96, 138; on character masks 73, 92; *Crack Capitalism* 60–1, 163; on cracks in capitalism 55, 60, 61, 63; on revolution 54, 113
hooks, bell 4, 104
hope: collective 83–4; and critique, contrast 9–10; and democracy 7, 117; and despair 107; essence of 157; versus fatalism 59; and Occupy movement 9,

11; and popular education 55; and possibility 96; and radicalism 1, 11, 159; and trust 7; Webb on 2; *see also* possibility
horizontalism, Occupy movement 18

Illich, I. 156; on learning 131
individualism, and conditioning 99
intelligence, equality of 71, 73, 74, 104, 114, 131, 149, 158, 167
intertextuality: bricolage 46–7; and data 50; definition 46
interviews: and knowledge production 47; mutual benefits of 47, 48, 49; power inequalities 48; problem areas 43
The Invisible Committee 49, 151

Jacotot, Joseph 71
Jaramillo, N. 21
Johnston, R., on popular education 8

Kane, L. 153
Katsiaficas, G. 64, 68, 96
Kincheloe, J.L.: and Berry, K.S. 31, 32, 37, 39, 40, 41, 49, 51, 139, 142, 146–7; and Tobin, K. 40, 46, 48, 154
knowledge: as commodity 132; Freire on 89; and organisational structure 127; in process, and bricolage 90; producers of 70; valorisation of 131
knowledge production: and bricolage 9, 32, 41, 147; co-production of 136, 147; in context 109; continuum of production sites 136; and interviews 47; and power 41; as revolutionary political project 136; and spaces 136; students 125–6
Kvale, S., and Brinkman, S. 43, 46, 47, 48, 51, 52

learning: and activism 144; collaborative 120, 122; collective 75, 77; conditions for, and pedagogues 75; connections, Occupy movement 138; and conviviality 108; critical 134–5; faux 121; Illich on 131; landscapes 136; loops, Occupy movement 147, 163; outputs versus outcomes 127; sites of 152
life, and education 136
Lincoln University 115, 135; *see also* Social Science Centre (SSC); Student as Producer (SaP)
London Stock Exchange camp *see* Occupy LSX

market values: dominant ideology in academia 132; in SaP initiative 132–3
Marx, Karl 91; on changing the world 31
Marxism, open 5, 38, 69
meaning, construction of, Castells on 97
Merrifield, A. 61, 63–4, 68–9, 141
methodology, bricolage as 162
multitude notion 14, 32; bricolage of 156; and critical mass 90; and schooling 35, 76

Neary, Mike 21, 22, 23, 24–5, 26, 115–16, 117; and Amsler, S. 133–4, 135, 136, 143, 153; on collaborative learning 120
negation, acts of, and rebellion 63–4
neoliberalism 90; as enclosure 53–4
networks: Occupy LSX 84; of trust 97
New Social Movements 2
Newman, M. 130, 134–5, 150
Nocella, A.J., *Academic Repression* 56

occupation, dimensions 140, 160
Occupiers, and organic pedagogy 79
'occupy', as empty signifier 160, 164, 165
Occupy London movement 2, 3, 6, 12, 13, 98, 164; case study 29; government reaction 90; organic pedagogy 161; *see also* Tent City University (TCU)
Occupy LSX (London Stock Exchange) camp 2, 12–13, 29; discourses 88; educational experience 86; epistemological curiosity 89; escapism 21; gender issues 92–3; General Assemblies 16–17, 81–2, 82–3, 84, 149; hierarchy, lack of 109; internal conflict avoidance 102, 103; lessons from 113; networks 84; organisation 15–16; and Paternoster Square 15; praxis development 85–6; revolutionary potential 96; solidarity 20–1; tensions within 85, 104–5; in virtual space 84; *see also* Tent City University (TCU)
Occupy movement: bricolage in 142; democratic pedagogy 74; and Freire's philosophy 56; and hope 9, 11; horizontalism 18; inequality within 117; learning connections 138; learning loops 163; origins 13; and popular education 4; and possibility 141; research approaches 30–1; services 17–18; significance 14; slogan 18–19; and social media 20, 84; solidarity, search for 142; as space of

slippage 69, 141; spread 13; tensions, internal 162
Occupy Oakland protests 15
Occupy Research Collective (ORC) 43, 100, 146; attitude to researchers 102; research guidelines 44–5
Occupy Wall Street 13
Ollis, T. 144–5, 156
oppression: consensual 70–1; uncovering of 166
oppressors and the oppressed, Freire on 82
organic pedagogy 87–8; and Occupiers 79; Occupy London movement 161; problems 79–80; versus schooling 79

paranoia: and trust 94; and undercover police 93
patriarchy 112
pedagogical moment 158
pedagogues: and conditions for learning 75; emancipated 74; as facilitators 149–50; and revolutionary education 148; *see also* teachers
pedagogy: democratic, Occupy movement 74; emancipatory 76; myth of 71–2; in popular education 135; of space and time 135; theories of 71; *see also* organic pedagogy; power sharing pedagogy
pepper spray, use of 15
Peters, M.: and Freeman-Moir, J. 142; on utopianism 153–4, 155
police, undercover, and paranoia 93
politics: of critique 94; dialogue of 65; of possibility 94–5; pre-figurative 63
popular education (critical pedagogy): and action 144; challenging nature of 4; and choice 130; and co-learning 149; and critical thinking 58; definitions 3, 59; documentation of 8; and hope 55; Johnston on 8; and Occupy 4, 134; pedagogy in 135; and power sharing pedagogy 149, 151; process 3–4; purpose 59–60, 155; in SaP initiative 126, 127, 129, 134; and self-awareness 50–1; and SSC 22, 60, 123; and transformation 56, 58
Popular Education Network (PEN) 3
possibility: and bricolage 138, 139, 147; and hope 96; and Occupy movement 141; politics of 94–5; *see also* hope
power, and knowledge production 41

power sharing pedagogy: and countervailing discourses 166; and popular education 149, 151; Shor on 97, 113, 163; SSC 97, 118, 120, 121–2, 147, 151
praxis development, Occupy LSX 85–6
proximity, and communication 20
public spaces: creation of; definition 14; uses of 15
Pusey, A. 123, 124

radicalism, and hope 1, 11, 159
Rancière, Jacques 5, 38, 72–3; *The Ignorant Schoolmaster* 69, 71, 91, 149, 161; universal teaching 97, 104, 131
reality, and sloganisation 102
rebellion: and acts of negation 63–4; and revolution, Freire on 148
reclamation: and bricolage 142; of self 143
research: as activism 156, 161; approaches, Occupy movement 30–1; bricolage paradigm 146, 153, 161, 162, 167; desirable outcomes 51; guidelines, ORC 44–5; militant co-research 33; motivation for 4; researcher's engagement 31, 34, 45–6; transgressive 34; *see also* action research; bricolage; grounded theory
revolt, of doing 65
revolution: Holloway on 54, 113; as present reality 69; and rebellion, Freire on 148
Rose, M. 76

School of Barbiana 71
schooling: education, distinction 4; essentialism of 61; Freire on 57; and multitude notion 35, 76; versus organic pedagogy 79; *see also* education
Schostak, J., and Schostak, J. 4, 28, 32, 34, 41
post-Seattle movements 2, 18
self: divided 66, 99; reclamation of 143; reinvention of 113; and the social, Freire on 59
self-awareness: and popular education 50–1; *see also* consciousness
sexism 93; dealing with 98–9
Shantz, J. 140, 146, 154, 164
'sheeple' 104; meaning 102, 103

194  *Index*

Shor, Ira 5, 54, 57, 58, 59, 69, 74–5, 76–7, 82; on education 108, 157; on power sharing pedagogy 97, 113, 163; on teachers' role 137; *When Students Have Power* 74
Shukaitis, S., and Graeber, D. 33, 38, 48
Sitrin, M. 18
sloganisation, and reality 102
social action, and education 4
social centres 123–4; *see also* Social Science Centre (SSC)
social change, and Student as Producer (SaP) initiative 130
social life, enclosure of 143
social media, and Occupy movement 20, 84
social movement 151; education as 116–17; SSC as 117
social movements: Castells on 117; as sites of reproduction 158; as sites of slippage 157–8
social relations: alternative 83, 92; enclosure of 8; reimagining of 80, 112; and SaP initiative 131; and society 156
Social Science Centre (SSC) 2, 3, 115, 116–25; with business 118; Constitution 118–19; as emergent institution 21–2; experts in 121; and 'higher learning' 24, 120; membership 119; networking potential 23; as part of the city 23, 124; and popular education 22, 60, 123; portability 167; potential 142; power sharing pedagogy 97, 118, 120, 121–2, 145, 151; purpose 22, 24, 117, 124–5; roots 122–3; as safe place 118, 122, 123; as site of slippage 69, 120, 123; 'Social Science Imagination' course 24, 121; teachers/students, tensions 22–3, 118, 120, 123, 167–8
social structure, and change 128
society, manipulation by capitalism 53
solidarity, Occupy LSX (London Stock Exchange) camp 20–1
space and time, pedagogy of 135
spaces: and knowledge production 136; of slippage: Occupy movement 69, 141; SSC 69; virtual, Occupy LSX in 84; *see also* public spaces
Steinklammer, E., on education 58, 110, 153, 155
Stenhouse, L. 29
storytelling: as bricolage 139; in higher education 139
Strategic Optimism, University for 154

Student as Producer (SaP) initiative 2, 3, 115, 125–37; as anti-curriculum 136; and choice 130, 133; Creative Commons licenses 135; facilitator 130; features 25–6; funding 26; and grounded theory 136–7; 'key aspects' 130; learning outputs versus learning outcomes 127; literary output 130; market values in 132–3; popular education in 126, 127, 129, 134; potential 142, 165; purpose 25; research-engaged teaching and learning 126, 129, 131, 132, 134–5, 153; site of potential slippage 125; and social change 130; and social relations 131; student motivation 128
students, teacher, shared authority 77
Sturman, A. 28

Tahrir Square, Cairo 13
teachers: role, Shor on 137; students: distinction 22–3, 118; shared authority 77; tensions 22–3, 118, 120, 121, 123, 167–8; *see also* pedagogues
tensions: need for 105; in Occupy LSX 85, 104–5, 107; teachers/students 22–3, 118, 120, 121, 123, 167–8
Tent City University (TCU) 2–3, 13, 15–16, 37, 92, 166; and experts 90–1, 113; ownership 87; purpose 16, 101; and self-criticism 97; significance 60; slogan 104; *see also* Occupy London movement
textual public 32
theory, and data 37–8
time, free, use of 63, 86
TINA (There is No Alternative) syndrome 61; escape from 139
transformation, and popular education 56, 58
transgression: and bricolage 141–2; Foust on 34, 35, 141, 142
trust: as guiding principle 98; and hope 7; networks of 97; as organising principle 61, 67; and paranoia 94; problems with 104

UK Uncut 95
university education: counter-culture need for 135; as public good 132, 133; *see also* free universities; higher education
unrest, global 8
utopianism, Freeman-Moir and Peters on 153–4, 155

values, and education 82
Van Stekelenburg, J. 19
von Kotze, A. 151

Walton, J.K. 132
Webb, D., on hope 2

Whitehead, J., and McNiff, J.
 39, 50
Williams, J. 2013
Williams, R. 1

Zapatistas 113, 151

# Taylor & Francis eBooks

## Helping you to choose the right eBooks for your Library

Add Routledge titles to your library's digital collection today. Taylor and Francis ebooks contains over 50,000 titles in the Humanities, Social Sciences, Behavioural Sciences, Built Environment and Law.

**Choose from a range of subject packages or create your own!**

**Benefits for you**
- Free MARC records
- COUNTER-compliant usage statistics
- Flexible purchase and pricing options
- All titles DRM-free.

**Benefits for your user**
- Off-site, anytime access via Athens or referring URL
- Print or copy pages or chapters
- Full content search
- Bookmark, highlight and annotate text
- Access to thousands of pages of quality research at the click of a button.

**REQUEST YOUR FREE INSTITUTIONAL TRIAL TODAY** — **Free Trials Available** We offer free trials to qualifying academic, corporate and government customers.

## eCollections – Choose from over 30 subject eCollections, including:

| | |
|---|---|
| Archaeology | Language Learning |
| Architecture | Law |
| Asian Studies | Literature |
| Business & Management | Media & Communication |
| Classical Studies | Middle East Studies |
| Construction | Music |
| Creative & Media Arts | Philosophy |
| Criminology & Criminal Justice | Planning |
| Economics | Politics |
| Education | Psychology & Mental Health |
| Energy | Religion |
| Engineering | Security |
| English Language & Linguistics | Social Work |
| Environment & Sustainability | Sociology |
| Geography | Sport |
| Health Studies | Theatre & Performance |
| History | Tourism, Hospitality & Events |

For more information, pricing enquiries or to order a free trial, please contact your local sales team:
**www.tandfebooks.com/page/sales**

 **Routledge** Taylor & Francis Group | The home of Routledge books

**www.tandfebooks.com**